Queer Religiosities

An Introduction to Queer and Transgender Studies in Religion

Melissa M. Wilcox
University of California Riverside

ROWMAN & LITTLEFIELD
Lanham • Boulder • New York • London

Acquisitions Editor: Natalie Mandziuk
Editorial Assistant: Courtney Packard
Higher Education Channel Manager: Jonathan Raeder

Published by Rowman & Littlefield
An imprint of The Rowman & Littlefield Publishing Group, Inc.
4501 Forbes Boulevard, Suite 200, Lanham, Maryland 20706
https://rowman.com

6 Tinworth Street, London SE11 5AL, United Kingdom

British Library Cataloguing in Publication Information Available

Library of Congress Cataloging-in-Publication Data
Names: Wilcox, Melissa M., 1972– author.
Title: Queer religiosities : an introduction to queer and transgender studies in religion / Melissa M. Wilcox, University of California Riverside.
Description: Lanham : Rowman & Littlefield, 2020. | Includes bibliographical references and index. | Summary: "Queer Religiosities is a comprehensive, comparative, globally-focused textbook that introduces students to queer studies in religion. It is organized in a comparative, thematic format that allows readers to approach the study of queer religion from a variety of angles while teaching key principles in the study of religion and the study of sexuality and gender. Queer Religiosities aims to make the rapidly growing research in queer studies in religion accessible to students"— Provided by publisher.
Identifiers: LCCN 2019046463 (print) | LCCN 2019046464 (ebook) | ISBN 9781442275669 (cloth) | ISBN 9781442275676 (paperback) | ISBN 9781442275683 (epub)
Subjects: LCSH: Gender identity—Religious aspects. | Queer theory.
Classification: LCC BL65.S4 W55 2020 (print) | LCC BL65.S4 (ebook) | DDC 201/.7—dc23
LC record available at https://lccn.loc.gov/2019046463
LC ebook record available at https://lccn.loc.gov/2019046464

This book is dedicated to all of the courageous, committed, and insightful scholars who have developed first gay and lesbian, then queer and transgender studies in religion over the past several decades, often at great risk and sometimes at great cost to their careers. May this book be worthy of your sacrifices, and may it live up to your expectations.

and

This book is also dedicated to the memory of my father, U.C. Berkeley Professor Emeritus of Forestry Dr. W. Wayne Wilcox. A talented, funny, and beloved teacher, he thought textbook writing mattered even if it damaged his career as it did, much to his disgust. Like my mom and my brother, I share his passion and his refusal to let the sticks and carrots of academic administration determine the focus of my work. Thanks for everything, Dad. We miss you more than you would have ever imagined.

Contents

Preface

Queer and transgender studies in religion are not only rapidly growing and cutting-edge areas of academic inquiry; they are also intensely relevant to contemporary social, cultural, and political issues. Where queer studies, and at times also transgender studies, have looked askance at religion, relegating it solely to the status of oppressor, and religious studies has often returned the favor by considering queer and transgender studies irrelevant or reducing them to a kind of "add queers and stir" approach, outside of the academy there are many who find the connections between queer folks, trans folks, and religion to be self-evident and important. Certainly, queer and transgender studies in religion can help us to understand the often complex and varied approaches to sexual, gender, and bodily diversity within many religious traditions, but they can also do much more.

These fields can shed light, for instance, not only on same-sex marriage rights but also on the use of homophobia as a citizenship test in some European countries in the early 2000s. They can help us to question assumptions that secular spaces are truly secular, or that religion and justice are necessarily opposed for queer and trans people. They can challenge our understandings of the global dynamics of power and help us to sort out what Pope Francis means when he talks about "gender theory" and why he calls that theory one aspect of "ideological colonization."[1] And they can help us to ask deeper questions about religion when it appears in queer and trans spaces, and about queerness and transness when they appear in religious spaces. Queer and transgender studies in religion are not rarified fields, even when they engage in fairly complex and dense theory. They're eminently accessible to interested nonspecialists, and they're widely applicable to everyday situations in which many of us find ourselves regardless of how we understand our gender, our sexuality, and our own religious practices and beliefs.

Far beyond a simple additive or identitarian approach, in which doing queer and transgender studies just means studying queer and transgender people, these fields of study offer analytical tools for thinking through complex dynamics of power, embodiment, fixity and lack thereof, the normative and its demons. In time, transgender studies and queer studies together have the power to radically reorient the study of religion. Religious studies, in turn, holds profound promise for greater nuance, inclusion, and breadth and depth of insight in transgender and queer studies. The fields may currently still be engaged largely in tiptoeing gingerly around each other or dismissing each other altogether, but those of us who work at their intersections understand the striking connections and similarities between them and are pushing for greater recognition of the promise that lies within those connections.

Queer Religiosities is designed to introduce a general audience of nonspecialist readers, both within and beyond the classroom, to these exciting and rich fields of study. Written to be accessible and engaging, the book doesn't presume a background in religious studies, queer studies, or transgender studies. Instead, it introduces readers to all three of these fields before moving on to explore the important new perspectives offered by their combination. In writing the book I have resisted oversimplifying concepts or glossing over more difficult theoretical ideas, attempting instead to explain, situate, and illustrate them in ways that will be comprehensible to readers new to these areas of study. Readers with experience in one or two of these fields will find in this book an introduction to the aspects of these areas of study with which they are less familiar, and insights into how the fields they know better can be applied in new ways. Those with existing experience in queer and transgender studies in religion will, I hope, gain new perspectives and insights from the syntheses and analyses of the field that are contained herein.

Queer Religiosities is both thematic and intersectional in its design, and these two aspects of the book are interconnected. Intersectionality, a term coined by legal scholar and critical race theorist Kimberlé Crenshaw in 1989 to name an approach to analysis that had already been in use by womanists and feminists of color and Marxist feminists for some time, refers to the idea that the lines along which power travels—class, caste, skin color, race, age, ability, gender, sexuality, nationality, language, religion, and the like—are neither parallel nor separate. Rather, they intersect so that any analysis of gender, say, is deeply impacted by dynamics of class or ability. Someone's experiences "as a woman" are always inflected by that person's experiences as a Muslim, or a white person, or a Ghanaian, or a person with a visible disability, or a cisgender (non-transgender) person. Any attempt to generalize about "all women" runs afoul of assumptions about who constitutes the category "woman," and in addition to being exclusionary is bound to be inaccurate. So, too, with generalizations about what it is to be Christian, Hindu, or a practitioner of one's ancestral indigenous traditions.

For this reason, then, the book avoids an older, and increasingly sharply critiqued, "world religions" model for conceptualizing the field. Although people have been describing the practices, beliefs, ancestral spirits, and deities of others for millennia, the idea that this wide range of approaches to understanding and engaging with the world could all be understood through the concept of religion is much newer, and as I explain in more depth in the introduction, it has a deeply fraught history. None of this is to argue that specific instances of religious practice cannot be compared, such as the strategies that contemporary queer Muslims, Jews, and Christians use to navigate through homophobic interpretations of the story of Lot/Lut. Rather, it means—as many transgender and queer practitioners of religion already know—that any writing that attempts to give a sum total overview of a specifically designated religion and its relationship to transness and queerness will inevitably center some approaches to that religion and silence others. Such centering and exclusion both reflect and reenact problematic effects of power that are not, in the end, conducive to the expansion of knowledge. They also make living religious traditions into fixed "things" that do not themselves intersect or blend with each other, that do not shift and change over time and between different cultural contexts. There is little room in a model like this for a queer African Christian who practices some aspects of his ancestors' traditions, for example, or a trans Jew who both observes Shabbat and finds their spiritual sustenance in Buddhist meditation, or a *hijra* who serves a Hindu goddess and understands herself as Muslim. Are those readers to learn more about their practices and traditions by reading several different chapters in a world religions book, when those chapters are likely to be silent about how common it is to blend and alter traditions in practice?

Rather than reiterate the world religions model, this book takes a thematic approach that has its roots in phenomenological methods but that moves beyond such methods out of resistance to their characteristic structuralism. A number of more recent textbooks in religious studies have taken a similarly thematic approach, offering in the process a more realistic, more inclusive, and in the end more accurate introduction to the field. Readers wishing to know "what Hinduism says" about queer and trans people will be frustrated by the thematic approach, which insists that there is no single or straightforward answer to that question, nor to any of its close relatives—"What does Christianity say . . . ," "What does Islam say . . . ," and so on. But readers who have tired of the limited representations of religious traditions, queerness, and transness—representations that often entirely erase the existence of queer and trans people in those traditions and focus instead on what straight, cisgender people have to say about them—may find the much more varied stories about religion in this book to be a welcome respite.

Themes, of course, are ideal types and constructed categories. The themes I have chosen for this book—stories, conversations, practices, identities, communities, and politics and power—reflect my own focus on lived religion and my particular interests in how people live out same-sex desire, gender variance, and religion. A more theoretically or theologically focused author would no doubt have come up with different themes; indeed, another scholar of lived religion would also likely have developed a different list. I have attempted, however, to weave other perspectives and themes into the ones highlighted in this book. More highly theoretical approaches make their way into most chapters, as does attention to the arts (part of practice, to be certain, but also of every other theme in the book), bodies, and senses. As I address at some length in the introduction and reiterate throughout the book, each theme intersects with the others, and many of the stories I tell to illustrate the theme of one chapter could have been told with a slightly different focus to illustrate the theme of another. In the end, then, the goal of this book—as in all of my teaching—is to leave readers not with all of their questions answered but with all of their answers questioned. In the process, I hope that those who read this book, regardless of their level of existing background in religious studies, queer and transgender studies, or even queer and transgender studies in religion, will come away from it with new perspectives, new tools, and most importantly, new questions.

TEACHING THE BOOK

Queer Religiosities is designed for use in both lower-division and upper-division undergraduate courses, as well as in graduate teaching. At the lower-division level it may be fruitfully combined with other introductory books in survey courses on such topics as religion, gender, and/or sexuality. At the upper-division level, where I have taught my own Queer Religiosities course for nearly two decades, the book can either serve as a foundational text for explorations of transgender and queer studies in religion or it can complement other sources in an advanced engagement with a variety of approaches to the study of religion, gender, and sexuality. At the graduate level, it provides grounding in important and increasingly popular subfields that are not typically a mandatory part of the curriculum, and it can provide a framework for graduate students in the fields of transgender and queer studies in religion as they develop their own knowledge base and interests and as they begin to think about teaching in these areas. The bibliography at the end may be useful for designing doctoral exam reading lists.

The book contains several tools of which teachers—and students, whether in the classroom or of life in general—should be aware. There is a glossary in the back, and all terms included there are in boldface when they first appear in the book. Each chapter ends with fact-based study questions, which help students to review the chapter, and more expansive, often applied, discussion questions. The former can be helpful in assessing students' comprehension of the readings, while the latter can be worked into out-of-class assignments and in-class activities to solidify and deepen students' understanding of the concepts covered in each chapter through application and analysis. Each chapter also concludes with a short list of recommended texts for further reading, drawn generally from the texts mentioned in the chapters. While some readers may pounce eagerly on these lists, others will not. Teachers who wish to encourage their students to read more expansively might consider an assignment asking students to engage with one or more of the works in these lists; alternatively, the book can be paired with selections from these lists in class reading assignments in order to expose students directly to research in the field. Finally, the appendices to the book also include an annotated filmography. There is a plethora of films available on transgender and queer studies in religion, most of them documentary but some of them fiction, and I hope that this filmography will assist teachers in selecting the right films for their students' interests and their own pedagogical goals.

I find these thriving new subfields to be enriching and exciting; I hope you do too. Welcome to the profoundly queer and genderqueer world of studying religion.

NOTE

1. I owe my awareness of this topic to the work of Danielle Dempsey, and am grateful for the education I've received from her in this area.

Author's Acknowledgments

This book was composed on occupied land; as a settler and the descendant of a long line of settlers in North America, I acknowledge my debt and responsibility to the ancestral and contemporary caretakers of the land and to all Native peoples. The following is the acknowledgment of land collectively developed for those of us who work at UC Riverside, and used here with permission:

> In the spirit of Rupert and Jeanette Costo's founding relationship to our campus, we would like to respectfully acknowledge and recognize our responsibility to the original and current caretakers of this land, water and air: the Cahuilla, Tongva, Luiseño, and Serrano peoples and all of their ancestors and descendants, past, present and future. Today this meeting place is home to many Indigenous peoples from all over the world, including UCR faculty, students, and staff, and we are grateful to have the opportunity to live and work on these homelands.

Queer Religiosities is indebted to many of my students and colleagues over the years. I began teaching the course with the same title in 2002, and I'm grateful to the sociology department at UC Santa Barbara for supporting its initial iteration. I've taught the class a total of nine times so far, at UCSB, Whitman College, and UC Riverside, and I've learned an enormous amount from all of the students I've had in the class over the years. I'm profoundly grateful for all of the ways in which my students have taught and continue to teach me.

At UCR, I've had the pleasure of learning with a number of graduate students and advanced undergrads who have interests in transgender and queer studies in religion. Thanks to Danielle Dempsey, Kathryn Phillips, Jessica Rehman, Aaron Brown, Allie Arend, Kori Pacyniak, Tessa Harmon,

Alina Pokhrel, J Selke, Kimberly Diaz, Hannah Snavely, Riley Leight, Lucas Lopez, and Lupe Palos—among others!—for always teaching me new ideas and perspectives. Adam Tyson did an independent study with me that focused on queer and transgender studies in Islam, and brought to my attention a number of resources I hadn't yet encountered. Thanks, Adam!

I'm also grateful for the support and insights of the "Undisciplined Normativities" research group in queer and transgender studies in religion at UCR. I especially want to name those who were most heavily involved in the group during its first and second years, when I was researching and writing this book: Allie Arend, Aaron Brown, Danielle Dempsey, Bárbara Navaza, Kathryn Phillips, Sherine Hafez, Tammy Ho, Wesley Leonard, Kori Pacyniak, Taylor Riley, Patricia Sazani, and Andrea Smith. I am still overawed by the opportunity to participate in a research group on queer and trans studies in religion, and I'm so grateful to all of you for making it happen. You've all taught me a great deal over the course of the past three years, and much of what you've taught me has ended up in this book.

This project was originally Sarah Stanton's brainchild. She approached me many years ago to write a textbook on queer studies in religion, and while I was interested I was also overwhelmed with other projects. She kept gently nudging me, and eventually we worked out a timeline that we could both manage. Sadly, that timeline was lengthy enough that Sarah had left Rowman & Littlefield for another position by the time the book was completed. Were it not for her, though, *Queer Religiosities* "the book" would never have become a reality. I am grateful to Rolf Janke, who took over from Sarah when she left, for his ongoing encouragement and for his patience in allowing me ample time for revisions. When his time at Rowman was also ended, Natalie Mandziuk saw the book through to completion and Alden Perkins handled the final details with aplomb. Extensive comments from my friend and colleague Erin Runions and from an anonymous reviewer also contributed enormously to the final product. All remaining errors and lacunae I have managed to create entirely on my own.

My greatest debt in writing this book is to the generations of colleagues in gay, lesbian, and more recently queer and trans studies in religion who have gritted their teeth, stuck their necks out, and stood their ground to bring this field into being. No small number of them suffered career setbacks or even the wholesale destruction of their careers in the academy, and serious threats to their health and well-being, because of their dogged commitment not to be silenced or to choose the "safe path" of studying something else. Some of them have served as my mentors and supporters over the years; others I have the honor and privilege of mentoring and supporting in turn, to the best of my abilities. I have learned from all of them regardless of rank, seniority, and position, and have been honored to work side-by-side with them over the years. Not all of them are included in this book, purely because of limitations of space. I wish I could have written about everyone's work, and I apologize to those whose writings have not been directly covered. For whatever it's worth, my own ideas have been formed by the writings of every author in the bibliography, and many more than that since that list, too, is painfully limited due to simple restrictions on space and on human capacity. My friends, you all have my deepest respect and gratitude, and this book is dedicated to you.

As I was finalizing the revisions to this book, news spread of Donald Boisvert's passing. That loss hit hard—Donald was among those in queer studies in religion who welcomed me into the larger field of religious studies as a new colleague rather than an aberration. That welcome meant the world, and Donald was among my touchstones in those early years during and after graduate school. We keep losing our elders before they even really get to become elders. May the day come when the battles against homophobia, transphobia, sexism, racism, and so many other sources of marginalization ease up and we can all not just survive but thrive.

My work benefits the most from my embeddedness in family, both family of origin and chosen family. This book is also dedicated to my dad, Wayne Wilcox, who died as I was preparing to write it. I learned to teach by watching, talking with, and listening to both him and my mom, Margaret Wilcox. Though both worked for research universities, both put teaching first as I do. I began teaching simultaneously with my brother, Wynn Gadkar-Wilcox. I've learned alongside and very much from him as a teacher, and also from my sister-in-law Sujata Gadkar-Wilcox (teaching runs in the family!). An drea Fazel and Lynnette Hawkins are stalwart friends (and also educators!) who've walked through life with me for more years than any of us care to count at this point in time, and I'm always grateful for their love and support. And Nicole Pitsavas, the love of my life, is always there for me through it all—I am forever grateful. Cathy Albanese taught me always to thank my four-legged family as well: Tukéenen, whom we lost just as this book was going to press, Max, Raven, Kestrel, and the equine family members Diamond and Lily. They keep me sane, if somewhat sleep deprived, and remind me that there is more to life than work—a lesson I need to learn repeatedly.

A tip of the forever-broken heart to the child and the dogs who are lost but not forgotten.

Introduction

As Cherokee **Two-Spirit** scholar Qwo-Li Driskill notes, citing Miami and Shawnee scholar Malea Powell, "Theory and scholarship are always stories about how the world works."[1] Feminist scholar Adrienne Rich points out that the stories others tell can have a profound impact on us: "When someone with the authority of a teacher, say, describes the world and you are not in it," she writes, "there is a moment of psychic disequilibrium, as if you looked into a mirror and saw nothing."[2] Stories, as we'll see in chapter 1, can make the world, unmake it, and remake it in a different form. They can erase people, places, and events or add them in, elevate or downplay their importance, retell or reinterpret them. We all know this, or we wouldn't speak up so loudly—sometimes—when someone gets a story about us wrong.

This book is a series of stories about how the world works, woven together from the stories others have told about the stories that still *others* have told to *them*. These are stories about religion, same-sex desire, and **gender** variance, but they're also stories about how thinking about things from new angles—telling stories from a new starting point, for instance, or shifting the protagonist—can significantly change the plot. Learning to do **transgender** and queer studies in religion means learning to ask new questions, to notice what we're taking for granted and wonder why, to trace the lightning pathways of power and privilege through unfamiliar territory illuminated only in fragments, and to find new stories along the route.

Since even categories can tell stories—lumping a world of differences, disagreements, and even warfare into a single category of "Christian," for instance, or dividing **sex** and gender each into only two possibilities—the stories in this book trace a set of carefully chosen themes, avoiding older tendencies to name religions, sexualities, and genders as restricted sets of "isms" and "ities." This is not a book about "What Islam (or Judaism, or

1

Buddhism) says about homosexuality and transgenderism," for several reasons. First, the terms *homosexuality* and *transgenderism* are contested. Many people consider them offensive, words made up by outsiders to describe an identity or a community as a disease. Some people do claim these words for themselves, but many others reject them and choose less medicalized terms that describe their identities as part of whole people—"queer person," "gay man," "transgender woman," "nonbinary human being," and the like. Still others find the terms and the ideas they reference to be completely irrelevant to their lives.

Second, as a former colleague of mine is fond of saying, religions can't talk.[3] "Islam," "Judaism," and "Buddhism" say nothing about anything! But people, texts, communities, traditions, practices, arts, histories—*those* may have things to say. Once we're thinking about such a wide range of sources, we can also understand that there's no singular representative for any religion. In fact, sometimes the very idea that such a wide range of practices and beliefs all count as the same religion is a recent development—like the idea that many of the religions of India can be understood as a single religion, "Hinduism," an idea and a name that were invented by the British during their colonization of South Asia. Even in a religion like Roman Catholic Christianity, which has a single figure (the pope) as its official leader, "what Catholicism says" about anything can range from what a specific pope thought to the varied opinions of Catholic theologians to the lived realities of everyday Catholics in places as varied as São Paulo, Manila, and Montréal and time periods from the first century of the Common Era (CE) to the present. Any story about religion, then, is bound to be partial. Stories that present themselves as partial at least help you to understand what they are and aren't saying; stories that are partial but claim to be complete, at least as an overview, make it harder to see what's left out. All too often, among the things that get left out are the lives, even the existence, of same-sex desiring and gender-variant people.

Rather than tell stories about "Hinduism," "Christianity," "Buddhism," "Islam," "Judaism," and the like, or about "homosexuality," "bisexuality," and so on, this book tells stories that come together around themes that are relevant to the lived experiences of same-sex-desiring and gender-variant people, but that are also relevant to many forms of human existence and experience. Like any themes, although these were chosen for a reason, they're also not the only possible choices. They help to tell a fairly broad range of stories about queer and transgender studies in religion, but other themes could tell equally interesting and valuable stories. There are also no clear, unbreachable boundaries between themes. As you'll be able to tell throughout the book, stories that appear in the context of one theme could easily have appeared in another with just a slightly different focus. All of the themes are about stories, yet stories are also a theme. People have conversations about stories and in communities; all of these shape identities; practices may relay stories, bring together communities, form or undo identities, and change politics; and organizations can encompass, foster, resist, or reject any of these processes. As you read through the book, think about how each theme intersects with the others and about what other themes you can see emerging from what you're learning. How else might we tell these stories? What other stories would different themes allow us to tell? What stories would be less obvious within those themes? If "theory and scholarship are always stories about how the world works," what stories does this book tell? What stories remain untold? How will you tell them?

Queer and transgender studies in religion is a field of study, or two closely related fields depending on your perspective, that combine the insights of queer studies, transgender studies, and religious studies in order to gain new perspectives not only on gender, sexuality, and religion but also on less obviously related issues such as the subtle presence of biblical themes in ostensibly secular political debates and the complicated connections between colonialism and gay rights. These three areas of study—religious studies, transgender studies, and queer studies—are grounded in similar understandings of human worlds and lifeways, even as they also have significant differences that allow them to enhance and sometimes also to challenge each other. In this introductory chapter we'll go over each of these fields separately, learning a little about their origins and their core ideas and methods before exploring how they come together in queer and transgender studies in religion.

RELIGIOUS STUDIES

Religious studies is the oldest of the fields that inform transgender and queer studies in religion. Yet its history only dates back to approximately the middle of the nineteenth century, and its roots stretch back roughly one to two hundred years farther. There's no established single origin for religious studies, but it began to grow out of two developments in European cultures: the Protestant Reformation and the rise of European colonialism.

The major split in Western Christianity that was initiated by Martin Luther is known as the Protestant Reformation, so named because people who left the Roman Catholic Church to join the new religious movement did so in *protest* against and to *reform* various Catholic ideas and practices. As the movement became more powerful it experienced more and more concerted resistance, sometimes even violence, from Catholic leaders, rulers, and laypeople; Protestants sometimes responded with or initiated similar violence. Moreover, Protestant-Catholic tensions quickly became tied to other struggles for power on the continent, with rulers picking religious sides strategically as they angled for more land, wealth, and power. The bloodshed led some thinkers to plead for recognition of the similarities between the two religions—after all, these peacemakers argued, both are Christian.

Many of these thinkers were part of an intellectual movement in Europe known as the Enlightenment. At its most radical, Enlightenment thought stressed the equality of all human beings, although all too quickly cultural biases, greed, and political power plays led many to create exceptions to this rule. "All men are created equal," reads the US Declaration of Independence, which was powerfully influenced by the Enlightenment. Yet only white males who owned land were allowed voting rights in the early republic, and those of African descent could be enslaved. Native Americans, Africans and African Americans, and others whose ancestors were not European found themselves quickly defined out of the seemingly expansive equality of much of Enlightenment thought through scientific racism, which sought supposedly scientific proof of the inequality of people of color to white people. If all men were created equal, this backward reasoning went, but people of color were obviously not equal, since some were enslaved and others were being systematically deprived of their lands as well as their lives, their health, their rights, and even their history and culture, then people of color must not be men.

This logic tied directly into—in fact, often existed to support—the growing European colonial enterprise through the eighteenth and nineteenth centuries. Its legacy lives on in contemporary racism, neocolonialism, and ongoing **settler colonialism**. As Europe's population expanded and its rulers built increasingly powerful military forces, trading relationships—however unequal—with countries in Asia and northern Africa turned into full-blown colonization. Extracting increasing amounts of resources from these countries, and eventually taking over their governments and their lands, European governments created empires that stretched across the globe. In their race for ever-greater wealth and ever more land, they crossed oceans and deserts and found lands and peoples they had never known of before—and they occupied them too. While the more radical forms of Enlightenment thought would have argued (and did sometimes argue) for egalitarian relationships with these peoples, both existing cultural biases and the lure of wealth and power overwhelmed such arguments. Perspectives like scientific racism shored up ideas that colonized peoples were unable to rule themselves and that they needed the "parental" guidance of Europeans for their own good.

While women of color fared no better than men, and gender-variant people often fared worst of all under these systems, white women at least had their ancestral origin—increasingly called their race—in their favor. Yet here, too, while some radical Enlightenment thinkers argued that all *humans* were created equal and that white women lacked only access to education in order to become the intellectual equals of white men, all too quickly ideas about sex and gender shut down such progressive perspectives on gender equality. Science had a role to play here, too, since by the nineteenth century some (male) scientists were opining that because the human body contains a finite amount of blood, educating women would make them infertile. Sending too much blood to the brain by encouraging women to think, they argued, would deprive their wombs of blood and prevent them from bearing children. Not only was this perspective a clear example of scientists grasping for evidence to support cultural biases, just like with scientific racism, but it also assumed that bearing children was the most important function for all women.

So where does religion come in to these intellectual developments? Recall that Enlightenment thinkers were arguing, at least in principle, for the equality of all human beings. Some of them were trying to convince Protestants and Catholics that they were more alike than different, since they were all Christians (even though each group tended to flatly deny that the other could possibly be Christian). Some went so far as to argue that Judaism, whose members had long suffered under severe repression in many Christian European countries and had even been forced to leave or convert to Christianity in Spain, Portugal, and some of their colonies, was also a religion, and that it might even be equal to Christianity. For most Christians at the time, the claims made by these thinkers, especially those of the Haskalah, or Jewish Enlightenment, were nothing short of blasphemy. Furthermore, Christian missionaries frequently traveled together with or even in advance of military colonial forces, and Christianity was often used for colonial functions ranging from ideological pacification to outright cultural and physical genocide. But while the Enlightenment ideal of equality for all was slow to catch on, especially among white, Christian men, the idea that at least some subset of human societies around the planet had something called religion that could be identified and even compared began to take root. It was especially attractive to two groups of people: scholars and Christian missionaries, some of whom were one and the same.

When Christians thought about other religions, they had traditionally divided those "others" into three categories: those they thought were worshipping false gods, whom they usually termed *pagans* or *heathens*, from Latin and English words for rural people; those they thought were worshipping the Christian god falsely, whom they termed *heretics*; and those who claimed to worship the same god and recognized Jesus as a historical religious leader, but denied him the status of Christ—the Anointed One—and savior of humankind. The latter groups, mostly Jews and Muslims, were labeled with various epithets over the years but often were treated by Christians as special categories, either especially close kin to Christians because they worshipped the same god, or especially evil because Christians believed that Jews and

Muslims had had the opportunity to embrace Christianity and had turned it down. Sometimes there has been a fourth category for those whom Christians believed to be worshipping Satan, and sometimes the lines have blurred between those whom Christians have deemed to be devil worshippers and some of these other categories. At times in Christian history, for example, pagans have been accused of worshipping the devil; at times heretics have been accused at least of being misled by him; and at times Christians have accused both Jews and Muslims of being in league with Satan.

For Christian missionaries, whose main task has traditionally been to bring Christianity to non-Christians, these categories have directed both where they focus their efforts and how they do so. Those people deemed to be worshipping false gods, for instance, might be seen as good prospects for learning about the deity whom Christians consider to be the true god; on the other hand, those in league with Satan may be much more challenging, even dangerous, to approach, and those whom Christians believe have already rejected Christ may not seem worth the trouble of approaching again. But an understanding of religion as a shared human phenomenon, one that can not only be understood but even be compared with other religions—that idea offered missionaries an important tool for their work. If they could under-stand the religions they considered false, they believed, then they could speak more convincingly to the followers of those religions by discrediting them and proving the superiority of Christianity. Soon the project of studying and comparing religions was driven by questions like "What is this religion's Bible?" and "Who is this religion's Jesus?"

Meanwhile, scholars—many of them from Christian backgrounds if not practicing Christians themselves—were asking similar questions for different reasons. The nineteenth century was an era of universalizing structure and order in the European intellectual world. This was the time period that gave us Linnean classification, in which every single being that scientists consider to be living has its own category, its place in that ordered system delineated by kingdom, phylum, class, order, family, genus, and species (and, in some cases, subspecies, breed, or—as with humans—race). Charles Darwin's ideas about evolution were sparking intellectual explorations into other contexts where his theories might apply, and scholars interested in human cultures were offering up theories of social Darwinism, which argued that entire peoples and cultures evolved in the same ways that different species did, adapting to their environments or dying out. Some cultures seemed to these scholars to be destined to die out, and some scholars even tried to help them along in that process; other cultures, they thought, had already mostly died out, or at least had degenerated, and still others were evolutionary remnants from earlier times, akin to prehistoric fishes found deep in isolated oceanic trenches. At the top of the social Darwinist evolutionary tree, in these theo-ries that often went hand in hand with scientific racism, were of course the northern and western European cultures. Nonetheless, scholars of human cultures followed in the footsteps of their biologist colleagues, seeking to create an evolutionary tree of humanity by studying the various cultures that they believed to be forerunners of their own, in their eyes the most highly evolved culture. This project inevitably included religion.

With Christianity, and often the highly text-focused Protestant branch of that religion, as their model, these early scholars of comparative religion set off in search of the ancient scriptures of each religion. Where ancient scriptures did not readily present themselves, as in oral cultures, the religion was deemed less highly evolved; where they did, the scriptures were avidly studied and contemporary societies judged by the fidelity of their adherence to those scriptures. As you might imagine, most were found wanting. This was part of the story of **Orientalism**, which was a central pillar of European colonialism: Whereas many cultures in North America, South America, and sub-Saharan Africa were simply considered unevolved due to their common reliance on oral rather than written tradition for passing on their cultural heritage and their histories, those in North Africa, southeastern Europe, and Asia (and a few in the Americas) were considered precursors to Europe's current greatness.

European intellectual and military leaders began to refer to these cultures, mostly located to the east of Europe, as *Oriental*, an older word for "Eastern." Once lumped together in this way they could be treated as a sort of cultural Linnaean genus, studied both separately and together but always with the understanding that they were at their roots similar or the same. By the same token, the scholars and artists who came to be called Orientalists often understood these varied cultures to be very different from, even actively opposed to, Occidental ("Western") cultures. Such perspectives still shape the world today through Orientalist analyses like Samuel Huntington's ideas about the "clash of civilizations" between the so-called West and East—ideas that regularly present themselves as unquestioned truth in the speeches of politicians and intellectuals alike. [4]

Orientalist scholars in the nineteenth century told a story about colonized cultures in North Africa and Asia that went something like this: Once proud and powerful nations with superior technologies and highly developed intellectual traditions, including religious systems, each of these cultures eventually fell into disarray, usually due to self-indulgence, and declined to the point of confusion and chaos. Europe, clearly in its cultural prime as far as these scholars were concerned, had a duty to support these fallen cultures and to bring the unevolved ones up to speed. In other words, many Europeans and their descendants around the world believed they bore what the English poet Rudyard Kipling called "the white man's burden": the solemn responsibility to conquer and control the rest of the world for its own good. Christian missionaries generally agreed, although they were saving souls for

Christ, not societies for civilization, and it's within this nexus that religious studies came into existence.

The comparative study of religion as a human phenomenon, known in its current form as religious studies, was developed by philosophers who believed in a shared human nature; by scholars of language called philologists, who were fascinated by ancient texts from other civilizations; and by theologians who were curious about the beliefs of other peoples. Many were Orientalists. As academic specialties developed and divided from one another, archaeologists, anthropologists, sociologists, and historians joined in. Early forms of the field clearly showed its colonial and Christian roots, as well as the influence of nineteenth-century Western science in its persistent comparison of religions with an eye to determining which was the most advanced. As you might imagine, Christianity—and especially Protestant Christianity—reliably came out on top.

But another aspect of the Orientalist movement in European thought, influenced by the Romantic period in the first part of the nineteenth century, lauded at least historical and sometimes even contemporary aspects of some North African, southeastern European, and Asian cultures. As Orientalist perspectives came to characterize some attitudes toward the indigenous peoples of North and South America and some parts of the Pacific Islands, this romantic admiration extended to their cultures as well. Not that admiration was necessarily beneficial to those being admired; it often led to other forms of colonialism and to the theft of cultural heritage. But this admiration also began to change the Western academic study of religion. From a goal of conversion and colonization began to develop a goal of cultural sharing—a more global version of the Enlightenment plea for Protestants and Catholics to stop killing each other. In service to this new goal, as intellectual historian Tomoko Masuzawa has written, was developed the idea of "world religions."[5]

The world religions concept began to be promoted especially publicly with the first World's Parliament of Religions, held as part of the 1893 Chicago World's Fair. Represented at the parliament were most of the traditions we would name today under the "world religions" rubric: Christianity, of course, in its Protestant, Catholic, and Eastern Orthodox forms; Judaism; Islam; Hinduism; Buddhism; and Jainism. The Baha'is were also represented, as well as some newer religious movements developed largely in the United States, including Christian Science and Spiritualism. Sikhs were conspicuously absent, and it may be worth noting that Islam was represented by a white convert to that religion. Indigenous religious traditions, on the other hand, were deemed "culture" or "natural history," not religion, and were located in zoo-like exhibits where indigenous peoples from around the world were represented "in their natural habitat," as the colonizers understood it. Colonial logics and scientific racism were amply evident at the Chicago

World's Fair, and they continued to have a major influence on the academic study of religion for decades to come; some would say they still do. The World's Parliament of Religions, for its part, was revived on its hundredth anniversary in 1993 with broader representation of different religious traditions, and it continues to meet today.

Religious studies, then, has its roots in intellectual and political developments that many religious studies scholars today disagree with and even dedicate themselves to working against. And while these roots continue to inspire debates among scholars, such as those over how the descriptive/ analytical/historical branches of the field relate to specialties like theology and ethics, they've also been left behind in much the same way as other intellectual traditions and social movements have left behind disproven or unsavory aspects of their own histories. What does the field of religious studies have to offer today?

Although we still debate over how to define what it is we study, many religious studies scholars today recognize that this debate happens because the idea of religion as a universal human phenomenon that can be compared across cultures is a **social construct**. The concept of **social construction** is one that religious studies shares with gender and sexuality studies, of which queer studies and transgender studies are two parts; all of these areas of study use the methods of many different scholarly fields—like history, literary studies, linguistics, art history, anthropology, and others—to study an aspect of human experience that these fields consider not to be a part of human essence—not inborn—but an aspect of human culture. But when we say that religion, gender, or sexuality is a social construct, we don't mean that it's not real. Theories about social construction, also called **constructivist theories**, tell us that something socially constructed can still be very real in its effects; this is one of the most important and most commonly misunderstood aspects of this school of thought. For example, the idea that there are deep and fundamental differences between all humans with penises and all humans with vaginas (and that no humans have any combination of these two organs) is a social construct; a social and cultural choice has been made to divide humans along this particular binary set of categories and to assign all kinds of other traits to them—such as aggression, compassion, strength, weakness, intellect, and stupidity—based on that division. But sexism, which is one effect of the social construct of gender, is very real and is visible in everything from differential health outcomes between men and women to the persistent gap in earning power between them. The relative invisibility of **intersex**, transgender, **genderqueer**, and **nonbinary** people, and the violence that attends many of their lives, is further evidence of the realities created by social constructs. If sex and gender are conceived of as binary models (males and females, men and women) in which sex predicts gender (all males are men and all females are women) then there's no space for anyone who doesn't fit neatly within that culturally constructed binary.

Sex and Gender: What's the Difference?

Sex and *gender* are terms that have come to be used interchangeably in much of anglophone popular culture, as though *gender* is the polite word for *sex*. But they have importantly different meanings. Sex refers to embodiment and is described by words like *female*, *male*, and *intersex* (having physical aspects of both femaleness and maleness). For some people, *transexual* is also a word that describes sex. The sex of most human beings is assigned by various authorities at or even before birth, usually through observation of genitalia or genetic testing. Some intersex newborns are still forced to endure literal sex assignment, as they are subjected to genital surgery to make their bodies conform to the contemporary scientific expectation that humans (should) come in only two sexes.

Gender refers to identity and sometimes to expression (since people don't always express their gender identity publicly), and is described by words like *woman*, *man*, *feminine*, *masculine*, *genderqueer* (combining aspects of multiple genders), *nonbinary* (refusing the binary of "man" versus "woman" or "feminine" versus "masculine"), **agender** (not identifying with gender at all), *transgender* (referring typically to someone who identifies with a different gender from the one they were assigned at birth based on their perceived embodiment, sometimes including people who are genderqueer, nonbinary, or agender), and **cisgender** (referring to someone who does identify with the gender they were assigned at birth based on their perceived embodiment). *Two-Spirit* is a term that some Native American and First Nations people use to describe both gender variance and same-sex desire, alongside a commitment to their ancestral traditions and their Native identities.

As a result of assignment to a specific sex at or before birth, in many cultures (but, importantly, not all) gender is also assigned at or even before birth. When a doctor or midwife pronounces the sex of a fetus or an infant, for instance, most relatives immediately assign gender and begin calling the fetus or the child "her" or "him"; the so-called gender prediction kits that you can buy over the counter in places like the United States are basically kits for assigning a specific sex and gender to a fetus based on the presence or absence of a Y chromosome. And in most countries today, transgender people seeking gender affirmation treatment must have their gender officially assigned to them by a psychological or psychiatric authority figure who writes the medically required letter of approval for treatment. What appears to many people to be basic biological fact turns out to be a powerful network of social constructs, reinforced by both medical authorities and marketing directors. See the section on gender and sexuality studies for more information.

To understand the concept of religion as a social construct is to understand that *the idea of religion as a universally shared, identifiable, and comparable aspect of human culture is invented*. This is not the same as saying that individual religions are invented, that people make up beliefs and then try to fool others into believing them. Religious studies scholars generally don't weigh in on whether or not a particular way of understanding the world is true. Instead, what we're focusing on here is the social construction of the idea that there is a thing we can call *religion* in every human culture, and that this thing called religion is similar enough from one culture to the next that it warrants being called by the same word and it can be compared across cultures. That idea is invented. How do we know? First of all, we can trace the process of invention. The word *religion* is older than the eighteenth century, but its use in the "world religions" sense is a modern development. Second, there are languages in various parts of the world that have no word that can translate *religion*. If religion is a universal human phenomenon that takes comparable forms around the world and across history, then every human culture must recognize something like religion. But the concept doesn't even exist in some cultures. No wonder even scholars can't agree on a definition! If the concept of religion is a social construct, though, then we don't need to try to find the ultimate, perfectly accurate definition. Instead, it may work better to determine how the word is being used in the specific contexts we study—or whether it's being used at all. Understanding that your subject of study is a social construct can be challenging when it forces you to realize that you're not tracking down some shared aspect of humanity on the basis of which we can all get along and bring about world peace, but it can also be freeing when you let go of the need to find those similarities and focus instead on specific cases of human engagement with the world beyond the human, or the sacred, whatever that may be.

Understanding religion, then, like understanding gender and sexuality, means accepting that even the terminology we use is a tool to help us understand, not a fixed description of a universal truth. It means doing our best to comprehend a person's or a group's understanding and experience of the world around them from the inside. Writing in the early twentieth century, the Dutch scholar Gerardus van der Leeuw described a paired approach to understanding religion in this way, using the terms **epoché** and **Verstehen**. The first term, *epoché*, is a Greek word that means "suspension." Van der

Leeuw used it to mean a suspension of our own beliefs when we study those of someone else. He felt that it wasn't very helpful for religious studies scholars to respond to something they learn about a religion by thinking, "Well, of course *that* can't be true." Practicing *epoché*, importantly, doesn't mean eradicating our own perspectives on the world and accepting those we study. That would be pretty confusing if we studied more than one religion! It doesn't mean that religious studies scholars have to be atheists or agnostics, either—after all, those too are forms of belief. Some scholars also argue that practicing *epoché* doesn't mean setting aside our values. It simply means that in order to proceed to van der Leeuw's second step, *Verstehen*, we need to temporarily suspend our own belief or disbelief.

With our own understandings of how the world works temporarily suspended, van der Leeuw thought, we can better approach a deep understanding of the religion we're attempting to study. *Verstehen* is a German word meaning "understanding," and van der Leeuw thought of it as a form of *empathetic* understanding. More than just intellectual comprehension, empathetic understanding implies that scholars should try not only to comprehend what those who practice other religions *think*, but also to sense what they *feel*.

One of the founders of a twentieth-century school of thought called the phenomenology of religion, van der Leeuw was particularly interested in describing and classifying religious phenomena. In a way, his work and the work of other phenomenologists of religion was similar to that of Carl Linnaeus and his intellectual descendants in its focus on sorting and organizing data. Today, religious studies scholars still rely on approaches like van der Leeuw's *epoché* and *Verstehen*, but they use their empathetic understanding to help them analyze what they learn in light of larger aspects of human experience like politics, literature, history, art, power, and, of course, gender and sexuality.

There are differences of opinion among religious studies scholars about whether their analysis should be directed at understanding problems solely in the human realm or whether it can also address questions about the world beyond the human. Some scholars term the first approach *nonconfessional* and the second approach *confessional*. Although its history goes back to the nineteenth century and it now appears in scholarly settings around the world, the divide between confessional and nonconfessional approaches to religious studies seems to have taken its sharpest form in the United States, where two Supreme Court decisions in the early 1960s affirmed that the comparative (that is, nonconfessional) study of religion could—and perhaps even should—be taught in public schools, but simultaneously clarified that the First Amendment to the US Constitution forbade those same schools from mandating or supporting religious indoctrination or practice. This decision deepened the divide between confessional and nonconfessional religious studies in the country and fully separated the two from each other in all public schools, including public colleges and universities. Since most scholars hold college and university positions, these court decisions impacted the shape of the field itself in the United States.

More recently, a growing number of scholars have been arguing that the stark separation of nonconfessional from confessional studies of religion imposes its own worldview on scholars while claiming to be neutral. They suggest that what is sometimes called methodological atheism forces all scholars who pursue work outside of theology and ethics to separate their academic work from the rest of their lives. Given that more white people than people of color are atheists, some have also pointed out that methodological atheism may privilege the perspectives of white scholars and marginalize scholars of color and those from the Global South/Global East. This sharp divide places intellectual historians who study (but don't develop) theology and ethics, and ethicists who don't work within a specific religious tradition, in a gray area. Are they confessional or nonconfessional scholars? Should it matter?

Debates over the confessional/nonconfessional divide in religious studies edge over into debates over what some scholars call normative scholarship. When used in this sense, *normative* means something like "based in values or norms," and this debate stems from older arguments over the concept of objectivity. In popular usage, *objective* often means "fair" or "unbiased." When used in the context of scholarship, it means something closer to "neutral." People who pursue objective scholarship as a goal usually do so because they believe that a scholar's own perspectives can lead that person to false conclusions, and that only by setting aside those perspectives and working from a neutral, in some ways blank, space can a scholar discover the truth. Sound a bit like *epoché*? It should—they're similar and closely related ideas.

The opposite of objective is *subjective*, literally meaning "involving the subject, or the self," but often used to mean "biased" or "not based on fact and reason." But many feminist, antiracist, and anticolonial scholars have argued that it's impossible to remove all of one's assumptions and to set aside all of one's beliefs. From this perspective, both objectivity and *epoché* are impossible, and those who believe they've achieved either of these ideals are simply denying their own perspectives, not suspending them. Instead, these scholars have suggested, we should each pay close attention to how our learning and our analyses are impacted by our perspectives on the world. We should make these impacts, and the strengths and limitations that they bring with them, clear when we communicate our analyses. Taking things even further, many of these same scholars argue that in some scholarship, objectivity can serve as an excuse for standing by and refusing to take sides in the face of injustice. These scholars, including most scholars of gender and sexuality studies, not only believe that objectivity is impossible, they believe that scholars have a responsibility to do normative scholarship in the interest of making the world a more just and equal place.

While many scholars who take a nonconfessional approach to religious studies continue to see normative and confessional scholarship as one and the same thing, and to separate themselves from both, many others are exploring and exploding the boundaries between these approaches. Their work brings us back to van der Leeuw with questions. Is *epoché* the same as objectivity? If so, is it valuable? Is it even possible? Can we use an understanding of knowledge (also called an **epistemology**) that's based on social location to achieve *Verstehen* by understanding how our own world concepts and experiences shape our engagement with those of others? After all, *Verstehen* speaks of understanding, not agreeing with—of empathy, not sympathy. Gaining an empathetic understanding of (not sympathy or agreement with) world concepts that lead to gross injustices like colonialism, racism, transphobia, and genocide may be the only effective way to work toward halting such ills in the world. In most areas of gender and sexuality studies—including transgender and queer studies—knowledge isn't generated just for its own sake. In these fields, the purpose of scholarship is to change the world for the better. For scholars of queer and transgender studies in religion, the line between confessional and nonconfessional approaches to religious studies may be blurrier than it is for many of their colleagues. *Epoché* may need to be a partial practice, in which we don't suspend our beliefs but rather highlight them so we can understand their impact on our perception of other practices and beliefs and thereby understand those practices and beliefs better on their own terms. *Verstehen* may be the most important aspect of religious studies methodology for such scholars; indeed, it might even be one of the contributions religious studies can make to other fields.

GENDER AND SEXUALITY STUDIES

The field of gender and sexuality studies has its roots in feminist and women's studies and in feminist social movements from the nineteenth century onward. Although much of mainstream feminism in the late nineteenth and early twentieth centuries was rooted in an **essentialist** perspective that understood gender to be based in an innate biological or psychological essence of men and women and that accepted but revalued cultural assertions about women's gentle and nurturing natures, this approach to feminist activism and scholarship was also challenged nearly from the beginning by more radical feminist perspectives from Quakers, Marxists, women of color, and anticolonial activists and thinkers in places like Egypt and Japan, who linked sex-based oppression to class oppression, racial oppression, colonialism, and empire. Analyses that we today term intersectional have a long, but some-times erased, history in feminist thought.

With the work of French existentialist Simone de Beauvoir, constructivist ideas about gender began to become more established. Beauvoir famously wrote that "one is not born, but rather becomes, a woman."[6] In Beauvoir's analysis, a baby who's born with an identifiably female body is assigned by members of society like doctors, parents, teachers, and friends to the catego-ry of "girl," with pronouns like "she" and "her," and learns how to inhabit that category from her interactions with other people. Through lessons from her family, her friends, and her culture, she learns to be a woman. From Beauvoir's perspective, then, women are not naturally nurturing, soft, kind, gentle, reticent, strong, or anything else. They are female-bodied people who are taught from birth to be the way their culture expects female-bodied peo-ple to be.

Published in French in 1949 and in English in 1952, Beauvoir's work initially drew a limited response outside of philosophical circles. It slowly caught on, though, and it became an important theoretical work for many in the growing feminist movements of the 1960s and 1970s. As part of those movements, some feminists—especially but not solely women—began rais-ing questions about how women are represented in educational materials. Like civil rights and Black Power activists, like members of the Chicano Movement and the American Indian Movement, and as members of these various movements, feminists began to point out that textbooks, course mate-rials, and established canons of literary, artistic, and philosophical works focused exclusively or nearly exclusively on white men. Jewish activists pointed out that when Jews (again, mostly Jewish men) were actually in-cluded in positive ways, their Jewishness was often erased; they too were invisible in the texts. As the gay and lesbian, and eventually the bisexual and transgender, movements developed, they noticed that most or all of the peo-ple in the textbooks and the canons were also heterosexual and cisgender—or were represented that way. All of these groups began to push back, resulting in the founding of departments and programs in women's studies, Black studies, Chicano studies, Native American studies, Asian American studies, and gay and lesbian studies. In many schools, these departments and pro-grams have developed today into gender and sexuality studies programs and ethnic studies programs, and as these fields have grown they've developed their own interdisciplinary and transdisciplinary methods for studying gen-der, sexuality, race, and ethnicity.

Interdisciplinary or Transdisciplinary?

In the context of academia, a discipline means an area of study, typically one that's widely recognized and characterized by certain accepted methods. Disciplines usually have a focus for their work, but often the methods they use are as central to defining the discipline as the focus, and often the focus is broad. Chemistry, for instance, is a discipline in the natural sciences that focuses on the chemical makeup and structures of the physical world, including the bodies of plants and animals. It uses a variety of techniques grounded in the scientific method, from lab experimentation to advanced imaging to theoretical work to computer simulations and more, to better understand chemical compounds and reactions, and sometimes to create new ones. Sociology is a discipline in the social sciences that focuses on the study of societies, using a variety of quantitative (numbers-based) and qualitative (description-based) research methods to learn more about how societies function and how they impact each other and the individuals and smaller social units (families, communities, and so on) that are part of them. Philosophy is a discipline in the humanities that uses a variety of analytical and historical methods to better understand the work of existing philosophers and to develop new philosophical perspectives in response to contemporary challenges.

But some fields of study, such as ethnic studies, cultural studies, and the like, draw from across these disciplinary boundaries in their methods and sometimes in their focus. When these fields first developed, they were called interdisciplinary, meaning that they worked between the disciplines. Many people still use that word today. Often, though, the word *interdisciplinary* refers to research done by multiple researchers who have each been trained in a different discipline. The researchers themselves aren't interdisciplinary; their collaborative research is. So what should we call entire fields of study that weave together multiple disciplines, in which many scholars are trained in multiple methods? Some people have suggested that the word *transdisciplinary*, which implies bridging across or transcending disciplines, might be a better word for such fields.

Is religious studies a humanities discipline, as it's often categorized? Is it an interdisciplinary field? Is it transdisciplinary? What about gender and sexuality studies—are they a social science, as they are sometimes categorized? Are they interdisciplinary? Transdisciplinary? What do you think? Why?

Initially, many of these fields took a corrective approach. Faced with the near-total erasure of intellectuals, scientists, artists, political leaders, and the like who were women, gay, Native, and/or people of color, many scholars labored to tell a new story by adding the people who were missing. Over time, though, they realized that telling the same story with new characters wasn't enough, because the ways the stories were being told were part of the problem. Remember the passage at the start of this chapter claiming that "theory and scholarship are always stories about how the world works"? Feminist, queer, and ethnic studies scholars realized pretty quickly that they needed to tell new stories, not just to add characters to old stories, and doing that meant creating new theories as well as new scholarship.

Four developments in the late 1980s and early 1990s created crucial turning points in this process. Critical legal studies scholar and critical race theorist Kimberlé Crenshaw coined the term *intersectionality* to describe the analytical approach that feminists of color and antiracist white feminists had been taking for decades, and by naming and describing the approach she encouraged more scholars to use it. Philosopher Judith Butler published her landmark book *Gender Trouble*, which introduced the concept of performativity as a way of thinking about the social construction of gender and opened the door for the development of gender studies. Transgender activists and scholars like Sandy Stone, Leslie Feinberg, Kate Bornstein, and Susan Stryker published articles and books that sparked the transgender rights movement and transgender studies. And literary scholar Teresa de Lauretis coined the term *queer theory* to describe an intersectional and constructivist approach to the study of sexuality, then repudiated the term when it failed to live up to her vision. Yet within a decade of its founding, queer theory had turned in new directions that led it toward what de Lauretis had envisioned after all. Let's take each of these ideas and movements in turn.

Womanism, Feminism, Intersectionality

As we've seen, some feminist thinkers have combined their analyses of sexism with an awareness of class, race, and colonial oppression since the nineteenth century. Those thinkers, though, have often been marginalized by the mainstream of feminist thought and activism. Sometimes this was because they were themselves women of color, working-class women, and/or women from colonized nations—including Native American and First Nations women—and white, elite feminists were often just as susceptible to racist, classist, and nationalist ideas as their antifeminist counterparts. Sometimes even feminists who opposed racism, classism, capitalism, and imperialism worried that their struggle for women's rights was hard enough without having to also battle these social ills. In making this judgment, of course, they were forgetting that women's rights include the right of women to be free from racism, poverty, and colonial appropriation of their lands, bodies, lives, children, and cultures. In both early (nineteenth and early twentieth century) and later (1970s onward) forms of feminist thought and activism, some feminists relied on a perspective of "sisterhood," through which they suggested that women around the world were more alike due to their oppression by men than they were different. All too often these narratives of sisterhood erased the ways that mainstream feminists were complicit in racial, class, and colonial (and as others began to point out, ableist, homophobic, and transphobic) forms of oppression. The prevalence of this narrow focus in the feminist mainstream led scholar and novelist Alice Walker to coin the term *womanist* in her 1984 book of collected writings, *In Search of Our Mothers' Gardens*, and the term came to be used by many women and some men of color—especially but not only African Americans—to describe their inextricably intertwined commitments to racial, class, sexual, and gender justice.

In a series of articles in the late 1980s and early 1990s, critical legal scholar Kimberlé Crenshaw, one of the originators of the school of thought that came to be known as critical race theory, put a name to this longstanding but persistently marginalized method of study: *intersectionality*. The concept of intersectionality relies on a metaphor of social power and privilege traveling in channels, or tracing lines across the social landscape, that intersect with one another. Visually, you can imagine this like a graph with intersecting x, y, and z axes—but with far more than three axes and with intersections in many different places. Another way to imagine intersectionality is the game of pick-up sticks, where a handful of slender sticks is thrown down on a flat surface. The feel or the image of those scattered sticks, overlapping each other every which way, is another way to understand the intersections in intersectionality.

Another important concept for understanding intersectionality is that of unmarked categories. An **unmarked category** is typically the dominant, or assumed, one. For instance, in white-dominant cultures and subcultures, when people describe other people they often include race in the description only if the other person is a person of color; if the other person is white, they'll describe physical attributes like hair color and eye color, but they usually won't say the person is white. Whiteness is the unmarked racial category in white-dominant societies. Likewise, in many cultures heterosexuality is an unmarked category. When was the last time someone told you, "I went to a straight wedding this weekend"? On the other hand, if the two spouses were both men or both women, it wouldn't be unusual for a wedding guest to tell friends or family that they'd been to a gay wedding.

A Riddle

This popular riddle stumps many people because it relies on unmarked categories. Can you figure it out? The answer is at the end of the chapter.

> One wintry night, a man and his son were driving home from an evening event when their car hit a bad patch of ice, slid off the road, and collided with a tree. Both men were injured and were taken to the hospital. The son needed emergency surgery for his injuries. The surgeon rushed into the operating room, ready to get started, looked at the patient, and walked back out, saying, "I can't operate on this man; he's my son."

How is this possible?

Crenshaw explained that an intersectional perspective helps us to understand that when we try to analyze one axis of power—gender, in her example—separately from others like race or class, we end up analyzing only how gender affects the unmarked category. Using her research on legal cases involving violence against cisgender women of color, Crenshaw pointed out that these cases challenged many feminist theories about women's experiences of violence and the strategies needed to prosecute perpetrators in court. Those theories had been developed without an intersectional analysis, and that process had resulted in ideas that fit only the experiences and the cases of middle-class and elite white women. Intersectional scholarship today has also pointed out that similar drawbacks affect scholarship that ignores sexual identity, ability, age, nationality, gender identity and expression, immigration status, and many other factors.

So, does intersectionality mean that we have to somehow study all people with different experiences, and all of the varied axes of power, every time we want to study something? No. It means that when analyzing power—whether through the perspective of sexuality, gender, religion, or something else—we also have to be thinking about the ways that other aspects of power—like ability, class, race, and so on—affect what we're studying. Intersectionality also doesn't mean that we have to study only nondominant groups. After all, the whole point of a concept like unmarked categories is that we tend to ignore the dominant groups *as groups*. White people have a race; middle-class and elite people have a class; males have a sex; straight people have a sexual identity; cisgender people have a gender. The perspective of intersectionality insists that we need to consider the impact of all of these factors, even for dominant groups, in our analyses.

Performativity and the Social Construction of the Body

Judith Butler's work in the late 1980s and the early 1990s, especially her famous book *Gender Trouble*, introduced a new way of thinking about gender as *performative*. Frustrated with the essentialist approaches to gender in most of the feminist work she read in the 1980s but also dissatisfied with the limitations of Beauvoir's approach to constructivism, Butler based her own understanding of gender on theories about language. She drew on the work of mid-twentieth-century philosopher J. L. Austin, who was interested in forms of speech that he called performative—speech that not only said something, it *did* something. A ritual pronouncement, such as "I now pronounce you married," is one example of performative speech. It doesn't just say to the people being addressed, "Hey, you're married!" When spoken by a ritual leader, that sentence *actually marries* the people in question. Before the sentence they were unmarried; after the sentence they were married. Performative speech *does* things. Gender, Butler thought, is like that. So saying that gender is performative isn't the same thing as saying that gender is a performance. That's a common misunderstanding of Butler's ideas, especially because she certainly does say that one enacts gender. But that enactment of gender, importantly, also *does* something: It creates the appearance, the illusion, of a stable, internal, gendered essence. Enacting gender, for Butler, constructs the self.

We also don't enact gender in a vacuum; rather, we replay norms of gender, and, in so doing, most people reinforce those norms. In an article written for *Theatre Journal* a few years before the publication of *Gender Trouble*, Butler likened gender not to a theatrical performance but to a role. A playwright writes the original script and creates the role. The first actor to play that role shapes it in certain ways; perhaps now people think of that character as always dressed in red, or tall, or carrying a flower, or speaking in a particular accent. In following the script, in playing the role, the actor has both perpetuated and altered the role. Likewise, each generation and each person perpetuates but also—sometimes—alters gender norms through repeatedly reenacting them. Each subsequent actor (or person) will be shaped by the role (or the gender norm) and will shape it in turn, and it's in this potential for shaping that the possibility of resistance lies for Butler.

The challenge, though, is that unlike in theater, with gender there is no stage, no sign that one is playing a role. Imagine seeing a friend play a cruel person on stage; after the show you'd probably congratulate your friend on a great acting job. But now imagine that your friend acted cruelly to someone else, with no warning or context, at a party. Wouldn't you want to know what was wrong with your friend? With no stage in sight, when we enact gender roles—when we reiterate and thereby reinforce these norms—we convince others that we're carrying out our gendered nature, our essence. We even convince ourselves, and that's how, in Butler's theories, gender is performative: It makes things. The performative reiteration of gender norms makes social constructs: It makes gender into an essence and it makes the self into a form that is essentially gendered. Through this process, it produces the fervently defended idea that one of the most important differences between human beings lies between their legs, and that human sexes only come in two varieties, despite the widespread presence of intersex people in both historic and contemporary cultures around the world. So Butler, in a way, reverses Beauvoir's form of constructivism. Where Beauvoir argued that people are assigned to a sex at birth and then gender training starts, Butler suggests that the constant performative reiteration of gender norms produces the illusion of binary sex as a central, defining element of humanity—and that illusion is necessary for the assignment of sex to matter, maybe for it to take place at all. It's kind of a chicken-or-egg question—which came first?—but to at least some extent Butler's argument indicates that gender precedes sex.

The performative reiteration of gender norms, for Butler, also creates **heteronormativity**: the cultural assumption that only different-sex desire and eroticism are normal, natural, and beneficial to society. In addition, it defines certain forms of different-sex desire and different-sex sexual activity as "normal," thereby establishing that other forms of different-sex desire and eroticism are not heteronormative. Rooted in a concept that feminist essayist and poet Adrienne Rich dubbed ***compulsory heterosexuality***—a cultural assumption that all people are naturally heterosexual and a cultural insistence that all people should live out that "natural" heterosexuality—heteronormativity relies, like compulsory heterosexuality, on the ideas that human bodies come in only two forms, that those two forms match only two genders that should never be confused or combined with one another, and that those matching bodies and genders complement each other emotionally, physiologically, and even anatomically.

But human beings don't come in only two sexes. Intersex people's bodies express aspects of both femaleness and maleness through chromosomes, hormones, sexual organs, and/or secondary sexual characteristics. During the intense focus on categorizing and classifying that took place in some nineteenth-century intellectual circles, and especially in the natural sciences, scholars claimed that most intersex people (they used the word *hermaphrodites*, which is considered offensive by many intersex people today) were really defective males or females. Over the course of the next century, extensive medical interventions were developed to "fix" these "defects," starting just after birth and often continuing throughout an intersex person's life. Intersex activists have objected strenuously to these interventions, which historically have often been initiated without the knowledge or the informed consent even of an infant's parents, because they are by definition nonconsensual (an infant doesn't have the cognitive development to consent to medical procedures) and because they often cause physical scarring, lifelong pain, and severe emotional trauma. The performative effect of these decades of involuntary surgeries, like the performative effect of enacting gender roles, is to create the appearance that there are only two sexes and only two genders, and never the twain shall meet—except in heterosexual sex.

Queer Theory

The connections that Butler drew between sexuality, bodily sex, and gender made her an important founder not only of the new approach to gender—now a part of gender studies—that developed over the course of the 1990s and subsequent decades, but also of the new approach to sexuality called queer theory and, eventually, queer studies. Gay and lesbian studies had been developing fairly steadily, despite encountering the same sorts of resistance faced by women's studies, Black studies, Chicano/Latino studies, and similar fields over the course of the 1970s and 1980s. But like those fields, it had done a lot of much-needed corrective and additive work—adding gay and lesbian figures to histories, literary canons, theoretical development, and the like. More theoretical and analytical work had been developing all along, as it had in related fields, but it had not been at the core of the scholarship.

What's in a Name? Naming Sexual Identities

People use many different terms to name sexual identities, and some resist using terms because they object to having their desires be made into a part of their identity in the first place. *Straight*, or the more formal *heterosexual*, is a familiar term for many people that refers to those who are solely or predominantly attracted to people of a different sex. In some cultures, people who are attracted to others of the same sex use the term *homosexual*; others find that term to be too medicalizing and consider it offensive. Some use terms like *gay*, which can refer solely to same-sex-attracted men or can refer to same-sex-attracted people of all genders; some women use the term *lesbian*. *Bisexual* is a common word used by people who are attracted to both men and women; those who find "men and woman" to be too restrictive a description of humanity and who object to the binary nature of that description may prefer words like **pansexual**. And it's important not to forget that some people don't experience sexual desire; they identify as **asexual**, sometimes shortened to **ace**. Those who don't experience romantic attraction, who may or may not also be ace, are **aromantic**, or **arrow**. People who are same-sex attracted, attracted to all sexes and genders, asexual, or aromantic; and those who participate in less heteronormative forms of sexual practice such as **BDSM** (bondage, discipline, dominance, submission, and sadomasochism), sometimes use the term *queer*. To some people queer is an all-encompassing term, one that resists boundaries and divisions. To others it's a political term, indicating not only a sexual identity but also a commitment to a progressive or even radical politics of sexuality. Some black queer folks use the term *quare*, and in Latin America *cuir* is increasingly in use as a term that brings together political and sexual expression. Finally, some people prefer descriptions of what they do over names for who they are, using terms like *same-gender loving* or **SGL**.

Around the world, there are many different ways of understanding, conceptualizing, and experiencing desire and sexuality. People may change terms depending on the context, using *gay*, for instance, when communicating with Western nongovernmental organizations (NGOs) or international visitors who may not understand local terms but switching when among friends to a traditional, regional term. Some traditional conceptualizations separate desire from gender; others combine them. While it's important to remember, for instance, that transgender is not a sexual identity, nor does transgender identity predict anything whatsoever about a person's sexuality, some Native people use the term *Two-Spirit* to refer to both their gender and their sexuality (and others use it only to refer to their sexuality).

In February 1990, building from a small amount of theoretical writing that was starting to take an intersectional approach to gay and lesbian studies, literary scholar Teresa de Lauretis organized a conference that she called Queer Theory. The phrase had never been used before. Striking a political tone by joining activists in reclaiming a once-derogatory term, de Lauretis explained that her use of the word *queer* was "intended to mark a certain critical distance" from gay and lesbian studies, to "transgress and transcend . . . or at the very least problematize" the identity-based language of that field. The term was picked up rapidly, especially in literary studies circles, but not—or rather, not initially—in the way de Lauretis had intended. Whereas her introduction to a 1991 special journal issue on queer theory, which introduced the concept and contained a number of the papers from the conference, lauded the promise of the new theoretical turn, by 1994 de Lauretis had repudiated queer theory, remarking caustically that it "ha[d] quickly become a conceptually vacuous creature of the publishing industry."[7]

Yet despite her dismissal, queer theory continued to grow. While never simply a "conceptually vacuous creature of the publishing industry," it did fail in its early years to live up to de Lauretis's vision. Early queer theorists were typically cisgender white men whose writing focused on other cisgender white men as literary authors and as literary characters. Their work usual-

ly didn't consider race, gender, or class in any significant depth, as de Lauretis had hoped the turn to the more radical term *queer* might encourage the
new queer theorists to do. Little surprise, then, that she was disillusioned by
the immediate fate of her creation.

Yet already by the late 1990s, queer theory was beginning to take on a
new form with the arrival of a new generation of scholars on the scene.
Involved in self-identified queer activism, often considering *queer* to be a
political term more than an identitarian or a scholarly one (much as de
Lauretis had argued), and influenced by struggles over gender identity in
feminist circles, feminism in queer circles, and race in all of these locations,
scholars such as J. Jack Halberstam, José Esteban Muñoz, Siobhan Somerville, and Roderick Ferguson, among others, pressed queer theory toward
intersections with feminist theory, critical race theory, and the nascent field
of transgender studies. Others followed rapidly, and queer theory broadened
into queer studies with the inclusion of postcolonial theory, critical disability
studies (at an intersection often termed *crip theory*), and settler colonial
studies. Today, these branches of queer studies have also come to inform
scholarship at other intersections, such as the influence that queer of color
critique has had on the development of critical ethnic studies.

Like gender studies, especially in the wake of Butler's work, queer studies moved away from the more essentialist approach to sexuality that had
characterized some of gay and lesbian studies up to that point. To be sure, as
with feminist theory in the 1970s and 1980s, not all of gay and lesbian
studies in that time period was essentialist. But the initial move to correct the
heterosexism of existing scholarship by adding gay and lesbian narratives
made a certain amount of **essentialism** difficult to avoid. The words *gay* and
lesbian are modern, Global North/Global West terms, at least in their origins
and in their current usage (after all, at one time Lesbian simply meant someone from the Greek island of Lesbos).[8] They also reference a particular
understanding of homosexuality that was developed when that word was
invented in nineteenth-century Europe. Can we say that someone from a
culture that doesn't use terms like *gay* and *lesbian*, or concepts like homosexual, *is* gay, lesbian, or homosexual? Only if we decide that those words are
culturally specific terms for a universal human phenomenon—only, that is, if
sexual *identity* (not just desire) is innate. You'll notice in this book that I
alternate between using terms like *same-sex attracted* and *gender variant*,
and using terms like *queer* and *transgender*. When I'm talking about people
who use, or are likely to use, contemporary Global North/Global West gender and sexual identity terms, I'll often use terms like *transgender* and *queer*
for them. But when I'm talking about people who generally don't use such
terms, I'll either generalize with a phrase like *same-sex attracted* and *gender
variant* or I'll use the chosen identity term for that community.

Queer theory and queer studies have taken a much more fluid and constructivist approach to sexuality than gay and lesbian studies did. Drawing not only on the legacy of that field but also on the psychoanalytic theories developed by Sigmund Freud, his students, and their students in turn; on **materialist analysis** as developed by Karl Marx, Friedrich Engels, and their intellectual descendants; and on philosopher Michel Foucault's work on power and social institutions, queer studies spends less time on an "add queers and stir" approach to scholarship and more time on thinking about how sexuality can appear in unexpected places and unexpected forms. In studying such disruptions of the norm, even and at times especially when they appear within the norms themselves, queer theory seeks to both expose and unsettle normative models of sexuality and, in its best, most intersectional forms, many other channels or axes of power. In its older uses before it became a derogatory, then an activist, then simply an umbrella, term for nonheteronormative sexuality, *queer* meant things like strange, odd, or suspicious; untrustworthy or dishonest; or, as a verb, to cheat, put out of order, or unsettle. Queer studies reclaims these meanings of queer, seeking to unsettle and put out of order existing norms and assumptions about sexuality and desire and to learn from normative accusations that queer people, places, objects, and cultures are strange and untrustworthy. From the perspective of queer studies, even cheating looks like a pretty good goal—if by that you mean cheating heteronormativity of its power to dismiss and diminish queer lives.

Transgender Studies

Sometimes separately, sometimes in conversation or in concert with the development of gender theory and queer theory in the 1990s and the 2000s, transgender studies also began gaining momentum. As with gender studies and queer studies, transgender studies has roots that stretch back beyond the formation of the field in the early 1990s. As with the other fields, in fact, and for similar reasons, some of those roots lie in the nineteenth century.

As scientists from Europe and its settler colonies busied themselves in the nineteenth century with classifying things, categorizing them, and determining their causes, as they classified human beings into races and sexes based on minute scrutiny of their anatomies, these scientists also turned their attention to sexuality and gender. Pondering why some people were sexually attracted to others of the same sex, these sexologists wondered whether perhaps such desires weren't simply tastes, akin to a fondness for honey or finely cooked seafood, but rather were innate. As scholars have pointed out, the sexologists were not the first to consider same-sex desire innate in some people, but in Europe they were the first in many centuries to do so. For much of European history, at least since the arrival of Christianity as the dominant religion on the continent, European cultures had tended to treat same-sex eroticism as a vice. Sometimes it wasn't a very serious one, just a little bad behavior, like having too much wine or fooling around with your fiancé before you were married. At other times it was considered a serious crime, and people were even executed for engaging in same-sex erotic acts. Sometimes they were burned at the stake, which is where the epithet *faggot* comes from; a faggot, in older British English, is a fire starter. But in all of these cases, it was not something innate about the person that was being punished, or in more lenient times gossiped about in the town square; it was their tastes and their actions. In Europe in the nineteenth century, it was a more unusual move to suggest that people with same-sex desire might be born that way.

In keeping with the compulsory heterosexuality that was a part of European cultures at the time, and that was also deeply embedded within scientific assumptions, some sexologists theorized that people who experienced same-sex desire might actually be members of the "other" sex. In order for a man to be attracted to another man, they thought, he must actually be a woman, and a woman attracted to other women must actually be a man. Sexologists who suggested this theory called these people *inverts*.

For these scientists, it seems, the idea that a man could be attracted to anyone other than a woman was so unthinkable that it made more sense for him to be really a woman despite being male. Such is the power of compulsory heterosexuality! But wait—there's a problem with the logic here, isn't there? If a man attracted to other men is really a woman, then in a male-male couple both are women. But by the same logic, a woman attracted to another woman is a man. So they're both men. Gender becomes completely unstable in this system. The sexologists solved this theoretical problem by explaining that in any same-sex pairing, one person was an invert and the other was simply sexually adventurous (if male) or tragically misled (if female). So each pairing contained an "invert" and a "normal," thus restoring the heterosexual order in the face of same-sex desire through the invention of inversion.

Feminine men and masculine women—or male-bodied women and female-bodied men—were hardly an invention of nineteenth-century European sexologists. In fact, gender variance, diversity, and fluidity have been recognized in a wide range of cultures around the world for thousands of years, and, as historian and queer studies scholar David Halperin argues, the sexologists may even have gotten some of their ideas from ancient Greek understandings of adult male citizens who enjoyed being penetrated by other men.[9] Associations between male femininity and male-male desire among adult men also had a few centuries of history in some parts of Europe by the late nineteenth century. But at least two aspects of the sexologists' ideas were different, perhaps even novel: first, that only certain combinations of sex and gender were possible, and therefore that inverts were "in the wrong body"; and second, that, as some of them began to suggest (over the objections of other sexologists, some of whom were themselves same-sex desiring), inversion was pathological. Same-sex eroticism went from being a sin to being a sickness that might or might not be curable. We'll see later in the book that by the 1970s, in some parts of the world like certain subcultures of the United States, same-sex eroticism had reverted back from sickness to sin.

The Legacy of the Invert

Though it had largely fallen out of favor in scientific, medical, and political circles by the final decades of the twentieth century, the inversion model has left a lasting legacy around the world. It underlies religious ideas about "permanent homosexuality" versus "temporary homosexuality" (the former is a newer way of referring to inversion; the latter refers to those "normals" who are drawn to inverts) and persistent stereotypes of gay men as feminine and lesbians as masculine. It provides the basic framing for most "conversion therapy," which encourages clients to enact their genders in more normative ways in the expectation that gender change will eradicate their same-sex attraction. It drives transphobia among cisgender heterosexuals and cisgender queer folks alike—in the latter case, because much of assimilationist gay and lesbian politics relies on claims to normativity through, in part, the enactment of cisgender identities. It likely also played a key role in the fact that gender variance became a recognized psychiatric diagnosis just as same-sex attraction ceased to be one. The invert remained in the diagnostic handbooks, in other words, but switched names and populations. By the late twentieth century, the specter of the invert had been largely transferred from gay men and lesbians to transgender people, except among medical, psychological, and religious practitioners who still look to an older version of psychology where desire and gender were intertwined. The invert has changed names and faces over the years, but the inversion model refuses to fade into oblivion because of the ways it reinforces heterosexual, cisgender power and privilege.

As the field of psychology developed in the late nineteenth century and into the twentieth century, the name *invert* gave way to the newly invented, more scientific-sounding term *homosexual*, but the concept of homosexuality retained within it the idea of gender inversion, and "true" homosexuals were said to be recognizable by their gender variance. People who experienced same-sex desire, for their part, increasingly embraced the new term and began to form communities around it. They might have disagreed over questions of gender variance, and certainly many objected to being pathologized, but at least some embraced and even celebrated the **inversion model**, holding drag balls and establishing subcultures in which butch-femme (masculine-feminine) relationships were the norm for both gay men and lesbians, while others challenged the idea that gays and lesbians were gender variant. By the early twentieth century, researchers such as sexologist Magnus Hirschfeld, founder in 1897 of the LGBT rights organization known as the Scientific Humanitarian Committee and cofounder in 1919 of the Institute for Sexual Sciences in Berlin, began to separate same-sex desire from gender variance, naming the latter *transsexualism*. Hirschfeld and his colleagues at the Institute for Sexual Sciences developed the earliest medical technologies for gender affirmation treatment.

After World War II, which brought the Nazi destruction of the Institute for Sexual Sciences and the deaths at Nazi hands of many of the scientists and LGBT people who worked there along with those they served, academic work on gender variance followed two main pathways: a scientific and medical one, in which mostly cisgender, heterosexual scientists sought to better understand what they called transsexualism or transsexuality and to develop better treatments for what they considered a pathological condition; and a more social scientific and humanities-oriented one, in which largely gay- and lesbian-identified scholars, following the inversion model, sought their own ancestry in gender-variant figures from the past, from cultures other than their own, and from literary texts. Rarely at this time were self-identified transsexuals (or, to use the newer term that developed sometime in the 1980s, transgender people) able to publish their own research on gender variance, largely because of the stigma that severely restricted their lives and their opportunities.

This state of affairs underwent a major change starting in the early 1990s, with several events that historian Susan Stryker identifies as the beginnings of transgender studies.[10] In 1991 scholar and activist Sandy Stone wrote a searing indictment of the tendencies of essentialist feminisms to marginalize, excoriate, and even deny the existence of transgender people and especially transgender women. Far from considering transgender women to be among those women whose rights feminists were fighting for, the cisgender women in these branches of feminism denied that transwomen were even women, considering them male wolves in sheep's clothing. "The *Empire* Strikes Back: A Posttransexual Manifesto" evoked both the (then-recent) *Star Wars* film and feminist Janice Raymond's 1979 transphobic and transmisogynist screed *The Transsexual Empire*, which had personally attacked Stone. In this article, Stone challenges both medicalizing and feminist discourses about transsexual people, insistently raises the voices of transsexuals themselves, and offers more nuanced and complex understandings of gender that contributed to the development of gender studies, transgender studies, and transgender activism. Other early influential writings in the formation of transgender studies include Leslie Feinberg's 1992 pamphlet "Transgender Liberation: An Idea Whose Time Has Come," which popularized the term *transgender* and defined it to include a wide range of gender-variant people regardless of embodiment or medical intervention; the various works of Kate Bornstein; and Susan Stryker's evocative 1994 article "My Words to Victor Franken-stein above the Village of Chamounix: Performing Transgender Rage." From these works of intertwined scholarship and activism has developed a field of study that, in Stryker's words,

> is concerned with anything that disrupts, denaturalizes, rearticulates, and makes visible the normative linkages we generally assume to exist between the biological specificity of the sexually differentiated human body, the social roles and statuses that a particular form of body is expected to occupy, the subjectively experienced relationship between a gendered sense of self and social expectations of gender-role performance, and the cultural mechanisms that work to sustain or thwart specific configurations of gendered person-hood.[11]

Transgender studies and queer studies are closely related, then, in that each looks to spaces, people, texts, bodies, arts, and events that disrupt the norm in order to understand and unsettle that norm. Both fields do so at the intersec-tions of gender and sexuality, but with particular emphasis on one or the other. Although they're separate fields, and rightly so because of queer stud-ies' tendency to erase transgender people or to absorb them into the category of "queer," at their best they overlap in generative and mutually informative ways.

QUEER AND TRANSGENDER STUDIES IN RELIGION

Sometimes it takes a religious studies scholar to notice this, but it can be startling to realize how often gender studies, transgender studies, and queer studies reference religious themes. Be it Judith Butler's repeated references to gender as a ritual practice, Sandy Stone's discussion of ceremonies and the "almost religious" character of Jan Morris's autobiography in "The *Empire* Strikes Back," or philosopher Michel Foucault's repeated invocation of Christian themes like confession, religion appears to haunt gender, queer, and transgender studies—yet these fields hardly ever engage religion direct-ly. Religion remains the ghost flitting through the curtains in most trans and queer academic spaces. Religious studies, for its part, has been equally resist-ant to engagement with gender studies, queer studies, and transgender stud-ies, despite their clear importance to the study of religion, perhaps at least in part because of a widespread cultural assumption that sex and religion don't go together but also because of century-old assumptions that queer and trans folks and religion don't go together. Scholars in queer and transgender studies in religion have been working to change these situations.

If you've been reading closely, you may have noticed that there are some striking similarities between religious studies, gender studies, queer studies, and transgender studies. All of these fields, for example, are primarily constructivist in their contemporary approaches to their subject of study, asking not what the essence of gender, sexuality, or religion is but rather what forms each takes in the lives of individual people, texts, arts, cultures, and subcultures. Each field seeks a deep understanding—what some religious studies scholars would call *Verstehen*—of how the people, texts, artworks, or other aspects of their study understand and enact religion, gender, or sexuality. Each has roots it might now wish to separate itself from in the nineteenth-century scientistic and colonialist urge to categorize, catalog, and above all, rank human existence and to pathologize existences that rank low on the scale. Each has a history in which authorized, dominant elites have spoken for the people under study, rather than those people being recognized for engaging in scholarship themselves about their own communities, even as some always have done exactly that. Each still struggles with that legacy, even as each continues (with varying degrees of success) to overcome it. As primarily constructivist, transdisciplinary fields that focus not on a specific method but rather on a specific aspect of human experience and the varying ways that different people and cultures comprehend those experiences, religious studies, gender studies, queer studies, and transgender studies have more in common than most scholars in these fields are aware or are willing to admit. What, then, can they learn from each other? This is one of the driving questions of this book, and one I hope you'll ask along with me as you read through it. In order to set up some initial answers to the question, though, let's start with a brief overview of the history and the roots of queer and transgender studies in religion.

In some ways, these subfields are not as new as they may seem, because some scholars have worked at the intersections between gender and sexuality studies and religious studies right from the beginning. It was Quaker activists, after all, who connected feminist, antiracist, economic justice, and anti-imperialist struggles back in the nineteenth century, and one of the earliest works of feminist studies in religion (which didn't draw the connections the Quakers drew and has since been criticized for its racism and xenophobia) was Elizabeth Cady Stanton's *The Woman's Bible*, published in two volumes during the 1890s. Contemporary feminist studies in religion dates back to the late 1960s, and gay and lesbian studies in religion began not long after that.

Although few people initially took it up, it's fair to say that queer studies began to make its way into the study of religion within a few years of de Lauretis's 1990 conference, most clearly with the publication of Howard

Eilberg-Schwartz's book *God's Phallus and Other Problems for Men and Monotheism* in 1994. While Eilberg-Schwartz was working in the areas of Hebrew Bible studies and Jewish studies, in the realm of Christian theology Robert Goss's *Jesus Acted Up: A Gay and Lesbian Manifesto* (1993) drew on the radical queer activism of ACT UP (AIDS Coalition to Unleash Power) to make profoundly queer theological arguments and also contributed to the rise of queer studies in religion. Goss's next book, the 2002 work provocatively entitled *Queering Christ*, showed queer studies in full swing in theological circles, as did Marcella Althaus-Reid's daring, intersectional, and still profoundly influential books *Indecent Theology: Theological Perversions in Sex, Gender, and Politics* (2000) and *The Queer God* (2003).

Jewish studies, too, rapidly developed additional work relevant to queer studies after the publication of *God's Phallus*, including such books as Daniel Boyarin's *Unheroic Conduct: The Rise of Heterosexuality and the Invention of the Jewish Man* (1997) and the edited volume *Queer Theory and the Jewish Question* (2003). Mark Jordan's early queer studies work, such as *The Invention of Sodomy in Christian Theology* (1997) and *The Silence of Sodom* (2000), brought queer theory into Christian studies, and Janet Jakobsen and Ann Pellegrini's *Love the Sin: Sexual Regulation and the Limits of Religious Tolerance* (2003) was the first book to successfully build a bridge between queer studies and religious studies that scholars crossed in *both* directions. Jakobsen and Pellegrini were the first to convince some queer studies scholars that studying religion might be important and useful, although such arguments remain an uphill battle despite the influence of these two scholars' ongoing work. The field has expanded since these early books to such an extent that even the partial bibliography at the end of this book lists nearly 150 books. A bibliography that included articles as well would probably contain close to a thousand entries. The number of works published annually in this area grows each year, demonstrating both the health and the importance of the field.

Transgender studies in religion is just beginning to see a similar pattern of growth, even though it too dates back into the 1990s thanks to articles written by transgender theologians and religious leaders. Virginia Ramey Mollenkott's *Omni-Gender: A Trans-Religious Approach* (2001) and Justin Tanis's *Trans-Gendered: Theology, Ministry, and Communities of Faith* (2003), both at least partly theological works, were the first book-length studies to appear from religious studies scholars that addressed transgender studies in religion. Prior to those works, a few anthropologists had taken up the intersections of gender variance and religion in the context of India (Serena Nanda's *Neither Man nor Woman: The Hijras of India* [1990]) and of Native American and First Nations people (the edited volume *Two-Spirit People: Native American Gender Identity, Sexuality, and Spirituality* [1997]). Although it's not clear whether the editors of *Two-Spirit People* saw connections between their work and the growing movement in transgender studies, they followed the same principles espoused by transgender studies in creating space for gender-variant people to speak for themselves instead of simply being spoken about. In 2018 a special issue of the *Journal of Feminist Studies in Religion* offered an important overview of and contribution to the increasing growth of transgender studies in religion.

With this all-too-brief background, then, we can begin to ask another question that will occupy us for the rest of this book: What does it *mean* to do queer and transgender studies in religion? At the most basic level, it means to bring the methods and the insights of these three fields together, to discover what we can learn from the places where they align and what new insights can be found for each field at the points where they disagree, the places of productive tension. Scholars working in transgender and queer studies in religion have taken several different approaches, often in combination. These include, but are not limited to: (1) studying the experiences of gender-variant and same-sex-desiring religious people in the past and the present, in order to learn how they might inform religious studies (including theology and ethics), gender studies, and queer studies; (2) discovering queerness and transness where they might not be expected, through queer and trans readings of sacred texts, art, rituals, and other aspects of religion; (3) discovering religion where it might not be expected, through reconsideration by religious studies scholars of practices and beliefs that are recognized as queer or trans but that may not be understood as religious; (4) unsettling norms by studying them, bringing queer and trans studies perspectives to normative religious practices and traditions in order to expose them as norms, examine their social construction, and challenge their dominance, and enacting the same critique in the opposite direction by bringing religious studies perspectives to bear on normative genders and sexualities; and (5) exploring how the insights of queer and transgender studies can impact the study of religion and vice versa.

Moving forward in this book you'll see each of these approaches, often in combination, in our considerations of the themes. We begin with stories, both because, as Driskill and Powell teach us, all theorizing is a story, and because stories, or beliefs, are often the first thing many people in English-speaking cultures think of when they think about religion. From stories we move on to conversations, then to practices, identities, communities, and politics and power. Each of these themes presents us with a focal point for entering into a consideration of transgender and queer studies in religion. None is exhaustive; taken together they do not tell the whole story of queer and transgender studies in religion. Nothing can, because the story isn't yet complete—and perhaps it never will be.

As you read on, keep the following methodological principles in mind:

- *Verstehen* (empathetic understanding): You don't have to agree with anything you read. You don't have to believe it, either. But you need to understand that many of the religious world concepts and experiences you'll read about, as well as the self-understandings of the people in this book, are just as real to them as yours are to you. If you cannot comprehend that reality, if you cannot in some way understand what it might be like to inhabit it, you will find religious studies—and probably gender and sexuality studies—difficult if not impossible to do. Use your imagination!
- Social construction: These fields of study generally hold that there is no objectively provable, preexisting, universal human nature or experience called "womanhood," "manhood," heterosexuality," "gayness," "transness," or "religion." Each of these concepts is understood differently and is of greater or lesser importance—or none at all—in different cultures, different subcultures, different time periods, and even among different individuals. Part of what these fields are interested in learning, often, is how understandings of sex, gender, sexuality, and the sacred are structured, understood, and named in a given context, how they interact with and shape each other, and how they change over time or across geographical areas. That said, claiming that something is socially constructed isn't the same as claiming that it's not real. Social constructs have very real effects in the world, and those effects are part of what we study.
- Creativity: Queer and transgender studies in religion are deeply creative fields, not just in the sense that they make or create things, but also in the sense that they're willing to consider things from new perspectives, to think outside of the normative boxes. Think you're finding sexuality, or gender, or bodies, or religion where you didn't expect them? Trust your instincts. There aren't many right answers here, just well-argued analyses.
- Intersectionality: Transgender and queer studies—in religion or otherwise—are at their best when they're intersectional. As you read through this book, and as you try out transgender and queer studies for yourself, consider whether you're taking into account race (even if you're studying white people), and gender (even if you're studying cisgender men), and class (even if you're studying elites), and ability (even if you're studying fully abled people), and so on.
- Complexity: My students know that one of my favorite sayings is, "Occam's razor doesn't apply to humans." Occam's razor is a principle of logic that holds that the simplest solution to a problem is the best one. But human beings are complicated creatures! To study humans and really get things right, as most scholars in gender studies, queer studies, transgender studies, and religious studies know, we have to remain open to complexity, to what many religious studies scholars call "messiness." Religion is

messy; so are sex, sexuality, and gender, in lots of ways! But in the mess is where the most interesting aspects of all of these things lie. Don't fear the mess. It contains both beauty and insight—and a heck of a lot of queerness.

STUDY QUESTIONS

1. What are some problems with questions like "What does Christianity say about homosexuality?" What better questions might we ask instead?
2. What two developments in European culture most strongly influenced the origins of religious studies? How did they shape this field? What is the Enlightenment, and how did it play a role in these processes?
3. What is scientific racism? How did it impact the nascent field of religious studies?
4. This chapter explains that "the idea of religion as a universal human phenomenon that can be compared across cultures is a social construction." What does that mean?
5. What are confessional approaches to the study of religion? Why can such approaches not be taught in public schools in the United States?
6. What objections have feminist, antiracist, and anticolonial scholars raised to the idea of objectivity? How might these objections apply to Gerardus van der Leeuw's concept of *epoché*?
7. What is intersectionality? What does it mean to do an intersectional analysis? Give one example.
8. What does Judith Butler mean when she says that gender is performative? (*Hint:* She doesn't mean it's a performance!) Can you think of an example?
9. Describe the five current approaches that scholars take to queer and transgender studies in religion.

FOR FURTHER THOUGHT

1. Consider the quotation from the beginning of this chapter: "Theory and scholarship are always stories about how the world works." What stories have been taught to you about how the world works in terms of religion, gender, and sexuality? Whom do those stories include and exclude? Do those stories include you? What impact do such stories have on people's lives? What impact have they had on your own?
2. This chapter has emphasized the idea of social construction, and also the fact that social constructs can be very real in their effects. What social constructs are you aware of? What effects do they have in

society? In individual people's lives? What do you think of the idea that gender and sexuality are social constructs? Why?

3. How should we approach the study of religion if the very idea of religion is a social construct? What kinds of questions about religion become hard to ask and answer if religion is socially constructed? What kinds of questions become easier? What do you think of the idea that the concept of religion as a universal, comparable human phenomenon is socially constructed? Why?

4. What do you think of the divide between confessional and non-confessional religious studies? Is it useful? Problematic? Both? Where might people who advocate for this divide classify your own interests in the study of religion? If you're reading this book for a course, how might they categorize that course?

5. What is your opinion about the critiques of objectivity? Is objectivity possible? Is it good? What about *epoché*? Explain and support your answers.

6. Try out an intersectional analysis on something you've encountered in your daily life, whether it's something you've experienced or something on the news. What do you learn about this case from analyzing it along a single axis of power, such as gender or race? What do you learn when you analyze it intersectionally?

7. Butler argues that the enactment of gender produces the illusion of an innate, gendered essence. What do you think of that idea? Why?

8. This chapter discussed five approaches that scholars in transgender and queer studies in religion currently take. Which of those five approaches most appeals to you, and why? Can you think of other approaches not listed here, either ones that you've already seen or ones that you can imagine?

ANSWER TO THE RIDDLE

The answer to the riddle about the surgeon is that she's a woman. Most people—even those who know women doctors—have trouble figuring this out because in many societies around the world "man" is the unmarked gender category for doctors. (Nurses, on the other hand, are usually marked as female—think about how often people talk about a "male nurse" but don't specify a "female nurse.") Did you miss the possibility that the surgeon was a woman, and decide instead that the son has two dads? Lots of people choose that answer to the riddle, and it's true that same-sex parenting and blended families (both possibilities in the case of a man with two fathers) are also not the culturally valued form of family in most places; different-sex couples and so-called intact families (such an insulting term to the many other forms of family!) are also unmarked categories. But consider for a moment that these solutions to the riddle might be easier to come up with because of how resistant many of our cultures are to the idea of women being emergency room surgeons. Even if we would ourselves fiercely defend women's right to be surgeons, many of us are so strongly (if unconsciously) affected by unmarked gender categories that we will introduce two dads into the riddle in order to avoid seeing the surgeon as a woman! Food for thought, huh?

RECOMMENDATIONS FOR FURTHER READING

Butler, Judith. "Performative Acts and Gender Constitution: An Essay in Phenomenology and Feminist Theory." *Theatre Journal* 40, no. 4 (1988): 519–31.

Crenshaw, Kimberlé. "Mapping the Margins: Intersectionality, Identity Politics, and Violence against Women of Color." *Stanford Law Review* 43, no. 6 (1991): 1241–99.

Hall, Donald E., and Annamarie Jagose, eds. *The Routledge Queer Studies Reader*. New York: Routledge, 2012.

Halperin, David M. *How to Do the History of Male Homosexuality*. Chicago: University of Chicago Press, 2002.

Masuzawa, Tomoko. *The Invention of World Religions: Or, How European Universalism Was Preserved in the Language of Pluralism*. Chicago: University of Chicago Press, 2005.

McGuire, Meredith. *Lived Religion: Faith and Practice in Everyday Life*. New York: Oxford, 2008.

Stryker, Susan. "(De)Subjugated Knowledges: An Introduction to Transgender Studies." In *The Transgender Studies Reader*, edited by Susan Stryker and Stephen Whittle, 1–17. New York: Routledge, 2006.

Stryker, Susan, and Stephen Whittle, eds. *The Transgender Studies Reader*. New York: Routledge, 2006.

Stryker, Susan, and Aren Z. Aizura, eds. *The Transgender Studies Reader 2*. New York: Routledge, 2013.

Walker, Alice. "Womanist." From *In Search of Our Mothers' Gardens*, xi–xii. New York: Harcourt Brace Jovanovich, 1984.

NOTES

1. Qwo-Li Driskill, *Asegi Stories: Cherokee Queer and Two-Spirit Memory* (Tucson: University of Arizona Press, 2016), 4. Driskill's quotation cites Malea Powell, "Rhetorics of Survivance: How American Indians *Use* Writing," *College Composition and Communication* 53, no. 3 (2002): 399.

2. Adrienne Rich, "Invisibility in Academe," in *Blood, Bread, and Poetry: Selected Prose, 1979–1985* (New York: Norton, 1986), 198–201.

3. Thanks to Jon Walters for this pointed turn of phrase.

4. Samuel P. Huntington, *The Clash of Civilizations and the Remaking of World Order* (New York: Simon & Schuster, 1996).

5. Tomoko Masuzawa, *The Invention of World Religions: Or, How European Universalism Was Preserved in the Language of Pluralism* (Chicago: University of Chicago Press, 2005).

6. Simone de Beauvoir, *The Second Sex*, trans. H. M. Parshley (Harmondsworth, UK: Penguin Books, 1972), 267.

7. Teresa de Lauretis, "Queer Theory: Lesbian and Gay Sexualities, An Introduction," *differences* 3, no. 2 (1991): iii–xviii; Teresa de Lauretis, "Response: Habit Changes," *differences* 6, no. 2–3 (1997): 297.

8. I use the phrase "Global North/Global West" throughout the book, with thanks to the organizers of Queering Paradigms VIII, "Fucking Solidarity," in Vienna in 2017. Their point, and mine, in using this turn of phrase is that just as much as "Western" really doesn't describe the geography of global power dynamics and "Global North" may be more expressive, the latter term erases oppressed groups who live north of the equator but east of centers of power. Although it's a little unwieldy, "Global North/Global West" and its correlate, "Global South/ Global East" fruitfully combines the advantages of the term pairs "Western/non-Western" and "Global North/Global South."

9. David M. Halperin, *How to Do the History of Male Homosexuality* (Chicago: University of Chicago Press, 2002).

10. See Susan Stryker, "(De)Subjugated Knowledges: An Introduction to Transgender Studies," in *The Transgender Studies Reader*, ed. Susan Stryker and Stephen Whittle (New York: Routledge, 2006), 1–17.

11. Ibid., 3.

Chapter One

Stories

Religious studies scholar and Reconstructionist **rabbi** (Jewish religious leader) Rebecca Alpert opens her classic book *Like Bread on the Seder Plate: Jewish Lesbians and the Transformation of Tradition* with a story about the Jewish student organization Hillel; Chabad (or Ḥabad), which promotes the traditional observance of Judaism; and a rebbitzin—the wife of a rabbi but also often a religious leader in her own right, especially for other women:

> In the winter of 1979, the Jewish Women's Group at the University of California Berkeley Hillel invited the rebbitzin from the campus Ḥabad House, Hinda Langer, to speak on the subject of "Women and Halakhah [Jewish law]." Out of simple curiosity, one of the organizers asked Langer for her opinion about the place of lesbians in Judaism. Langer treated the issue as a minor matter. She suggested that it was a small transgression, like eating bread during Passover. Something one shouldn't do, but for which there were few consequences.
>
> Some time later that spring when some members of the Berkeley group were planning a Passover seder [a ritual meal], Langer's comment surfaced. But for them, Langer's explanation did not mesh with their reality. In their experience, lesbianism was much more problematic and transgressive in a Jewish context than Langer's comment suggested. So they chose that year not simply to eat bread during Passover but to place a crust of bread on their seder plate in solidarity with lesbians who were trying to find a place in Jewish life.[1]

Over time, Alpert explains, this story changed, was written down, changed again, made its way into art—until the crust of bread became an orange, the rebbitzin became a man, and the argument became one over women rabbis. The lesbians, and the powerfully transgressive symbolism of leavened bread on the seder plate, disappeared.

Alpert's telling of this story nearly twenty years after it took place and my retelling of it another two decades later resonate differently because of our time periods (late 1990s versus 2020), our audience (readers specifically interested in Jewish lesbians versus readers interested more generally in queer and transgender studies in religion), and our context (a specialized study versus a textbook). Maybe the story is different, too, when told by a rabbi than when told by someone who is neither Jewish nor a religious leader—even though we're also both professors. Telling the story is different now, when a quick internet search yields a range of queer Haggadot (orders of service for a seder), from telling it when Alpert wrote in a time of brand-new growth in queer Jewish studies, and her telling was different from when the Jewish Women's Group first asked the question, before any branch of Judaism fully and openly welcomed gay men and lesbians, much less bisexuals and transgender people.

Moreover, this is a story about a story—or better yet, a story about a story about a story. Alpert is telling a story about how the story of lesbian Jews being like eating bread on Passover became a story about women rabbis being like oranges on seder plates. But the seder itself tells a story, too. Feminist and queer Haggadot, along with other innovative versions of the ritual text, adapt that story to be more inclusive, to be the story they believe truly suits the spirit of Judaism, the history of the Jewish people that is told during the seder, and the story of the seder itself. Woven together in Alpert's story about a story about a story—and in my retelling of it here—are tales of the sacred, tradition, community, exclusion, invisibility, erasure, inclusion, marginalization, invention, innovation, history, and much more. As any religious studies scholar—or transgender or queer studies scholar—will likely tell you, stories are both powerful and malleable. This chapter opens with a consideration of some approaches to stories in religious studies, queer studies, and transgender studies. It explores how these different approaches to stories might be woven together, then moves on to some specific examples of types of stories within transgender and queer studies in religion.

RELIGIOUS STUDIES: SACRED STORIES

What kinds of stories do religions tell? If your answer to this question is "myths," you're not alone. Many people associate the word *myth* with religious stories, and you can easily buy books and find websites about the myths of various groups of people—ancient Greek myths, ancient Roman myths, ancient Norse myths, ancient Celtic myths, ancient Near Eastern myths.

Wait a minute.

Where are the contemporary religions in this list? Sure, many neo-pagans are reviving the practice of some ancient traditions, but in general and except for a few academic books, it seems like *myth* refers to religions that are no longer practiced. Maybe that has something to do with the other use of the word to mean "false story." "That's just a myth!" you might scoff at an elder who tells you not to make faces because your face will get stuck that way, or a friend who worries about getting pregnant from a toilet seat.

Some religious studies scholars still use the word *myth* to refer to the stories that religions tell, but others have moved away from that word precisely because of its other meanings. Some people prefer the term *sacred story*, because it indicates that these stories have a lot in common with other types of stories but also that they're special, since many of the people who tell them experience them as sacred and experience the sacred through them. Because we'll be discussing different thinkers in this chapter who use the word *myth* differently, you'll need to pay close attention to how the meaning of the word shifts. Our baseline term, though, will be *sacred story*. Watch for the times when *myth* means *sacred story*, and the times when it doesn't.

We could study sacred stories by learning about different ones from around the world. That would be interesting, but which ones should we include in a single chapter? If you practice a religion, or if you were raised in one, what story would you choose to represent the whole of your religion? Would other people from the same religion choose the same story? Would they tell it the same way? What parts of the religion might get left out if someone who knows nothing about your religion learned only that story? What would be missing? Analytically, it might be more useful to study how stories work. What do they do? You might forget any particular story you learn—or you might not—but the analytical tools developed and used by religious studies scholars to study sacred stories are ones you can use whenever you encounter any kind of sacred story. Let's start there.

Religious studies scholar Bruce Lincoln suggested back in 1993 that stories—which he called *narratives*—could be classified into four categories based on three criteria.[2] The first criterion he called *truth-claims*. Does a narrative claim to be true? Some stories don't, like the story that the moon is made of green cheese, whereas others do. Lincoln called stories with no truth-claims *fables*. The second criterion is *credibility*. If the story doesn't claim to be true, then probably few people find it credible. But if it does claim to be true, then it's important to know whether the people to whom it's told believe that it's true. Stories in the "tall tales" genre ("the fish was thiiiiiiiiiis big!") have truth-claims but not credibility. Lincoln called narratives like these *legends*. The third criterion is *authority*, by which Lincoln means a world-defining or ultimate sort of authority. A story with authority doesn't just tell you what happened in a particular place and time; it also tells you something bigger about the world in which you live. Stories with truth-claims and credibility, but not this kind of authority, Lincoln called *history*. Those with all three criteria—truth-claims, credibility, and authority—he called *myth*.

The interesting thing about this system for understanding narrative is that in different contexts stories can gain or lose any of these criteria. To go back for a moment to the ancient stories that nowadays are often called myths or mythology, in early Scandinavia stories of the Norse gods had all of these criteria. Tales of Valhalla not only entertained people but also taught them how to live and gave them hope for a life beyond death for themselves and their loved ones. These stories had *authority*; they gave meaning and order to the world. As Scandinavians converted to Christianity, though, these stories retained their truth-claims but not their credibility; they also lost their authority. Today they are sometimes even recounted without truth-claims, as fable rather than legend, although perhaps in the Marvel comics and films about Norse gods Thor and Loki the truth-claims—and maybe for some people even the credibility—have returned. For followers of the neo-pagan religion Asatru, though, as for practitioners of other, more eclectic neo-pagan religions that draw from many different sacred stories, these narratives retain all three elements, up to and including authority.

Lincoln's interest in narratives lies in their ability to stabilize, shape, and even revolutionize a society. New stories with authority, and old stories with new authority, can radically change people's ideas about how the world works. Think, for instance, about the challenge that Darwin's theory of evolution laid at the doorstep of religions whose sacred, authoritative stories held that the world and everything in it was created in six days. Changes like that can change the status of a narrative. Some religious people responded to Darwin's theories by denying the credibility of the creation story, and some expanded that denial to the religion as a whole. Others retained both the credibility and the authority of the creation story but reinterpreted its meaning. Some thought that the six days referred to six extremely long periods of time; others understood the story as a metaphor with profound meaning but not literal truth. And some denied the authority and even the credibility of Darwin's theories instead. In struggles over social power, people can also intentionally shift a story from one of Lincoln's categories to another, moving a story from myth to history by affirming its credibility but denying its authority to define the world or changing a legend to myth by claiming credibility and authority for the tale. If stories with authority have the power to shape the world and society, then adding or removing their authority can at times produce radical change.

But let's take a smaller-scale example by returning to Alpert's story of the bread on the seder plate. By asking a rebbitzin for her opinion about lesbians in Judaism, the members of the Jewish Women's Group were starting with a certain level of authority. A rebbitzin's opinion is not binding—neither is a rabbi's in most understandings of Judaism—but her interpretation of text and tradition is influential at the very least. In the context of a session on Jewish law, the question invoked stories with great authority, especially those of the

Talmud, a collection of commentaries on the **Torah** (Jewish scriptures) written by ancient rabbis. And in answering, the rebbitzin evoked other authoritative stories—those told during Passover. But in reflecting on her answer as Passover was approaching, the group members thought that the rebbitzin's answer was lacking in credibility. Weighing it against what they knew of lesbians' experiences in predominantly heterosexual Jewish communities, they altered the story to be more credible. They thought that heterosexual Jews were treating lesbians not like people who ate leavened bread on Passover, but like people who committed the more serious ritual violation of putting leavened bread on the seder plate. Then they took another step. Wanting to symbolize the creation of space for Jewish lesbians in their own seder, they intentionally placed a crust of bread on the plate. With the truth claims and credibility of Jewish lesbians' experiences, and the authority of the Jewish tradition, this story and the actions that told it—as well as the story they told during the seder about the crust of bread—changed the world, if only (for the moment) in their own ritual space.

But the story had authority. It had the power to change the world in ways that some people wanted to see. It was repeated, retold, written down. Others found the intentional ritual violation of placing bread on the seder plate to be too provocative—after all, this gesture had authority; it *did* something; it was, to borrow Butler's terminology, *performative*. So they made it an orange. Maybe the story changed too many things too quickly for some people; it retained its truth-claims, its credibility, and its authority, but it slipped away first from the bread and then from the lesbians, ending up as a story about oranges and women rabbis. Lesbians in Judaism, like bread on the seder plate, were too much at the time for some people to handle; the story changed the world too radically for them. But when Alpert corrected the record and retrieved the original story in the highly public space of a book about lesbians and Jewish tradition, more people were ready for the power of the story—or at least for the inclusion of queer and transgender Jews. Queer Haggadot today continue to add a new element to the seder plate to symbolize the inclusion of, as one Haggadah puts it, "all of us, regardless of gender, gender identity, or sexual orientation."[3] Interestingly, that element continues to be an orange, not a crust of bread.

Sacred stories—myths, in Lincoln's terminology—can take many forms. They aren't just stories that are recognizably religious, like the story of the Passover that's told during a seder. Some family stories carry authority in Lincoln's sense. They authorize the way the family is now, or the life path of a particular family member—or they deauthorize them. Think about the power of these small statements: "We are a proud military family going back four generations"; "our family has been Muslim since your great-great-grandfather came to Indonesia"; "no one in our family has ever been gay."

In many cultures today, scientific stories carry immense authority. It's this authority that the practitioners of some religions find profoundly troubling when scientific stories directly conflict with the stories of their religions. Faced with conflicting stories that both have truth claims, credibility, and authority, what is one to do? Sometimes people remove the authority and even the credibility of one or the other. This story of irresolvable conflict is the dominant story told across much of the world today about the relationship between science and religion. It's a very authoritative story in itself; how does it change the world?

But that story of conflict is just one small part of the larger story of the relationships between science and religion. In many cultures, after all, religion and scientific inquiry have gone hand in hand. Even in Europe, where people often think first of the Roman Catholic Church's condemnation of Galileo Galilei for his heretical claim that the earth orbited the sun rather than the other way around, the founder of modern genetics, Gregor Mendel, was a Roman Catholic monk.

Scientific stories not only have the power to authorize or deauthorize religion, though; they also have the power to make and unmake the world in other ways. Scientific racism, for example, provided the authority for slavery and colonialism. Psychological theories of homosexuality as a mental illness under the inversion model provided the authority for treating gender variance and same-sex eroticism as pathologies, for criminalizing these so-called deviant behaviors, and for subjecting gender-variant and same-sex-desiring people to violent and inhumane "treatment" intended to "cure" them. Complicating this story is the fact that, still in 2020, healthcare providers hold the authority to allow or deny access to treatment for transgender people who are medically transitioning using hormones or surgery. Demedicalizing transgender identity tells an authoritative story that transgender people are not sick, but it may also tell healthcare providers and national health services an authoritative story that medical transition is unnecessary and should no longer be paid for by the state or by private insurance. As Lincoln saw clearly, stories have everything to do with power.

Transgender studies scholars have noted for years the power of stories both to empower and to erase trans people. Stories of gender variance appear around the world and across history. Some of them are religious stories; in fact, in some the sacred beings themselves change gender or sex. In some sacred stories gender variance is a sign that one has been chosen by a deity for a special role, but this chosenness isn't always enviable. Other sacred stories cast gender variance as willful defiance of the sacred order, which is represented as exclusively cisgender. But there are also many sacred stories about transgender people—again, myths in Lincoln's sense of having authority—that aren't so clearly religious. Some carry the authority of science, and these range from stories that transgender identity is part of the natural beauty of human variation to stories that insist that sex and gender are binary and are inextricably tied to each other and to one's chromosomal makeup (it's usually unclear what explanation these stories have for intersex people).

There are authoritative stories in less expected places as well, such as literature, film, comedy, and other aspects of popular culture. The transphobic "woman who's really a man" story was a standard gag in Hollywood films for many years, even as British comedy relied regularly on the figure of the (ostensibly) straight, cisgender man in drag for a laugh. The latter story drew on and authorized a cultural narrative that no "man" who wore women's clothes could ever be serious about it, and if "he" was, then "his" sanity should be questioned; the former story authorized a deadlier narrative about the threat that transgender women pose. At its height, the "woman who's really a man" story described a threat to the masculinity of any man who found himself attracted to her, and this false sense of threat underlies much of the violence—up to and including murder—against transgender women still today. More recently, for reasons that are beyond the scope of this chapter, the sense of threat in this story has shifted to portray transgender women not as sexually voracious gay men in disguise but as rapacious straight men seeking to attack innocent women. Both narratives function as sacred stories; both carry the authority to unmake and remake the world; and the world they seek to make is one without trans women in it.

There are similar stories about transgender men and masculine-presenting gender-variant people more broadly. As with stories about feminine-presenting gender-variant people, these sacred stories range from those that create and sustain a world wherein masculine-presenting gender-variant people are a part of the sacred cosmos, to ones where they are simply not "real" (for instance, stories claiming that masculine-presenting gender-variant people are simply women seeking to escape from sexism or from the threat of sexual assault),[4] to ones where they are a threat. And as with stories about feminine-presenting gender-variant people, these stories about threats also authorize violence against masculine-presenting gender-variant people, making a world in which transgender people must struggle not only for recognition but even for life itself.

Both queer studies and transgender studies recognize other functions for stories as well, though, because not all stories of same-sex desire and gender variance are told by heterosexual and cisgender people. Three of the most discussed genres of story told within these communities are history, autobiography, and the coming-out story. Although all three generally make truth-claims and have credibility, most stories in these genres do not carry the same authority as the sacred stories we've been discussing above; some, however, do come to hold that level of authority.

Despite Lincoln's use of *history* to mean stories without the ultimate authority that makes a narrative into myth, perhaps it's because of the authority that history has sometimes held over transgender and queer people that such communities have so eagerly sought images of themselves in the past. In many cultures, for some reason, to be true, valued, even acceptable, a practice must also be long-standing. Even new religious movements often defend their legitimacy by claiming to be a reemergence, rediscovery, or reclaiming of an ancient truth. Quo-Li Driskill explains this necessity in the context of Cherokee Two-Spirit people, who are barely legible within the largely destroyed precolonial Cherokee historical record: "The absence of such scholarship [on precolonial Cherokee traditions of gender and sexual diversity] and the lack of recovered archival documents regarding identities we might now call 'Two-Spirit' has been used by some Cherokees . . . to argue that Two-Spirit/LGBTQ people are, in fact, not a part of Cherokee 'traditions.'"[5] Those arguments have formed the basis for denials of and outright bans on same-sex marriage rights in Cherokee communities. Histories, given sufficient authority in Lincoln's sense, can in fact make and unmake worlds, and in the context of colonized peoples, stories about precolonial traditions carry significant authority. It is for these reasons that Driskill writes of "re-storying" as "a retelling and imagining of stories that restores and continues cultural memories," especially about Two-Spirit people.[6]

Sometimes one of the most important forms of re-storying is telling one's own story. In the face of erasure from history and from the present through silencing, incarceration, eradication through "cure," and emotional, medical, economic, psychological, and physical violence, simply speaking out—whether to a select few or to the world—can be powerful. So can hearing and reading the stories of others like you. As we'll see below, autobiography and biography are an important, and often the earliest, form of queer and transgender religious reflection, perhaps because of the authority granted to the self in many cultures that have been impacted by modern Western intellectual traditions. In addition, though, personal interactions with the sacred provide an ultimate authority that's difficult to challenge: If a sacred being reveals something directly to a person, by what authority can another human being disagree?

Early self-told stories of transgender and queer people that appeared in the wake of the medical/scientific invention of "inverts" and "homosexuals" as categories of humans were often routed through a second person's voice, likely due at least in part to the stigma surrounding homosexuality. Some self-writers were reluctant to be identified publicly; some knew that they were unlikely to be taken seriously as people deemed diseased and criminal, and needed instead to be represented by a more "respectable" authorial voice. Often, then, these early narratives were told by journalists and biographers, or they were told in fictional form by the authors themselves. Radclyffe Hall's *The Well of Loneliness* is one example of the latter; though the novel doesn't directly tell Hall's story, its protagonist, an "invert" who was assigned female at birth but lives as a man and is in a relationship with a woman, closely resembles Hall's own life, and the book is often considered to be semiautobiographical. As clear evidence of the risks Hall took even in publishing this story as fiction, it was banned in Hall's native Britain for thirty-one years after its 1928 publication.

Around this same time in Iran, as historian Afsanah Najmabadi recounts, the popular press was both delighted by and fascinated with intersex bodies, and reported on genital surgeries for intersex and transgender people interchangeably. Up to and through the middle of the twentieth century, Najmabadi explains, "transsexual surgeries emerged as a variant of the larger scientific marvel of sex change. In popular weeklies and national dailies, such operations drew on the same fascination as other wondrous spectacles of nature and achievements of medicine. . . . All these instances provided not only similar occasions for reflections on the wonders of nature/creation, but also moments of national pride and celebration of Iranian scientific progress."[7] Although these stories were told by others about intersex and transgender people, and although they made such people Others through making them into spectacles and marvels, they nonetheless also featured the voices of intersex and transgender people, made them a part of creation and therefore creatures of God, and showed transgender and intersex folks that people like them existed as part of "nature/creation."

These biographical, semiautobiographical, and, later, explicitly autobiographical accounts of intersex, transgender, and queer lives played a key role in the 1970s development of an emphasis within especially Global North/ Global West queer and, eventually, some transgender circles on the importance of "coming out." "Come out, come out, wherever you are!" was a rallying cry of 1980s queer activism, playing on the children's game of hide-and-seek. Underlining this ongoing emphasis in some circles, the 2008 film *Milk* features a scene in which 1970s San Francisco gay activist Harvey Milk pressures his fellow activists to tell everyone they know that they're gay. For a period of time, collections of coming-out stories—mini-autobiographies, if you will, that focused on people's experiences of discovering and telling their friends and families about their sexuality or (occasionally) their gender—filled the shelves of gay bookstores and queer living rooms. Some activist groups, most notably Queer Nation, used "outing" as a political tactic, accusing prominent antigay politicians and religious leaders of hiding their own homosexuality behind virulent homophobia, and going public with scandalous stories and images of secretive same-sex relationships.

But if outing others is a controversial political tactic—some say it's necessary, others say it's unethical—coming out is too. While *Milk* portrays its protagonist urging his fellow activists to put their battle for rights and freedoms ahead of their fears of family rejection, the film, and many still today who scorn queer and transgender people who remain "in the closet" or "stealth," ignore several important factors in the politics of coming out. For one, the emphasis on coming out relies on the individualist assumption that one's personal story and desires are the most important factor in a person's life. That is in fact true for some people, but it isn't for others, and the relative value that people place on individualism is often cultural. The value of coming out, in other words, may be at least in part a Global North/Global West value. Second, an emphasis on coming out assumes that frank and direct conversation about bodies and sexuality are always culturally appropriate, and that if they aren't, they should be made to be. Many cultures find it intrusive to ask *or* tell things about bodies and sexuality, yet they find other ways of acknowledging same-sex desire and gender variance. Even telling one's story, then, doesn't come in a one-size-fits-all format. Third, and again as represented so clearly in *Milk*, the emphasis on coming out assumes that one's "chosen family"—one's queer and/or transgender community—will be more than sufficient to sustain them if they come out and the family they grew up with rejects them. That works for people who can support themselves financially and who are part of groups embraced and accepted by the majority of their communities. But gay communities can be sexist, gay and lesbian communities can be transphobic, and any of these communities may be racist, Islamophobic, antireligious altogether, or xenophobic. Many "gayborhoods" are expensive to live in, so these communities are also classist, at least by default and often more directly, and they can be economically inaccessible for people with illnesses, disabilities, or responsibilities that prevent them from working full-time. Childcare and elder care can be hard to find, and historically child-friendly spaces in queer and trans communities have been in short supply, so parents also have struggled with inclusion at times. Risking the loss of your entire family and your entire heterosexual, cisgender community is hard enough when you're embraced and supported by a large queer or trans community; when you aren't, it can be potentially devastating. Some stories change the world in destructive ways, even when they're told by transgender and queer people, and at times coming out stories can have that effect.

QUEER AND TRANSGENDER RELIGIOUS STORIES

The relationships between queer people, transgender people, and religion are characterized by four types of story in particular. Two of them, sacred stories and personal stories, we've already encountered. Academic stories have also had an impact on religion in transgender and queer communities, perhaps more so than in most communities, and reframed stories have been an important way for transgender and queer people to create or broaden religious spaces for their lives and their communities. As with our chapter themes, these types of story aren't always clearly separable, and they often influence one another.

Sacred Stories

Sacred stories, as we've seen, come in many different forms. Some are recognizably religious, based on common understandings of what counts as religion; others, like the stories told by science or history, are less obviously religious but still have the powerful authority to make, unmake, and remake the world that designates them as myths in Lincoln's sense of the term. How do more recognizably religious sacred stories impact the lives and communities of transgender and queer people?

Part of the world-making power of sacred stories lies in their ability to determine ultimate truth, or truth as it exists (in some world concepts) beyond the realm of normal human experience and beyond human time. For many people, be they religious, spiritual, or even atheist, these times and spaces beyond individual human lives matter; sometimes they matter more than individual choices or preferences. So if an ancestor, say, or a sacred text, or a religious leader tells people that they ought to be doing something different in their lives, many people for whom that ancestor or that text or that leader matters will make such changes. By representing the ultimate world, what Christian theologian Paul Tillich called "the ultimate concern," sacred stories and their bearers also tell us who and what belongs in that world and who and what does not. That's pretty powerful stuff.

Let's take Buddhist sacred texts as an example. Do they represent same-sex-attracted and gender-variant people, and if so, how? As we covered in the introduction, we can't say that these texts—or any sacred texts written or related before the middle of the nineteenth century—are about homosexuality, or transsexuality, or LGBTQ people. Words like *homosexual, lesbian,* and *transgender*, and also words like *heterosexual* and *cisgender*, aren't just newer terms for an age-old phenomenon; they represent very specific ways of structuring and understanding same-sex desire and gender variance. In fact, even those words have changed since they were invented. Homosexuality, as we've seen, once included the idea of inversion. Although it still carries connotations of gender variance in some cultures, such as conservative Christianity, today being gay or queer doesn't necessarily mean that someone is gender variant, and being transgender means nothing about one's sexual identity. So, contrary to the claims of some activists, both queer and trans supporters and detractors, queer people, trans people, and the like aren't represented in any ancient sacred story. Gender variance and same-sex desire, though, may be, and three examples from Buddhist sacred texts show us how complicated these representations often are.[8]

1. *Shariputra*: In the *Vimalakirti Sutra*, a text from the Mahayana branch
   of Buddhism, a monk named Shariputra challenges an enlightened
   goddess about her female form, asking why she doesn't change into a
   male form since she's enlightened. His question references a belief,
   evident in certain other Buddhist texts, that male embodiment is more
   conducive to attaining enlightenment than female embodiment. The
   goddess replies that form is impermanent and therefore has no bearing
   on enlightenment, and as an illustration of her assertion she changes
   her body into Shariputra's body and Shariputra's body into her own.

2. *Pandakas*: Some Buddhist texts, particularly in the *vinayas*, or the
   rules for monastic communities, warn monks against ordaining a person called a *pandaka*. Most commonly represented as male-bodied,
   feminine-presenting people, but including a wide variety of intersex,
   gender variant, and same-sex-attracted forms, *pandakas* are a problem
   in a monastic setting not so much because of their gender but because
   of their sexual appetite. Said to be sexually insatiable creatures, *pandakas* wreak havoc in monastic communities by incessantly trying to
   seduce the monks and nuns.

3. *Chigos*: In medieval Japan up through at least the seventeenth century,
   some religious and **lay** (not religiously ordained) men's communities
   celebrated the figure of the *chigo*, or the beautiful male adolescent.
   Organizations such as monasteries and samurai orders relied on a
   close relationship between master and disciple, and those relationships
   at times became sexual. Stories from that time period in Japan speak
   of monks gaining important spiritual knowledge and even enlightenment through their relationships with novices—*chigos*—who sometimes have even been enlightened beings in disguise.

How should we interpret these stories in terms of their representations of
gender variance and same-sex desire? We could argue, for example, that the
story of Shariputra tells us that sex and gender are irrelevant. That could be
an empowering message for transgender and other gender-variant people
today, or it could be disempowering—it could be used, for example, to deny
transgender people access to medical treatment for transition on the basis that
sex and gender are impermanent and a focus on them can lead to harmful
attachment. Likewise, the stories of *pandakas* can be, and have been, used to
claim that both same-sex desire and gender variance are inappropriate for
practitioners of Buddhism, and especially for monks. But such interpretations
pay little attention to the fact that monks take a vow of celibacy and that
women are not allowed in monasteries. An interpretation of the *pandaka*
stories that took these factors more into account might be that the stories
recognize feminine-presenting *pandakas* as women, thereby recognizing
gender-variant people for who they are, and that *pandakas* are a problem not

because they are same-sex desiring but because they try to seduce monks into violating their vows of celibacy. Of course, even this reading still has to address the (trans)misogyny involved in portraying feminine people as sexually insatiable and women as a danger to a monastery.

The case of the *chigos* is even more complicated. Some readers—including Japanese commentators of the same time period as the *chigo* stories—immediately condemn these stories as tales of hypocritical monks who use enlightenment as a false excuse to violate their vows of celibacy. Modern readers, who often place significant value on egalitarian and fully consensual sexual relationships, have trouble seeing in the *chigo* stories anything but sexual exploitation and child sexual abuse. These aren't necessarily inaccurate readings, but another way of thinking about these stories is to apply the principle of *Verstehen* and consider that these relationships might in fact have been deemed acceptable by everyone involved. If they were, then we need to ask why. What logic might make it reasonable and ethical for a monk and a novice to have a sexual relationship? There are two pieces to the answer, and both have to do with how sexuality is socially structured in these stories and in the monastic culture that produced them.

Let's take the celibacy question first. If we assume for the moment that in this cultural and historical context sex between a monk and a novice didn't violate either person's monastic vows, then we need to ask with genuine curiosity how this was possible. The clear answer is that what we're calling *sex* didn't actually count as sex. Why? One possibility is connected to the fact that the Buddhist concern with sexual activity among monastics is connected to the goal of avoiding attachment. Attachment, in Buddhist world concepts, leads to continuing rebirth into the world of suffering. Giving up attachment makes it possible to come closer to release from rebirth, so it makes sense that monastics would try to avoid anything that creates attachment to the physical world. Since sex between men and women carries the possibility of producing children—a major source of attachment for many people—perhaps in these specific contexts celibacy for men meant not having sex with women.

What about the question of exploitation? This one is trickier, because again it relies on a series of cultural understandings of both sex and power. Of course any power-laden relationship can become exploitive in many different ways, and sexual exploitation is one of those. On the other hand, master-disciple relationships typically assume that the disciple will support the master in varying ways in return for the master's support of the disciple, and that such relationships can take consensual forms regardless of the power differential involved, whether we're talking about ancient apprenticeships, courtiers and royalty, or contemporary master-slave relationships in BDSM communities. Contemporary sensibilities are often undisturbed by a disciple paying fees to a master—in universities these are called tuition!—and also often accept the idea of disciples opening their homes to a visiting master, offering food, and the like. But sexual support seems to fall, for many contemporary observers, into another category. Yet this way of structuring sex between men, often termed *pederasty*, in which adult men form sexual and often loving relationships with male adolescents, appears in a number of different cultures, from the ancient Greek citizenry to the Muslim Ottoman imperial courts to medieval Japanese Buddhist monasteries. From the perspective of monk and *chigo*, then, perhaps the *chigo* stories are not artful falsehoods designed to romanticize unethical and exploitive sexual relationships between adult men and vulnerable adolescent boys, but rather stories that can tell us a great deal about how differently sex was structured in those monasteries than it is in our own cultures and our own times. And what the *chigo* stories offer to some readers are tales that counteract the *pandaka* stories by offering profoundly Buddhist narratives about the sacredness of male beauty and of male-male desire.

Personal Stories

As we've already discussed, personal stories in the form of biography and autobiography can be powerful for queer and transgender people in many different contexts. Storytelling can help people to feel included and understood, and to feel as though they aren't alone. Personal stories can also intersect in very powerful ways with sacred stories. Here's one example.

When I was doing research for my very first book, I spent time attending two congregations of the Metropolitan Community Church (MCC), an international Christian denomination that welcomes and even focuses on queer and transgender Christians. One of the congregations I attended was **charismatic**. The charismatic movement in Christianity, which began in Los Angeles near the start of the twentieth century, focuses on an experience that some of Jesus's early followers had after his death, as described in the book of Acts in the Christian Bible. As the sacred story describes it, the Holy Spirit descended on these followers and they experienced a number of spiritual "gifts," or abilities brought to them by the Holy Spirit, such as the ability to prophesy and the ability to speak languages they'd never studied. Toward the end of the nineteenth century, some Protestant Christians began to theorize that this experience wasn't just restricted to the early followers of Jesus; it could happen to any Christian, given the right circumstances. Soon they found those circumstances, and people began to have experiences resembling those described in Acts.

Since the early followers of Jesus had these experiences during the time of Pentecost in the Christian calendar, people who believe in the existence of these gifts of the Spirit were originally called Pentecostal Christians, or Pentecostals for short. In the latter part of the twentieth century, though, experiences of these gifts of the Spirit spread beyond Pentecostal churches, and an orientation toward these experiences within a congregation or on the part of an individual came to be described more generally as charismatic. Among the common gifts of the Spirit experienced by Pentecostal and charismatic Christians are the ability to prophesy, the ability to interpret prophecy, speaking in tongues, and the experience of being slain in the spirit. The gift of tongues is a form of speech that's unintelligible to most listeners, except those with the gift of interpretation. Early Pentecostals thought they were speaking foreign languages when they spoke in tongues, but they later came to the contemporary understanding that tongues are a personal prayer language or the language of the angels.

Someone who is "slain in the spirit," or simply "slain," has typically been prayed over, often for healing purposes, during a charismatic prayer service. The person frequently collapses, and at such services there will usually be spotters positioned to catch anyone who is slain and prevent them from being hurt as they fall. People often appear to be dazed or in a trance; some lie quietly while others shout ecstatically or speak in tongues. People often describe the experience of being slain as an intensely personal, close, and emotional experience of God.

The vast majority of charismatic churches are theologically conservative, and included in this conservatism is typically a flat and harsh condemnation of same-sex desire and gender variance as against the wishes of God, at the very least, or at the worst Satanic. In fact, in some Pentecostal healing services the prayer leaders attempt to release individuals from what they consider to be the demons of homosexuality. But anything can happen when you're alone with God, perhaps especially in the context of a queer- and trans-welcoming church, and some experiences of being slain in the spirit are far more affirming to queer and trans folks.

MCC developed a charismatic movement in the 1990s. Though the denomination was founded by a Pentecostal minister who had been defrocked (had his ordination revoked) when he came out as gay, and though many of its church services have the emotional feel of a Pentecostal service, charismatic practice had not been an explicit part of the church until this movement began. Some of the people who became involved in MCC's charismatic congregations were from Pentecostal or charismatic backgrounds; others found the emotional worship services to be fulfilling even though they were novel. Others, to be sure, left and found noncharismatic churches to attend. One person in the charismatic congregation I attended was unfamiliar with charismatic practice but stuck around and tried it out. At a healing prayer service, she told me, she was slain in the spirit. For her, it was an experience of being held in God's arms. As she laid there, tenderly cared for by the deity, God told her that she was God's child, just as she was, that God had created her as a lesbian and loved her as a lesbian. All of the guilt and shame she had carried from her homophobic Christian upbringing melted away as she lay there.

What force does someone else's interpretation of sacred texts have against such an intensely personal experience of the divine? Christians are divided on the question of whether the Bible forbids same-sex eroticism or gender variance. Some of the texts that would seem to address such questions are in the Hebrew Bible, the Jewish sacred texts that Christians call their Old Testament (meaning the sacred texts that predate, and Christians think predict, the coming of Jesus). But some Christian interpreters point out that Jesus made it very clear that his teachings superseded the Torah; this is why, for instance, most Christians don't follow Jewish dietary laws. Jesus himself says nothing in any of the Christian sacred texts about same-sex desire or gender variance. One of his early followers, Paul, wrote a few passages in his many letters to early Christian communities that some have interpreted as condemning same-sex eroticism and perhaps even gender variance, and in fact since 1946 some English translations of the Bible have anachronistically used the nineteenth-century medical term *homosexuals* to translate some of the words in those letters. Bible scholars, however, tend to point out that the words Paul used either referred to male self-indulgence—too much "wine, women, and song"—or were uncommon words whose meaning remains uncertain. Nevertheless, some Christian churches continue to hold that same-sex desire and gender variance are not permissible in Christianity, and many queer and transgender Christians suffer emotional, physical, and spiritual harm because of this interpretation.

Against this backdrop of contestation over the understanding of salvation (called **soteriology** in Christian theology) for transgender and queer Christians, charismatic experience played a profound role in the self-acceptance and the mental health of the woman I talked to that day. When God has told you directly that you are loved and cared for just as you are, how can another human being's interpretation of a contested text have any power? Certainly, had this person had the same experience in the context of a homophobic church, others in the congregation might have convinced her that she was being deceived by a demonic spirit that wanted her to commit sexual sin and go to hell. She was in a queer-supportive church because she already believed, at least at some level, that God accepted her, and both that belief and the supportive environment of the church no doubt created a space where she could both have and cherish that experience of being held by God, but in the end it wasn't the pastor, or the other congregants, or the queer-supportive Bible study that dissolved the guilt and shame; for her, it was a direct experience of God.

Direct experience of the divine has long been a potent source of authority for the voices and opinions of disempowered groups. Historically in Christianity, for instance, women have been considered insufficiently intelligent, educated, or even at times spiritually advanced to comment on the nature of God or on any other aspect of theology. From the earliest days of the religion through to the present, though, women have received an interested audience when their teachings come to them directly from God. Women prophets and visionaries have written theology, changed Christian thought, and even started whole new branches of Christianity like Seventh-day Adventism, the Shakers, and Christian Science through their visions and other mystical experiences. Likewise, other disempowered people have found a religious voice and religious credibility through direct revelation from the divine. Even Troy Perry, the founder of MCC, credits not his own drive and ingenuity but God for the impetus to start the church: God, he says, told him to do it. And such personal stories can change sacred stories, not just for the person experiencing God directly but for those who hear about that experience. Personal stories react to and interact with sacred stories, but they also create them. In Lincoln's terms, when they have divine or sacred authority personal stories can make, unmake, and remake the sacred world.

Academic Stories

Sometimes, academic stories *are* personal stories. They can also inform personal stories, and respond to or develop out of or engage with them. They can engage with and even alter or become sacred stories, too. Among the important examples of such interactions are the academic stories that have been told publicly about same-sex desire in the **Qur'an** (the sacred text revealed to the Prophet Muhammad, which forms the cornerstone of Islam) since at least the mid-2000s. Although scholars and **imams** (Muslim religious leaders) before him had taken queer-positive or at least even-handed approaches to questions of same-sex eroticism in Islam, religious studies scholar Scott Kugle was one of the first to directly challenge the common interpretations of the story of Lut as condemnation of "homosexuality," along with Amreen Jamal, on whose work Kugle draws.

The prophet Lut, known to Jews and Christians as Lot, lived among people who were far from upstanding citizens. Lut and his family were the odd ones out, trying to get their fellow townspeople to change for the better. Neither the Qur'an nor the Torah is particularly clear about what exactly was so bad about these folks—maybe because it was everything—although the examples given of their transgressions seem to indicate that they were cheaters and swindlers who abused strangers instead of treating them with hospitality. As the story goes, God sent angels to the town in disguise. Lut, being one of the only decent human beings in the place, invited them to his home to stay the night, but that evening the townspeople gathered at Lut's door and demanded that he send his guests out to be raped. Lut refused and offered his daughters instead, but the townspeople were clear that they desired only the guests. In light of this gross indecency God decided to destroy the cities after letting Lut (and, of course, the angels) escape. For centuries, the three religions that have this story in their sacred texts have frequently interpreted the sin of Lut's people to be a sexual one, and since the angels are presumably male and the townspeople are also presumed to be male, many have pointed not to rape but to same-sex eroticism as the sin in question.

"Hang on," said Kugle. "How did we get here?" He turns first to what he calls the "semantic analysis" of the Lut story offered by Jamal, who carefully parsed the Arabic words in all of the Qur'anic passages addressing the story of Lut. Jamal studied these words in their context—that is, what the text was addressing when it used them—and also looked for other occurrences of the same words elsewhere in the Qur'an, seeking through this method a more accurate understanding of the meaning the words had in the time and place of the Qur'an's revelation. To this semantic approach, Kugle adds a "thematic analysis" that gathers and compares the various appearances of the Lut story across the revealed text, seeking to gain from the collected passages a broader perspective on how to understand the story in its Qur'anic context. Kugle seeks, in this article and in later books, what he terms a "sexuality-sensitive interpretation" of Islam. As he describes it:

> Sexuality-sensitive interpretation is attentive to the fact that sexualities are always multiple in society. It is attentive to the fact that variation is always arranged in hierarchical orders of power, leading to marginalization and disempowerment of the nonnormative groups. . . . "Sexuality-sensitive" as a descriptive term for this kind of interpretation is a direct translation of the Arabic term *hassas*, meaning literally "a sensitive person" but used colloquially to denote "a homosexual person."[9]

Contrary to many interpretations of Islam, but in line with other scholars' and religious leaders' reconsiderations of classical interpretations, Kugle finds that Islamic texts are far less clear on the issues of gender variance and same-sex eroticism than many people—both Muslim and non-Muslim—tend to assume.

Other commentators, such as Dervla Sara Shannahan and Kecia Ali, have raised additional questions about Kugle's analysis, stressing from a feminist perspective that gender is not irrelevant to the story. Decentering gender is important to Kugle's argument because he's trying to make the point that the townspeople's sin was not same-sex eroticism but rape. As Ali, Shannahan, and others point out, though, we can retain a gender analysis while also making the same argument Kugle makes. After all, Lut presumably also had sons, and it's no accident that he never offered his sons to the clamoring townspeople. But this is not, Ali and Shannahan argue, because same-sex sexuality was abhorrent to Lut; it was because in a patriarchal culture like that of Lut's people, men controlled women's bodies in a way that they didn't control the bodies of other men. Lut's daughters, in this interpretation, were not the appropriate heterosexual alternative to raping (ostensibly male) angels; they were the sexual capital that Lut was able to give away in order to protect his guests from the inhospitable assault threatened by the townspeople.[10]

How can academic stories make, unmake, and remake the world? For queer and transgender Muslims seeking to bring these identities together rather than be forced to reject one in order to embrace the other, academic stories like Jamal's, Kugle's, Shannahan's, and Ali's can be inspiring, at times even lifesaving. They offer more inclusive, welcoming perspectives on sacred stories, and while the tales themselves may be profoundly familiar to those who encounter these academic stories, the knowledge that one does not have to read them through a transphobic or homophobic lens may not be so familiar, and the fact that a nonhomophobic, nontransphobic reading is also not new often comes as a surprise to many who engage with academic stories about their own sacred stories. Because scholars are often granted a great deal of authority, in some cases academic stories about sacred stories can become sacred in their own right, at least in their ability to unmake homophobic, transphobic versions of the world and remake the world into one that contains space for queer and trans religious practitioners. In so doing, academic stories engage with sacred stories in ways that support personal stories, offering people routes to understanding or explaining their existing knowledge of sacred inclusion and acceptance or opening the door, through remaking the world in an inclusive way, to personal stories that may previously have been foreclosed.

Reframed Stories

Academic stories also contribute to our final category: reframed stories. Through careful study and analysis, academic stories can reframe sacred stories, or they can offer the tools and the initial inspiration for more widely reframed stories. The crust of bread and the orange on the seder plate represent reframed stories because they add a new element to the story told over the course of the seder about Jewish history, oppression, and escape from bondage through God's intervention. Academic stories can also offer far queerer, and more playful, reframings of sacred stories. One example of this is Roland Boer's 2001 article, "Yahweh as Top," which is playfully subtitled "A Lost Targum."[11] Targumim (the plural of Targum) served, in the first several centuries of the Common Era, as both translations of and commentaries on the Torah in Jewish communities. The person reciting the Targum, which at least in some communities was not read from a text, both literally translated from Hebrew into a language the congregation could understand and also explained the text at the same time; you might say that Targumim are loose translations that show evidence of the translators' interpretations of the text. Boer's text, which tells a story including characters who would not be born for many hundreds of years after the creation of the Targumim, is not in fact a lost Targum. It's a reframed version of the story from the book of Exodus in the Torah in which Moses goes up to Mount Sinai to receive the Ten Commandments—the basic ethical principles on which both Judaism and Christianity are based.

The opening to the story sets the stage with minute descriptions drawn from God's instructions to Moses in chapter 25 of the book of Exodus regarding the building of God's sanctuary. Bringing together these detailed biblical descriptions with contemporary stereotypes of gay men as fussy metrosexual decorators, Boer adds that the figure sitting in the chair within this sanctuary

> appears slightly built, dark hair carefully curled, blow dried, sprayed and gathered in a loose ponytail, ear rings dangling on either side of a face made up in cool, icy colors. His moustache (no beard of course) is neatly trimmed to a flourish. Manicured hands hold daintily but firmly onto the cup, from which he sips with obvious pleasure. Although we might be dying to catch a glimpse of his body—is it lean and muscled, flabby, wasted?—it is entombed in a vast fur coat from his neck to his ankles, although a knee does poke out from his crossed legs.

Meet Roland Boer's vision of God. Soon Moses arrives, out of breath from the climb up the mountain. But he is not the only visitor; Boer's version of Moses's trip up Mount Sinai includes famed founder of psychoanalysis Sigmund Freud; Jacques Lacan, who took psychoanalytic theory in a new direction in the mid-twentieth century and is much cited in certain threads of queer theory; philosopher Gilles Deleuze; and sex radicals the Marquis de Sade, after whom *sadism* is named, and Baron von Sacher-Masoch, from whom we draw the term *masochism*. The conversation that ensues is an entertaining analysis that explores many of the sexual and symbolic dimensions of both the Hebrew Bible and the Christian New Testament, blurring in the end any idea of the nature, embodiment, gender, or sexuality of the divine.

To some readers, Boer's text is the height of blasphemy. To others, it's a creative exploration of alternative, very queer, and perhaps also transgender and intersex perspectives on Jewish and Christian sacred stories. Envisioning God as a fussy gay man hosting a tea party on the top of Mount Sinai creates space for at least some queer folks to see that the idea that humans are "made in God's image" includes them. Blurring the sex and gender of God creates space for intersex and transgender people also to be literally the image of God. And understanding God as a "top" (which could mean simply the penetrative partner in sex, but here also clearly refers to the dominant partner in BDSM play) opens up space for this form of queer sexuality to also be a part of the image of God. It may be that the story is blasphemous only to those whose understanding of what it means to be made in the image of God is less expansive, and this may well be part of Boer's point, even as the article goes much further than this in what is sometimes a complicated analysis despite being framed within the narrative of a short story.

A very different reframing of sacred stories, and one that's more visual than textual, takes place in the images of artist Alma López. A queer Chicana who has lived most of her life in Los Angeles, López creates feminist, queer, Chicana commentary through her art, her writing, and her teaching. In 1999 she developed the idea for a new art piece based on conversations she was having with other Latina activist artists in LA about a book of essays on the Virgin of Guadalupe. Understood by Roman Catholics to be a form of the Virgin Mary, mother of Jesus, who appeared to an indigenous man in Mexico during the early years of Spanish colonization, the Virgin of Guadalupe is a central figure in Mexican and Chicanx Catholicism; she is also important for some Latin Americans and Latinx people more broadly, and for other Catholics. In reading through the book, López recounts, she was especially drawn to an essay by writer Sandra Cisneros, whose anger at the use of Guadalupe's image to control the lives and bodies of girls and women López shared. Cisneros's essay explains how the writer came to a new understanding of Guadalupe by tracing the Virgin's image back to indigenous goddesses who, to her, were much better role models. "When identifying with [Guadalupe] as a brown woman with a real body like her own," López explains, "Cisneros wondered what La Virgen would wear under her exceedingly long dress and robe. My immediate response to her question was, 'Roses, of course!'"[12] When the local archbishop refused to believe that the Virgin Mary had appeared to an indigenous man, Guadalupe is said to have made roses miraculously tumble out of his cloak, so to López roses made perfect sense as Guadalupe's undergarments.

Fascinated by this image of Guadalupe as a powerful, real woman, López began to develop the image called *Our Lady*. She invited two of her friends, both fellow activist artists, to take part. The finished image, which has received widespread acclaim and sparked widespread controversy, shows the Virgin of Guadalupe as a proud, assertive Latina clad only in a bikini of roses. Her traditional cape has been transformed with the image of a stone carving of Coyolxauhqui, an Aztec goddess, to encourage viewers "to consider how tall and strong Our Lady must be to carry Coyolxauhqui on her shoulders like a floating cape."[13] Instead of the traditional angel at her feet holding the crescent moon (a symbol associated with the Virgin Mary, but in López's art also a reference to the moon goddess Coyolxauhqui), this Guadalupe stands on a moon that is supported by a bare-breasted angel with the wings of a viceroy butterfly. López explains that she uses the viceroy in her art because it looks like the monarch butterfly but isn't just like it. The monarch, unlike humans, migrates without restriction between California and Mexico. It follows its route not by its own memory but by a kind of ancestral memory, since the migration cycle takes multiple generations to complete. In addition to these references to migration and the injustices enacted by walling off indigenous lands, the viceroy (which looks like the migratory monarch but doesn't itself migrate) adds a queer reference for López. "In my visual vocabulary," she explains, "the fact that the Viceroy mimics the Monarch but is different means that it is 'queer.'"[14]

As you can tell from *Our Lady*, Alma López's queer, feminist commentary on sacred stories doesn't focus only on Catholicism. Although she has made a number of works of art that reframe sacred stories, a second piece that stands out is *Ixta*, which was created in the same year as *Our Lady*. In this work, López puts a queer twist on another popular image she saw around her when she was growing up in a largely Chicanx neighborhood of LA: the story of Popocatépetl and Iztaccíhuatl, or Popo and Izta (also spelled Ixta). This Aztec sacred story tells of two star-crossed lovers who were separated by war and then by treachery and miscommunication. Popocatépetl, a warrior, went off to fight against the Aztec Empire, which had colonized his people. He left behind his beloved Iztaccíhuatl, whom he was engaged to marry. But another man who wanted Izta for himself told her that Popo had died. Instead of marrying the rival, Izta died of grief. When Popo returned and found his beloved dead, he built a monumental tomb for her and knelt by her side. He stayed there so long that the two of them became the snow-capped volcanoes that grace Mexico City's horizon.

As beautiful as this story may be, it is also yet another story where a woman's entire existence revolves around the men in her world—in fact, where the men in her world determine even whether or not she continues to exist. López, again, wanted to see the story differently. Retaining the main story line, her image *Ixta* changes the narrative visually into a tale of two contemporary Chicanas, fighting not the oppression of the Aztec Empire but that of the United States and its 1848 annexation of northern Mexico (part of which was the city of Los Ángeles), and perhaps homophobia as well. With the classic image of Popo and Ixta as the backdrop, framed by the mountains they became but visually reversed as though in a mirror image, the modern-day Ixta lies draped along the border wall, the Los Angeles skyline arrayed behind her. Popo hovers over her in grief, her long, dark hair falling forward over her shoulders. As viewers, we might wonder what treachery has killed this Ixta, what battle this Popo was fighting that took her away from Ixta's side.

What is the power of the reframed sacred story for queer and trans people, for their allies, and for those who object to such reframing? Why did Alma López receive hate mail, even from children, and death threats after *Our*

Lady was exhibited at a gallery in Santa Fe, New Mexico? To answer these questions fully, we need the tools of both religious studies and queer and transgender studies.

QUEERING RELIGION/RELIGIONING QUEER

Alma López's work opens a door for us to begin considering one of the questions that threads throughout this book, and that we'll return to at the conclusion of each chapter: What do religious studies and transgender and queer studies have to teach each other? There's no better place to seek the answers to this question than a place where these fields intersect, and one of the clearest examples of this intersection is the reaction people often have when gender, sexuality, bodies, and religion get combined in ways they aren't used to seeing. Although such reactions range from delight to horror, they're typically neither neutral nor mild. Why? "Blasphemy," some people answer. But from a queer perspective, we might reply by asking, "What exactly *is* blasphemy? What defines it? More importantly, *who* gets to define it?"

Asking questions about who produced a story, who gets to define the "true" version of it, and who benefits (and who loses) from the way the story is told is part of an analytical technique called a ***hermeneutic of suspicion***. A hermeneutic is an interpretive strategy or technique, a way of interpreting a narrative. A hermeneutic of suspicion is one that refuses to accept the narrative at face value and instead asks "suspicious" questions about how the narrative came to be and why it's influential. Cisneros's critique of classic understandings of the Virgin of Guadalupe is based in a feminist hermeneutic of suspicion that asks *why* Mary is portrayed in this image with barely any hint of a physical form under her dress and why she is often used to teach girls and women to be subservient to men. Her questions about what Guadalupe wears under her robes challenge this portrayal, not out of a desire to disrespect Mary but out of a faith, perhaps, that Mary is a stronger and more powerful role model than she's often made out to be—not the subservient mother of God, but God herself. López's art goes one step further, making Mary not just a fierce Latina feminist role model but also a role model for queer people.

So why does a vision of Mary as a fierce, proud, queer Latina upset some people so much that they would send hate mail and death threats to the artist? Here Bruce Lincoln's theories become useful again: Perhaps it's because sacred stories—stories with truth-claims, credibility, and ultimate authority—can make, unmake, and remake the world. Perhaps seeing Mary as proud, fierce, brown, feminist, and queer—and sharing that vision in a public art exhibit—changes the world. Perhaps it unmakes a world where women who don't keep their eyes downcast, their bodies covered from head to toe, and their lives focused on men can be beaten, raped, murdered, cast aside, and thrown out of their homes, their families, and their churches. Perhaps it unmakes a world where women with brown bodies are less sacred than those with white bodies, where their bodies must be cloaked to be respected at all in a white supremacist culture. Maybe it remakes that world into one where women's bodies, Latina bodies, queer bodies, are sacred. That is an enormous change; no wonder it causes both delight and horror among those who view this small, unassuming image.

Transgender studies presses us to ask what it means for Popo to be presented as a cisgender queer woman in *Ixta*. It might also challenge us to consider whether the Virgin of Guadalupe changes her gender presentation when she moves from the traditional image in robes, hands folded and eyes downcast, to the way she appears in *Our Lady*, chin up, hands on hips, looking the viewer straight in the eye. It seems like part of the radical change in world-concept that this image creates is a change in Mary's gender. Despite critics' focus on the display of women's bodies in this image—the angel-butterfly's breasts, Guadalupe's bare skin—and the implication that sexuality is at the core of the violent reaction to *Our Lady*, it seems that sexuality isn't the only area in which this art unmakes and remakes the world. Sacred images of gender, too, are being overhauled.

Religious narratives—sacred stories—aren't just like any other narrative. But they also aren't entirely different, and they certainly aren't separate, set aside in a carefully delineated, clearly recognizable category all their own. The boundaries of the sacred are blurry, and sacred stories abound in apparently secular settings. The stories we tell about nations, for instance—national origins, special events in the life of a country, specific values we associate with that nation's culture—are sacred stories. Scientific stories are sacred stories in the lives of those for whom science is the (or a) guiding concept of the world. Histories that matter crucially to us—the origins of our ancestors, how we were named as babies, the roots of a practice or a profession that we care deeply about—these are all sacred stories. If sacred stories make, unmake, and remake the world, then they can make or unmake a world that includes the existence and the value of same-sex desire, same-sex eroticism, gender variance, and queer and trans people. If they exist not only within but far beyond the organizations people usually identify as *religion*, then these stories are potentially everywhere, changing the world or locking the status quo in place, enabling or erasing transgender and queer people's very existence. Where transgender studies, queer studies, and religious studies come together in the consideration of stories, they can help us to comprehend how stories can give life, and how they can kill. Those are powerful insights indeed.

STUDY QUESTIONS

1. Why do some scholars prefer the term *sacred story* to the term *myth*? As a scholar, which term would you choose, and why?
2. What are Bruce Lincoln's four categories of narrative? What criteria distinguish each one from the others?
3. What are the meanings of the orange that some queer, transgender, and feminist Jews place on their seder plate during this annual Passover meal? Where did this practice come from?
4. In what ways have biographies and autobiographies served as sacred stories for transgender and queer people?
5. How have coming-out stories helped some queer and transgender people? What are the problems with assuming that everyone can and should be publicly out?
6. How can direct communication with the divine make personal stories into what Lincoln called *myth*?
7. According to scholars like Amreen Jamal, Scott Kugle, Kecia Ali, and Dervla Sara Shannahan, what is the classical interpretation of the story of Lut in Islam? How do these scholars propose that the story should be read instead?
8. How do Roland Boer and Alma López reframe sacred stories? Why do they do this?
9. What is a hermeneutic of suspicion, and how does López use it in her art?

FOR FURTHER THOUGHT

1. What sacred stories are you familiar with? What kinds of worlds do those stories make? Are there ways that people might see same-sex desire and gender variance in those stories, places where transgender and queer people might find themselves? Has anyone ever reframed those stories, as far as you know? If so, how? If not, why not? What might a reframed version look like?
2. Have you ever experienced or known about a narrative that changed its status by losing or gaining authority, credibility, or truth-claims? If so, how did that change affect the world concepts of the people who used the narrative? If not, think of a situation in the world around you that you would like to see change. What narrative(s) uphold that situation and make it part of "the way things are"? What changes could happen to that narrative to alter the situation?
3. This chapter has discussed the importance of life stories—their own and others'—for queer and transgender people. In what ways have

stories like these been important in your own life? Does thinking about them through Lincoln's categories help you understand their importance in a different way? Are there other ways of thinking about these stories that might be more helpful than Lincoln's theories?

4. If academic stories can also be authoritative, and therefore can potentially unmake or remake the world, in what ways might this book have such effects? What worlds might it unmake, stabilize, or remake? Why?

5. As we've discussed, reframed sacred stories are often met with either delight or horror. How did it feel to you to read about Boer's and López's reframed stories? Why do you think you had these reactions (even if the reaction was just neutral interest)? What other reframed stories are you aware of? What do you think of them? Why?

6. Try out a hermeneutic of suspicion on a narrative familiar to you. Who produced the narrative? Whom does it benefit? Who suffers from this narrative? What can you conclude about the power dynamics mobilized by this narrative?

RECOMMENDATIONS FOR FURTHER READING

Ali, Kecia. *Sexual Ethics and Islam: Feminist Reflections on Qur'an, Hadith, and Jurisprudence*. Oxford: Oneworld, 2006.

Alpert, Rebecca. *Like Bread on the Seder Plate: Jewish Lesbians and the Transformation of Tradition*. New York: Columbia University Press, 1997.

Boer, Roland. "Yahweh as Top: A Lost Targum." In Ken Stone, ed., *Queer Commentary and the Hebrew Bible. Journal for the Study of the Old Testament* Supplement Series 334 (2001): 75–105.

Cabezón, José Ignacio. *Sexuality in Classical South Asian Buddhism*. Somerville, MA: Wisdom Publications, 2017.

De Alba, Alicia Gaspar, and Alma López, eds. *Our Lady of Controversy: Alma López's Irreverent Apparition*. Austin: University of Texas Press, 2011.

DeBlosi, Nikki Lyn. *Different from All Other Nights: A Queer Passover Haggadah*. New York: Bronfman Center for Jewish Student Life at NYU, 2013. Available online: https://www.keshetonline.org/resource/different-from-all-other-nights-a-queer-passover-haggadah/.

Faure, Bernard. *The Red Thread: Buddhist Approaches to Sexuality*. Princeton, NJ: Princeton University Press, 1998. See especially chapter 5, "Buddhist Homosexualities."

Gyatso, Janet. "One Plus One Makes Three: Buddhist Gender, Monasticism, and the Law of the Non-Excluded Middle." *History of Religions* 42 (2003): 89–115.

Kugle, Scott Siraj al-Haqq. "Sexuality, Diversity, and Ethics in the Agenda of Progressive Muslims." In *Progressive Muslims: On Justice, Gender, and Pluralism*, edited by Omid Safi, 190–233. Oxford: Oneworld, 2005.

Lincoln, Bruce. *Discourse and the Construction of Society: Comparative Studies of Myth, Ritual, and Classification*. New York: Oxford, 1992.

Najmabadi, Afsaneh. *Professing Selves: Transsexuality and Same-Sex Desire in Contemporary Iran*. Durham, NC: Duke University Press, 2014.

Pattanaik, Devdutt. *The Man Who Was a Woman and Other Queer Tales from Hindu Lore*. New York: Harrington Park Press, 2002.

Shannahan, Dervla Sara. "Some Queer Questions from a Muslim Faith Perspective." *Sexualities* 13, no. 6 (2010): 671–84.

NOTES

1. Rebecca Alpert, *Like Bread on the Seder Plate: Jewish Lesbians and the Transformation of Tradition* (New York: Columbia University Press, 1997), 1–2.

2. Bruce Lincoln, *Discourse and the Construction of Society: Comparative Studies of Myth, Ritual, and Classification* (New York: Oxford, 1992).

3. Nikki Lyn DeBlosi, *Different from All Other Nights: A Queer Passover Haggadah* (New York: Bronfman Center for Jewish Student Life at NYU, 2013), 14.

4. As Kathryn Phillips analyzes, for instance, in the context of female-bodied early Christian saints who presented as men.

5. Qwo-Li Driskill, *Asegi Stories: Cherokee Queer and Two-Spirit Memory* (Tucson: University of Arizona Press, 2016), 11–12.

6. Ibid., 3.

7. Afsaneh Najmabadi, *Professing Selves: Transsexuality and Same-Sex Desire in Contemporary Iran* (Durham, NC: Duke University Press, 2014), 38.

8. Some of the scholarship on these figures can be found in the academic essays at the beginning of Winston Leyland, ed., *Queer Dharma: Voices of Gay Buddhists*, vol. 1 (San Francisco: Gay Sunshine Press, 1998). The book is out of print, however, and can be difficult to find. Another resource is Bernard Faure, *The Red Thread: Buddhist Approaches to Sexuality* (Princeton, NJ: Princeton University Press, 1998), especially chapter 5. An important work in this area, which challenges some of the claims in the earlier articles, is Janet Gyatso, "One Plus One Makes Three: Buddhist Gender, Monasticism, and the Law of the Non-Excluded Middle," *History of Religions* 42 (2003): 89–115. For current and comprehensive coverage, see José Ignacio Cabezón, *Sexuality in Classical South Asian Buddhism* (Somerville, MA: Wisdom Publications, 2017).

9. Scott Siraj al-Haqq Kugle, "Sexuality, Diversity, and Ethics in the Agenda of Progressive Muslims," in *Progressive Muslims: On Justice, Gender, and Pluralism*, ed. Omid Safi (Oxford: Oneworld, 2005), 203.

10. Kecia Ali, *Sexual Ethics and Islam: Feminist Reflections on Qur'an, Hadith, and Jurisprudence* (Oxford: Oneworld, 2006); Dervla Sara Shannahan, "Some Queer Questions from a Muslim Faith Perspective," *Sexualities* 13, no. 6 (2010): 671–84.

11. Roland Boer, "Yahweh as Top: A Lost Targum," in *Queer Commentary and the Hebrew Bible*, ed Ken Stone, *Journal for the Study of the Old Testament* Supplement Series 334 (2001): 75–105

12. Alma López, "It's Not about the Santa in My *Fe*, but the Santa Fe in My *Santa*," in *Our Lady of Controversy: Alma López' Irreverent Apparition*, Alicia Gaspar de Alba and Alma López (Austin: University of Texas Press, 2011), 268.

13. Ibid., 272.

14. Ibid., 275.

Chapter Two

Conversations

Conversations, as we've already begun to see, are interwoven with stories. People have conversations about stories, like the conversations between Amreen Jamal, Scott Kugle, Kecia Ali, and Dervla Sara Shannahan about the Qur'anic story of Lut. Conversations can tell a story, as with Roland Boer's story about the conversation between God, Moses, the Marquis de Sade, Baron von Sacher-Masoch, Freud, Lacan, and Deleuze, and they can alter stories, as happened with the conversations that Rebecca Alpert recounts about lesbians in Judaism and bread on the seder plate.

Conversations also vary with regard to their participants and their audiences. Some conversations about same-sex eroticism and gender variance take place entirely among cisgender heterosexuals, as though transgender and queer people cannot or should not speak for themselves. For a while, in fact, this was the primary mode in which religious conversations about same-sex eroticism and gender variance took place within established religious institutions: People who identified as heterosexual and cisgender would gather and determine the fate of those within their religion who did not identify this way. Gender-variant and same-sex-attracted people have always had their own conversations too, of course. What has varied is how much influence those conversations have had outside of their own spaces—if they've been noticed at all. But sometimes, same-sex-attracted and gender-variant people lead the conversations for everyone. Their sexuality and their gender are either irrelevant or authorizing, giving them the authority to take the lead. Sometimes these conversations are religious or take place in religious settings; at other times religion serves as the backdrop or the underpinning for the conversation. Most such conversations also can't be fully understood without an intersectional perspective.

Communities of same-sex-attracted and gender-variant people in Indonesia, for example, are engaged in conversations both among and beyond themselves about topics ranging from religion to politics to fashion to popular culture. Like most of us, they change the tone, the focus, and even the language of the conversation depending on their conversation partner. Anthropologist Sharyn Graham Davies has written about these conversations as they take place among ethnically Bugis people in South Sulawesi, and her study can help us to understand the rich variety of conversations that people have about gender, sexuality, and religion.[1]

Although the majority of Indonesians are Muslims, the country has a long history of religious diversity, combination, and innovation. It's typical for religions that are new arrivals in any region to strike up a conversation with the existing religions there. Of course, sometimes those conversations are more friendly and sometimes they're less so; if a religion arrives at gunpoint, as Christianity did in some of the areas colonized by Europeans over the past several centuries, the "conversation" is pretty one-sided. But if a religion spreads through measures other than force it often engages with the local religions that are already present, and even when force is involved some blending of the two religions is likely—the Virgin of Guadalupe, who embodies aspects of Aztec and other indigenous Mexican deities, is an excellent example. So when Islam arrived in Indonesia, rather than replace the existing religious practices and world concepts entirely, it ended up in conversation with them.

In a number of regions of Southeast Asia and the Pacific Islands, there are indigenous traditions that understand people who are sexually or gender indeterminate—intersex people and people we might today call nonbinary or genderqueer—as conduits for the spirit world. In the Bugis language, people who can serve the community in this way are called *bissu*. Being intersex or gender indeterminate is necessary but not sufficient for becoming *bissu*; one must also be chosen by the spirits, follow strict guidelines for bodily purity that include celibacy, undergo extensive training and initiation, and demonstrate successful spirit possession through a special ritual. With its lengthy history, the role of *bissu* predates the arrival of Islam in Indonesia. And the *bissu*'s engagement with a populous world of deities and spirits would not sit well with any of the monotheistic religions present in Indonesia, since **monotheism** (literally, "one-god-ism") does not have room in its world concept for such a wide variety of generally benevolent deities beyond the human world. Yet most *bissu* are Muslim.

Moreover, one of the important functions of *bissu* in their communities is to obtain blessings from the deities and the spirits for others; among the common requests is blessings for the **hajj**, the pilgrimage to Mecca that all Muslims are encouraged to take part in at least once in their life if they're able to do so. So people who follow a religion that has only one deity, that generally doesn't recommend celibacy to its followers, and that currently struggles with questions about the permissibility of gender variance, seek out celibate, gender-variant religious specialists to communicate with other deities and with spirits in order to ensure blessings for an Islamic pilgrimage! At first glance, many outside observers would think these people are confused, or are bad Muslims, or are cynically trying to play the system and have the best of all worlds. But a *Verstehen* approach encourages us to think differently and to accept that if the *bissu* and their patrons say that the spirit world and Islam go together, then they *do*. And then we can begin to ask deeper and potentially more interesting questions about this example of religions in conversation over questions of gender variance.

Not that Islam and *bissu*'s practices have always or easily gone hand in hand. The sacred story that provided authority for the existence and the importance of *bissu* was challenged and delegitimized by Bugis elites who converted to Islam in the early seventeenth century, and in the mid-twentieth century, members of Islamic nationalist movements in South Sulawesi violently attacked *bissu*, killing many. In the 2000s, socially conservative Muslim leaders in the area condemned *bissu* and their clients as un-Islamic. Yet many *bissu* and their clients continue to consider themselves good Muslims and to combine their Islamic practice with their interactions with *bissu* deities and spirits. Some explain this by saying that *bissu* practices are part of their local cultural tradition and are therefore Islamically permissible; others feel no need to explain. Here we return to the question we considered in the previous chapter: Who gets to say? In this case, who gets to say who and what is Islamic?

If religions are in conversation around *bissu*, sometimes this leads to conversations over the heads of the *bissu* themselves—that is, conversations that take place solely among non-*bissu* people about the status of *bissu*. Such conversations take political, legal, and religious forms, when non-*bissu* politicians, judges, and religious scholars and leaders discuss the status and the fate of *bissu* without actually consulting them. Again, here we have the question of who gets to decide, why they are the ones who get to decide, and what the consequences of this decision-making structure are for those whose existence is being decided for them. But religious conversations also take place among *bissu*, about religious principles and about what it means to be *bissu*, and a form of conversation also takes place between *bissu* or those seeking initiation and their deity, since the latter is the final arbiter of who is and is not *bissu*.

Conversations are also part of the interactions between gender-variant people, same-sex-attracted people, and *bissu* in South Sulawesi. Some of these conversations focus on categorization, since *bissu* are not the only gender-variant people there. The distinction between the various categories of gender variance lies in how people navigate the underlying binary model of gender in Indonesia. When gender and sex are both conceived of as binary—woman and man (gender), female and male (sex)—where do intersex and gender-variant people fit in? *Bissu* understand themselves to be a combination of the two, sometimes so literally that they describe and present themselves as having a male half and a female half to their bodies. The binary remains, but it is troubled—queered, you might say—with the addition of the idea that the binary can be evident in a single body.

Another way of structuring or conceptualizing gender variance within a binary is through a model that retains the binary but includes the possibility that one's sexed position on the binary and one's gendered position on the binary might be related in various ways—for instance, a woman might be male-bodied and a man might be female-bodied. In Bugis, the former call themselves *calabai* and the latter *calalai*. Although a *calabai* might be married to a woman and a *calalai* to a man, it is generally understood that being *calabai* or *calalai* has implications not only for gender but also for desire, and that *calabai* (male-bodied women) desire men as part of their womanliness and *calalai* (female-bodied men) desire women as a natural part of being men. Both typically partner with gender-conforming people—female-bodied women (for *calalai*) and male-bodied men (for *calabai*). Furthermore, there are also same-sex-attracted people who are not gender variant (the partners of *calabai* and *calalai*, for example, but also those who choose same-gender partners). Conversations abound within and between these various communities about who actually belongs where—is a *bissu* actually a *calabai*, or a *calabai* a *bissu*? Some people claim more than one identity; some *bissu*, for example, also consider themselves to be *calabai*. Outsiders to the communities, including family and friends, engage in conversations with and over the heads of *calalai*, *calabai*, and *bissu* about whether someone really is one of these identities and whether the identities really do—or should—exist.

Finally, all of these traditional identities are in conversation with rapidly globalizing identities such as gay, lesbian, and transgender. Davies explains that the *calalai* and *calabai* she spoke with used many different words to describe themselves but generally avoided words like *transgender*, *lesbian*, and *gay*. In Indonesia more broadly, though, and especially in urban areas, some people do use these terms (or versions of them) even as others reject them as too medicalized, too sexual, and too Western. But in the context of a growing global conversation that often presumes that these words represent a fixed aspect of human nature, and in a context where the use of these words can often unlock political and economic support from powerful and wealthy Global North/Global West countries, engaging in a conversation about "gayness" or "transgender rights" or "LGBT people" may be an important strategic move. There are many more aspects of conversations at the intersections of gender, sexuality, religion, politics, and globalization in Indonesia, but with these few examples let's move on to consider the more general forms that conversations take, and the questions we might ask about them, in other religious traditions and in other parts of the world.

OFFICIAL CONVERSATIONS

Heather R. White, a historian of US religions, tells us that the first time the word *homosexuals* appeared in an English translation of the Protestant Christian Bible was in 1946.[2] Although Christians had argued for centuries over whether same-sex eroticism was worse than or similar to other nonmarital, nonprocreative forms of sex and had even, as one historian famously described, created bonding rituals for people of the same sex who were emotionally close to one another, the singling out of "homosexuals" in the Bible was a new development.[3] Blending two words in the original Greek text into a single word that had invented less than a century prior, the translators wove science's sacred story into their own. They were liberal Protestants, convinced that science would enhance religion rather than destroy it, and they were learning from the then-new field of psychology, which understood same-sex desire as a mental illness tied to gender variance in the form of the homosexual, once known as the invert. Based on the psychology of the time, they saw this pathology as totalizing, encompassing all aspects of the homosexual's life and essence through that unifying and centralizing organ known as the brain. They saw homosexuality as a condition, sometimes curable and sometimes permanent, that affected all human beings who were exposed to certain conditions; therefore, they understood *homosexual* to be a new word for a timeless problem. That their translation was anachronistic bothered them not one bit.

One of the key words in the ancient Greek versions of this text means "soft"; the earlier King James Version translated this term as "effeminate," thereby revealing the translators' assumptions that femininity is soft and that the Bible addresses only men, since the word *effeminate* is never used for feminine women but only for feminine men.[4] At the time when this text was written, though, the word referred to overindulgent men who partied too hard and had no time for their responsibilities as citizens of empire, and in fact White notes that "self-indulgent" was the common interpretation of this word prior to 1946. The other word continues to puzzle scholars, as it's a rare term and there's a lot of uncertainty about what it means. The King James Version, though, translated it as "abusers of themselves with mankind"—and remember that in this era *mankind* could mean all human beings regardless of gender. But armed with the idea of homosexuality as a gender inversion that caused an illness resulting in pathological sexuality, these translators saw "soft" and "abusers of themselves with mankind" as a clear indication that

Paul, the author of the text, thought homosexuals would be barred from heaven.

White tells us that conservatives scoffed at the replacement of sin with psychology. They had congregations of sinners to reform, and they weren't particularly interested in the new translation anyway. But over time they became convinced that the translation was correct, and by the time that liberals began to decide it had all been a terrible mistake, conservatives had decided that Christianity had always reserved a special place in hell for homosexuals. Queer and trans people were starting to think so too, and the liberals, for their part, conveniently forgot that they had ever played a role in the Christian rejection of trans and queer people. When held over the course of decades, conversations often get garbled.

Because of the fairly recent invention of the concept of homosexuality as a specific cultural way of structuring sexuality and sometimes gender, and because of the even more recent invention of the concept of transness and its gradual, if partial, separation from homosexuality, religious organizations have only recently begun to discuss on an official level questions related to the topic that most people call "homosexuality and religion." Predictably, queer and transgender people have typically not been a part of these conversations. In fact, prior to the 1990s there were very few conversations about transgender people in religion at all, largely because many people still associated gender variance with homosexuality. This is still true in some circles, most notably conservative Protestant ones, but there are also exceptions; in Iran, for instance, as the result of courageous advocacy by a transgender woman activist in the mid-1980s, the Ayatollah Khomeini himself released a **fatwa** (legal decision) declaring gender affirmation treatment to be Islamically permissible. Although transgender and queer people have begun to be included more broadly in these conversations about their own lives and their own value as human beings, in many religious settings queer and transgender people are still not allowed to determine their sexual ethics on their own but rather are welcomed to partner with the straight, cisgender people who are already doing it for them, in order to offer their special insights.

To say that religious groups began to discuss homosexuality less than a hundred years ago, though, and that most religious organizations only began to issue formal policies on homosexuality less than fifty years ago, is not to say that they were silent before that time on questions of the acceptability of same-sex eroticism and gender variance. Because the contemporary concept of homosexuality as a permanent human condition, whether pathological or normal, that affects many aspects of one's life and one's being is a recent invention, religious organizations haven't talked about it for long. They couldn't comment on it before it existed!

But we've seen lots of examples already of religious groups commenting on people's actions in terms of same-sex eroticism and gender variance.

Buddhists in sixteenth-century Japan extolled the beauty and the love of male adolescents; so did Muslims in the seventeenth-century Ottoman Empire. Buddhist texts tell of the danger of *pandakas* seducing monks and of an enlightened goddess who easily swapped her body with that of a male sage to prove the irrelevance of sex. Early Jewish rabbis considered how to apply binary gender-based legal principles to an intersex person; in a system that equated sex and gender, intersex and transgender would be quite similar identities, at least in their effects. In the same era, the rabbis concluded that sex between women was a fairly negligible offense, of concern only to the families of religious leaders. An Indonesian epic explains that *bissu* played a key role in the creation of the world. Other examples abound. While there are far too many to collect in a single chapter or even a single book, what's most important to remember about these varied statements is that no large and long-lived religion has been consistent in its treatment of gender variance and same-sex eroticism. In different time periods and different places, all have ranged from more positive approaches (varying from celebration to, at the very least, looking the other way) to harsh condemnation. Save for relatively recent or very small traditions, there is no religion with a singular, unvarying interpretation of same-sex eroticism and gender variance.

In the twentieth century, pressures to "modernize" affected both Global North/Global West cultures and Global South/Global East cultures, although these pressures affected each differently. As we've already noted, scientists had begun to distinguish what they did from the work of religion, and some of them used their ideas to challenge or denigrate religion. Something called *science* had become, in the nineteenth century, the mark of cultural advancement and sophistication. Hand in hand with science went *modernity*. To be the most admirable and the most powerful, a society (and individuals) had to be modern and scientific. Religious organizations struggled not to be left behind in this sea change, and many sought to weave scientific and religious perspectives together in order to create the most modern, advanced, and scientific religion. Sacred stories were subjected to scientific analysis, and as we've seen, even sin came to be interpreted through a scientific lens. Other religions reacted to these changes in the opposite way, by rejecting science and modernity as signs of the fall of Global North/Global West cultures. Some still see things like this.

If the concepts of science and modernity became tools for dismissing religion in the Global North/Global West, they became tools for justifying colonialism in the Global South/Global East. While some in the anticolonial movements that fought back against European occupation rejected the terms of this argument, others decided that in order to regain control of their countries they needed to prove the Europeans wrong—to prove, in other words, that they were scientific and modern. Even those countries that were not directly colonized by Europe or by European settler colonies like the United

States got in on this game, striving to prove their equality with the Global North/Global West through proving that they were modern and scientific. One of the ways to do this was to adopt Global North/Global West scientific approaches to same-sex eroticism and gender variance. While many colonized regions, especially those that were part of the British Empire, had antihomosexuality laws imposed on them by colonial governments, they retained those laws after decolonization and they developed both scientific and religious commentaries, often intertwined as in the Global North/Global West, on homosexuality and transsexuality. As a consequence, although the concept of inversion and its descendants, homosexuality and transsexuality, were invented by European scientists, these concepts made their way into most major religions and settled there by representing themselves as longstanding religious perspectives that had recently been given their proper name. Moreover, because any European influence was controversial in former European colonies, some people began to argue that not only the *concepts* but the *practices* of homosexuality and transsexuality were European imports, insisting that same-sex eroticism and gender variance were unknown vices prior to colonization. Nothing could be further from the truth, but what *is* true is that contemporary official religious attitudes toward same-sex eroticism and gender variance are in most cases a direct consequence of this interwoven history of the heavily loaded terms *science, modernity, homosexuality, transsexuality*, and *religion*.

So where do the various religious organizations stand now on the nature, religious status, and inclusion of queer, transgender, and other same-sex-attracted and gender-variant people? It would be impossible (and probably boring!) to discuss the answer to this question for each of the many thousands of official religious perspectives in the world, but some generalizations may be helpful. First, it's important to point out that different religious organizations have different levels of authority over their members and participants. Some, such as many branches of Christianity, have the authority to determine who is or is not a member of the religion, whereas others, like most branches of Judaism, determine only who can belong to a particular congregation and still others, such as many varieties of Hinduism, may have opinions about people's behavior but don't have membership rolls and therefore can't revoke people's membership at all. Second, most religious groups do have the authority to determine who can and cannot serve as a religious leader, but there are often resistant movements within those traditions that disagree and that will ordain religious leaders not ordained by the larger movement. Third, in the Global South/Global East, religious acceptance or condemnation of gender-variant and same-sex-attracted people is impacted by the argument made by some nationalists that homosexuality and transgender identities are Western colonial imports, and acceptance of indigenous forms of same-sex eroticism and gender variance often turns on whether or not those are also seen as imported and Western. Fourth, one can fairly easily say that more socially liberal religious organizations tend to be more likely to embrace gender-variant and same-sex-attracted people, whereas more socially conservative organizations are more likely to reject them or at least try to change them. Fifth, attitudes toward same-sex eroticism don't always predict attitudes toward gender variance, and vice versa. Sixth, and finally, for every group that rejects gender variance and same-sex eroticism, there is usually a group of people or an organization that defies that rejection, often a religious organization founded and run by same-sex-attracted and gender-variant people to support others like them. You can look up information about the specific official policies of many major religious groups online (but be sure you use an authoritative source or visit the organization's official website).

It's important to remember that official conversations about same-sex-attracted and gender-variant people are typically conducted without such people in the room. Any time a dominant group has a conversation by itself about the inclusion of a nondominant group, things tends to go poorly for the latter. This is part of the reason for the formation of so many queer and transgender religious groups by queer and transgender people, as we'll discuss further in chapter 5. However, restrictions on the participation of gender-variant and same-sex-attracted people in religious organizations don't entirely stifle such people's desire to join, and often to lead. Some seek ordination while fighting against identities that their religion says are wrong, and others have been so impacted by the condemnation of such identities that they aren't even aware of their own identities when they seek ordination. Most religious groups that ban the ordination of same-sex-attracted and gender-variant people, consequently, nevertheless have some such people within their leadership. Under the right conditions, a few of those leaders may go public with their identities; in other cases they work quietly behind the scenes.

Through their courage and their authority as religious leaders, these people who end up at the heart of conversations about gender and sexuality despite their organizations' efforts to keep them out can sometimes make profound change. Even when they're forced out or marginalized, some—like Troy Perry, who was removed from his pastoral position in his socially conservative Pentecostal church and went on to found the Metropolitan Community Church, or Rabbi Steve Greenberg, whose writings on Orthodox Jewish perspectives on same-sex eroticism have been profoundly influential for many people, or Joy Ladin, a transgender professor at Yeshiva University in New York City who transitioned publicly and who writes about transgender people in Judaism, or gay South African imam Muhsin Hendricks—go on to make a global impact in their religions. Such leaders show us another approach to conversations: the conversations that transgender and queer people have with their religious traditions and communities.

CONVERSING WITH TRADITIONS

In 1996, Indo-Canadian filmmaker Deepa Mehta released the first film in her Elements trilogy, which took up contemporary issues of social justice in India. *Fire* focused on questions of marriage and sexuality. Although it addressed a number of topics related to these themes, the film became famous—infamous, to some—for the love story at its heart that takes place between two sisters-in-law. Not least among the important factors in the controversy were their names: Radha and Sita.

Radha and Sita are two important and revered women in Hindu sacred stories. Radha is a *gopi*, or cowherd, beloved by the god Krishna. As the story goes, Krishna loves to visit Radha's group of *gopis* for flirtatious play, but Radha is his favorite among them. Krishna and Radha are often worshipped together, and some of Krishna's devotees, regardless of gender, imagine themselves as Radha in their devotion. Sita, although also deeply revered, has a very different story. The wife of Rama, the namesake of the *Ramayana* epic, Sita is exiled along with her husband in his stepmother's quest for power. While in exile, she's kidnapped by the demon king Ravana. Although Rama goes to great lengths to get her back, when Sita returns he doubts her fidelity to him. In desperation, she proves her purity through an ordeal by fire. When the flames don't consume her, Rama rejects her anyway, sending his pregnant wife out into the forest to bear their sons alone. Sita's part of the story ends when Rama accepts her sons as his own; she then begs her mother, the Earth, to swallow her up, and the Earth obliges. Because of this story, Sita is revered by many Hindus (and critiqued by many Indian feminists) as the epitome of womanhood.

While Sita and Radha aren't uncommon names for women in India, to frame a story about a relationship between two women in a clearly Hindu family and name the characters after these traditional role models for women raises the stakes of the film. For those Hindus who believe that same-sex eroticism is impure and un-Indian, associating Sita and Radha with lesbianism is quite simply shocking. As historian Mrinalini Sinha explains, Indian anticolonial nationalism has developed a significant school of thought that associates the Indian nation with Hinduism and the purity of that nation with the purity and gender traditionalism of Indian women.[5] Today that movement is known as the Hindutva, or Hindu nationalist, movement. As you might imagine, the followers of this political movement also believe that same-sex eroticism is a Western import to India, and they were especially upset by *Fire*. Protestors shut down a number of screenings and demanded that the film be banned, but although it was rereviewed by the censorship board in India, it was released again with nothing cut. Though Mehta and the actors who played Sita and Rahda all identify as heterosexual, nonetheless their feminist commitments led them to take the lead in this path-clearing conversation about same-sex desire in contemporary Hinduism. Lesbian activists, and probably even some who had not been activists prior to the film's release, turned out among many others in counterprotests supporting the film, and some queer women in India today still see *Fire*'s release as a turning point in their lives.

Similar tensions and conversations over same-sex desire, tradition, and colonialism exist in many parts of Africa, taking forms specific to the different political and religious contexts in the cities and rural areas around the continent. In Cape Town, South Africa, for instance, where openly gay imam Muhsin Hendricks has dedicated his life to fostering conversations about sexuality, gender, and Islam, LGBTQ rights are explicitly protected by the federal constitution that came into effect in 1997. A legal right to equality doesn't always translate to equal treatment, however, and despite the vocal support of such prominent religious leaders as Anglican archbishop Desmond Tutu, religion remains a significant source of discrimination and marginalization for queer and transgender people in South Africa. Imam Hendricks, one of only a handful of openly gay imams in the world, has spent decades in conversation with transgender and queer Muslims and with straight and cisgender Muslims about the inclusion of queer and transgender people in Islam. Though other religious leaders often dismiss his perspectives, there are laypeople who find them credible and helpful, and for queer and transgender Muslims his leadership has been especially important. Imam Hendricks is a key figure in the Inner Circle, which was founded in 1996 to support initially gay and eventually all queer and transgender Muslims, and he offers inclusive religious services such as Islamic same-sex weddings to people around the country.

Religious studies scholar Adriaan van Klinken, whose research focuses on religion in the lives of African queer and transgender people, has explored religious conversations among transgender and queer Africans and between those groups and larger religious organizations. He explains that Western activists and scholars are often surprised to learn how religious many African transgender and queer activists are, and he points out that such surprise is possible only "if religion is believed to be inherently homophobic and if religious commitment is considered to be a matter of individual choice and as conflicting with sexual identity."[6] Van Klinken's argument shows why the questions raised in the introduction are so important; sometimes, when we try to learn about cultures we're less familiar with, we come to that learning with assumptions about how those cultures work and we find what we expect rather than accurate information. This is perhaps especially true in the case of controversial topics such as religion, gender, and sexuality. In fact, van Klinken explains, many of the men he interviewed in Zambia claim belonging in the Zambian nation *because* they're religious: Zambia is a Christian nation, they explain, and they're Christian, and therefore they belong regardless of their sexuality.

We've shifted, over the course of this chapter, from considering conversations initiated by, and often limited to, official religious organizations to considering conversations initiated by queer and transgender religious people and groups that may or may not include larger, official organizations. Sometimes, though, for queer and transgender people to converse in useful ways with tradition they have to change or refuse the terms of the conversation that have been set by the official organization. In 2000, religious studies scholar Mark Jordan offered a profoundly insightful analysis of the limitations of conversations between queer and transgender people and powerful religious organizations in his book *The Silence of Sodom.*[7] Though the book ranges over a number of different topics relevant to the relationship between official Roman Catholicism and Catholic gay men, Jordan offers particular insights on conversations in a chapter about official church pronouncements.

Religious groups all have an organizational structure of one kind or another; especially in Christianity, the term used for these structures is *polity*. The Roman Catholic Church has an episcopal form of polity. Drawn from the word for bishop, an episcopal polity is hierarchical, with a single presiding figure at the top and larger numbers of each successive rank down to the lay members of the organization. In Roman Catholicism, the pope is the presiding figure. Traditionally a man, because the Roman Catholic Church does not ordain women into the hierarchy from which one can attain this rank, the pope is the ultimate authoritative voice for Roman Catholics. In fact, in the nineteenth century Pope Pius IX and the First Vatican Council that he convened declared that under certain circumstances the pope speaks infallibly: He cannot be wrong.

The pope doesn't run an enormous, worldwide church alone, though. When it comes to Roman Catholic **doctrine**, or official religious teachings, he's supported by an entire organization called the Congregation for the Doctrine of the Faith (CDF). Many official statements of Roman Catholic belief issue from this office, including the most influential statements about what the church calls "homosexuality." To date, the CDF hasn't issued any statements about transgender people, in part because the Roman Catholic Church is among the organizations that have tended until very recently to regard gender variance as an aspect of homosexuality and not a separate part of human experience (however, a related office, the Congregation for Catholic Education, released the church's first official document on gender identity in June 2019).

In critiquing Roman Catholic conversations about sexuality in *The Silence of Sodom*, Jordan engaged largely with CDF statements from the 1970s through the 1990s, most of them authored or directed by the man who became Pope Benedict XVI but was then known as Cardinal (another title in the church) Joseph Ratzinger. What's most important about Jordan's analysis for our purposes here is not his expert parsing of each of these documents so much as his overall argument in the chapter. As he sees it, the conversation between queer people and the Catholic Church has been entirely one-sided, directed and shaped by the church in such a way as to give the impression that the church is engaging with queer people when in fact it's preventing their full involvement in the conversation. Criticizing what he sees as "simplifications" at best and "caricatures" at worst in Catholic pronouncements on homosexuality, Jordan argues that such representations are not only inaccurate but actively harmful. "To study this kind of speech," he explains, "we need to step aside from its glare—or to look at it in rough reflection, as Perseus did with Medusa. We need to identify deceits about homosexuality without being deceived by them. So we cannot engage the documents 'on their own terms.' We cannot politely accept their categories, their rules of evidence, their patterns of argument. The categories, the rules, and the patterns enact much of the documents' forceful homophobia."[8]

Far from engaging in good faith in an open conversation with queer Catholics, Jordan suggests, the church is engaged in a one-sided, one-way conversation in which it speaks but doesn't listen. "What purposes are served," he asks, "by an authoritarian and highly repetitive moral speech?"[9] Not asking his readers to imagine what the church is *trying* to do, Jordan suggests instead that we consider the effects of such speech—not what it *says* but what it *does*. "One effect of the church's official discourse about homosexuality," he observes, "is just to keep dissidents busy rebutting [its statements]. Instead of building alternate forms of Catholic community, we spend our energy trying to explain, once again, why the latest Vatican pronouncement is unscriptural or self-contradictory or unscientific. . . . Another effect is to keep reinforcing certain categories for talking about homosexuality. . . . Yet another effect, perhaps the most dangerous, is to convince us that talk might actually lead to reform."[10] From Jordan's perspective, then, official doctrinal statements about homosexuality in Roman Catholicism are a form of conversation that functions to keep queer and, by extension, transgender Catholics too busy to fight back against their own marginalization.

While the other conversations with tradition that we've covered in this chapter—the film *Fire* in India, and conversations among queer and transgender Muslims in South Africa and gay Christians in Zambia—have been ways of engaging one another and the broader community to create religious change, Jordan's analysis reminds us that not all conversations with tradition are liberatory, and not all are worth engaging in. People who share his perspective often engage in new conversations instead, setting their own terms and developing innovative religious approaches along the way.

NEW CONVERSATIONS

Ethicist Thelathia Nikki Young brings newer insights to an already new conversation in her 2016 book on black queer ethics. We've learned about Alice Walker's creation of the term *womanist* to describe what would later be called an intersectional approach to feminism that already characterized the theory, writings, and activism of women of color and some antiracist white feminists. Scholars have taken up this term in various branches of religious studies; they've developed womanist approaches especially in theology and ethics. Among the important methodological focuses of womanist scholarship and its relatives such as *mujerista* ("womanist" translated into Spanish) scholarship in religion is a conversational, community-based approach to developing knowledge.

Given the history of academic knowledge as a site for the development of elite power—think, for example, of the role that Western intellectual perspectives have played in scientific racism and sexism, in colonialism, and in the creation and then the suppression of "the homosexual"—womanist thinkers are suspicious of the claim that "true" knowledge is the property of academically credentialed intellectuals. There are many types of knowledge, they point out, and they have similar concerns to Jordan's when it comes to the knowledge produced by groups in power about nondominant groups. In fact, many womanists argue, the most profound wisdom comes from living and reflecting on life; it can therefore be found in the perspectives and the lived realities of everyday people. Some womanists have found such perspectives in literature, looking especially to black women's writing for insights. Others have found inspiration in the same places as these writers often did: their communities. Womanist methods in theology and ethics, then, are strikingly different from the older and more established methods in these fields. Rather than turn to canonical texts written by elites and engage in written conversation with these written, dominant texts, womanists turn to the communities around them. The approach has roots not only in the works of women of color but also in both feminist and liberation theologies, the latter as originally developed by Peruvian Catholic theologian Gustavo Gutiérrez and based on his assertion that God has a "preferential option for the poor."[11] But womanists took these influences in new directions, drawing on community wisdom and seeing their roles as being creative compilers and observers of the theological perspectives and ethical approaches around them.

Despite Walker's principle that a womanist is "a woman who loves other women, sexually and/or nonsexually,"[12] womanist theology and ethics initially struggled to openly include lesbian perspectives, much less queer ones. There were a number of reasons for this exclusion. Many womanists were working in the context of Christianity, and few churches had yet moved to become openly inclusive of queer and transgender people. They were also often working within traditionally black churches, which have struggled with such inclusion. In the United States as elsewhere, slavery and racism have relied on sexual abuse and on racist characterizations of black people and other people of color as sexually depraved. One response to these racist tactics has been to avoid public discussion of black sexuality; another, which has gone hand in hand with the first, has been to stress black sexual purity. In the context of both religious and scientific debates over the acceptability of queer sex, and with transgender people being treated as simply another version of homosexuality, many predominantly straight, cisgender black communities found queer and trans issues too hot to handle. By the mid-1990s, though, some womanist theologians and ethicists were pressing the matter forward. Early leaders like Kelly Brown Douglas, Emilie Townes, and Traci West, among others, insisted on the necessity of inclusiveness in womanist theology and ethics—after all, they pointed out, lesbian and bisexual women were part of the community on whose wisdom womanists were seeking to draw.

Nikki Young builds on this history but also takes the womanist conversation in a new direction by bringing her own conversations with queer-identified black people into womanist ethics and bringing those insights into conversation with queer studies. "Black queer people," she writes, "are moral agents who enact family in ways that are simultaneously disruptive to current familial norms in our society, creatively resistant to the disciplinary powers at work in those norms, and subversively generative and imaginative in relation to establishing new ways of being in relationship."[13] For that reason, she argues, black queer people have much to contribute to the work of both ethics and theory—womanist, queer, and beyond.

It's not only scholars who raise challenges like Young's to the exclusion of black queer folks from religious spaces. Artists do this work as well. One prominent gospel singer, B.Slade, has been a high-profile activist in this regard since he came out publicly as gay in a 2009 interview. The son of a Pentecostal preacher, he grew up with not only gospel but other musical influences—including those from the music industry itself—in his San Diego area home. Under the stage name Tonéx (*"Pronounced Toe-Nay,"* as his first album title put it), he built a following as a creative and eclectic gospel singer from the mid-1990s through the 2000s. In 2009, though, a persistent interviewer and perhaps an artist tired of evasions led to Tonéx publicly revealing on a conservative Christian TV network that he was attracted to men, was sexually active with men, and saw nothing wrong with that. The gospel world dropped him.

By the end of 2009, Tonéx had changed his stage name to B.Slade and had turned his music in a new direction, agilely shifting the focus of his already eclectic art. Some in gospel music felt that he'd been unfairly treated, though, and continued to respect him and his work. In 2016 he was invited to take part in a service honoring two prominent gospel singers at an inclusive Oakland, California, church called Love Center Ministries. Although the audience was receptive, his performance was also livestreamed on Facebook, and some of the online commentators were harsh. No longer one to let homophobia go unchallenged, B.Slade fought back, releasing a video called "Conversation" that drew directly on Beyoncé's song, "Formation." "Conversation" challenged B.Slade's critics to talk with him as an equal, to have a real conversation, rather than dismiss him for not being what and who they thought he should be.

QUEERING RELIGION/RELIGIONING QUEER

Conversations, then, in the context of queer and transgender studies in religion are much more complicated than they might seem. While in its common usage the word *conversation* suggests a casual chat between equals, the attention to power that's central to queer studies, womanist thought, and transgender studies demands that we look more closely at such assumptions. Conversations can be one-sided, and usually it's those in power who do all the talking and none of the listening. Conversations can be controlling, coercive, or exclusionary. They can also be empowering, intellectually rich, and inspiring when held among transgender and queer people and their allies. Conversations can be provocative, like Alma López's art, B.Slade's music, and Roland Boer's "Targum," and they can build bridges when queer and transgender people come together in conversation with others who genuinely seek to learn and understand, as in much of Imam Muhsin Hendricks's work and that of many other queer and transgender religious leaders. So how can an analysis of conversations within queer and transgender studies in religion bring religious studies, transgender studies, and queer studies more into their own generative and egalitarian conversation? Some possible answers are offered by the authors considered above; in this section, though, we'll focus on meeting points between religious studies and queer studies in the area of contemporary social and political analysis, as demonstrated in the closely aligned work of three authors: Janet Jakobsen, Ann Pellegrini, and Erin Runions.

In the 1990s, ethicist and former policy analyst Janet Jakobsen and performance studies scholar Ann Pellegrini began to think together about rhetoric, or the language people use to talk about particular things. Both are also scholars of queer studies in religion, and they noticed religion and queerness being tied together in troubling yet influential ways in public conversations—in the media, for instance, in the written opinions of justices on the US Supreme Court, and in political speeches and ads. Together they wrote a book called *Love the Sin* that analyzed this rhetoric, drawing on insights from both queer studies and religious studies. [14]

Jakobsen and Pellegrini center their concerns in *Love the Sin* around questions of freedom and democracy, focusing on the sometimes-unnoticed roles that religion and sexuality play in these contexts. They ask, for instance, why sexual freedom isn't valued equally with other freedoms, such as freedom of religion, in the United States, but they also question whether religious freedom is truly practiced in the country. Pointing out the widespread cultural influence of Christianity, and especially Protestant Christianity, in US culture and politics, Jakobsen and Pellegrini argue that much of what passes for "secular" in the United States is in fact Christian. While we could easily point to examples of public spaces in the United States that are supposed to be secular or religiously inclusive but are not—the presence of a Christmas tree in the White House in December, for instance, or the opening of legislative sessions with a (nearly always Protestant Christian) prayer, or the Supreme Court decision that it's allowable in certain cases to post a copy of the Ten Commandments from the Hebrew Bible at a federal courthouse—Jakobsen and Pellegrini also point out subtler influences. In US Supreme Court cases involving homosexuality, for instance, they demonstrate that both opinions supporting LGBQ rights and opinions negating those rights often do so for reasons that are based in Christian, and specifically Protestant, concepts of the world.

Some of the clearest cases of Christian influence in Supreme Court opinions on topics related to sexuality are those that refer to traditions and values. Much of what people call "traditional values" in the United States stems from a very specific (and, as we've seen, relatively recent) interpretation of Christianity that presented itself inaccurately from the start as a timeworn truth of the religion. When someone argues that "traditional American values" include the idea that marriage is between one man and one woman, then, we have to ask whose tradition we're talking about, and why. Slaveholding men may have been married to just one woman, for instance, but many of them had no problem forcing their female and sometimes male slaves into having sex with them. In many cases slaves were not allowed to be married, and if they were married their marriages were treated as trivial by a slaveholding white society. For more than fifty years in the nineteenth century, the Church of Jesus Christ of Latter-day Saints, or Mormons, allowed men to marry more than one woman provided they had the financial ability to support a large family. Other Mormon groups still do. Some Native tribes, prior to colonization, welcomed their members to select different sexual partners at different points in their lives. Many of the Roman Catholics who first came to North America never married another human being, having dedicated their lives to God instead. So who counts as "American" in these references to the "American tradition" of marriage, and how secular is this tradition, really?

Yet justices who support LGBQ rights also draw on Protestant values to do so, especially in their reliance on the importance of privacy for establishing such legal rights as the right to marriage or the right to sexual activity between consenting adults. Starting in the late 1990s, a number of queer theorists have been interested in, and concerned by, the growing emphasis on privacy in both the gay rights movement and the larger US context. Lauren Berlant and Michael Warner asked in 1998 why queer folks were being pushed to "keep it in the bedroom" when straight sex was ever-present in the public sphere, and they warned that important aspects of queer culture and politics would be lost in this return to an emphasis on private propriety. [15] Lisa Duggan's 2002 article, "The New Homonormativity," raised further concerns about the problems inherent in paying for civil rights with promises of privacy. [16] A few years after the publication of *Love the Sin*, Jasbir Puar argued that queer privacy is a race-based and class-based privilege. [17] If queer and transgender rights are paid for in the currency of privacy, then some queers, it seems, can have no rights at all.

To this conversation, Jakobsen and Pellegrini added the crucial point that religion—and specifically Protestant Christianity—plays an important role in these political and legal developments. But how might Protestantism be linked to privacy? Ironically, through something called the "prayer closet." In the colonial period in the United States, through the Revolutionary War period and into the nineteenth century, Protestant ministers recommended that both men and women connect with God through private prayer. If one had a room to which one could retreat in order to be undisturbed while communing with the divine—even if it was only a closet—then all the better. Privacy, then, is a religious practice. It's hardly the sole property of Protestant Christianity, of course, but in the United States the cultural importance of privacy (for *certain* groups of people, as Puar points out) is based firmly in Protestantism. Arguing that the United States has a religious and a sexual establishment—a dominant group that gets to make the laws and determine the cultural rules that all other groups play by—Jakobsen and Pellegrini suggest that the country is characterized not by religious or sexual *freedom* but by religious and sexual *tolerance*, in which a group in power "generously" agrees to put up with other groups. This, they argue, is not justice, and it needs to change.

In 2014, biblical scholar Erin Runions wrote a book that extended Jakobsen and Pellegrini's argument into an analysis of the rhetorical roles played in US politics by the biblical city of Babylon. As Runions explains, "Invocations of biblical authority smooth the way for the continual attempts to reassert U.S. power in a world where national sovereignty must bow before the transnational circuits of capital and power." [18] For those recognized by a country or a people as belonging to their group, nationalism—identification with that country and that people, often above all else—has for several centuries been an important way of bringing order and meaning to the world. In fact, as we considered earlier, for some people nationalism functions like a religion. So perhaps it's not surprising to find the religion of the nation working hand in hand with the national religion—in this case, the US American nation evoking Christianity.

As economic systems, trade, war, and exploitation have become global, individual nations have become less powerful and have lost much of the control they once had over their own interests. War in one country can lead to economic challenges thousands of miles away, as other countries struggle to provide aid to the many civilians fleeing the violence. An economic crash in a country with a large economy can cause an economic depression halfway around the world. Profoundly affected by circumstances beyond their control, some people—especially those for whom this is a new experience, like groups that are otherwise dominant in their society—respond with various forms of nationalism, reasserting the primacy of the nation or, more accurately, *their* nation, over all else. Runions argues that the United States is in such a time in the first decades of the twenty-first century, and that in this context the biblical city of Babylon "represents what might be considered central fears within U.S. liberal democracy: that sexual, moral, ethnic, or political diversity will disrupt national unity or, conversely, that some totalitarian system will curtail freedom and force homogeneous unity."[19]

Runions traces what she calls "theopolitical" **discourse**—verbal and symbolic communication that blends religious and political themes—across US society and on both sides of the binary divide in much of US politics, arguing along with Jakobsen and Pellegrini (and numerous others) that the United States is not a secular but a Christian nation-state that promotes what Runions terms "theodemocracy," which incorporates "faith in the Christian God, democracy that distinguishes between civil and economic equality, and heteropatriarchal sexual regulation."[20] Whether they represent Babylon as a culturally sophisticated, modern city where people from around the globe speak many different languages yet work together to create technological innovation, or whether they represent it as a decadent urban environment full of sin and destined to turn from God, US leaders continually use this religious image to understand the role of their country in the world today. Runions's newest work, on biblical themes in the US prison system, promises to offer further insights about the deeply rooted roles of religion in an ostensibly secular political system and continues to build on the work of queer, transgender, and feminist studies scholars within and outside of religious studies to bring important queer and religious studies insights to profound questions of justice today.

What can the writings of these three scholars help us to understand about the insights that can come from an intersectional analysis of conversations at the junction of queer studies, transgender studies, and religious studies? In each of these works, queer and transgender studies bring the perspective that conversations always involve power. Religious studies adds the idea that power is rarely, if ever, secular—even when it appears to be at first. This is because religion is much more, and reaches much farther, than familiar religious institutions like churches, temples, synagogues, and mosques. Religion is a key conduit for power, but like other forms of power it often goes undetected when it's dominant. Where are religion and power in the conversations around you? Where are they present but unnoticed? What can we learn from spotting them in these unexpected places?

STUDY QUESTIONS

1. When and why did the word *homosexuals* first appear in an English translation of the Christian Bible?
2. This chapter has suggested that although religions have had conversations about same-sex eroticism and gender variance for many centuries, they started having conversations about homosexuality and transgender people much more recently. How is that possible? What's the difference between these types of conversation?
3. Name the six general principles listed in this chapter in relation to the official perspectives of religious groups on gender variance and same-sex eroticism.
4. In what ways does power affect religious conversations about gender and sexuality?
5. Why were Hindu nationalists so upset about Deepa Mehta's film *Fire*? What does this incident demonstrate about the connections between religion, colonialism, nationalism, gender, and sexuality? Do you think they would have been more or less upset if the film had been about two brothers-in-law with religiously significant names falling in love? Why?
6. How have queer scholars and artists challenged the marginalization of queer and transgender people in many black churches?
7. Why do scholars like Janet Jakobsen, Ann Pellegrini, and Erin Runions argue that the United States is not secular? On what do they base their argument?

FOR FURTHER THOUGHT

1. You've read the general principles about religious organizations' inclusion of gender-variant and same-sex-attracted people; now explore how these principles apply to a religion you're interested in. Start by finding out through online research, or by asking a religious leader, what official stance or stances that religion has taken, if any, and why. Then see whether there are other stances, for instance among subgroups or advocacy organizations within the religion, or in the absence of official stances whether there are groups that advocate such stances. What conversations can you find about these topics? On what bases do they make their arguments? What can you learn about the religion itself through answering these questions?

2. How might queer and transgender studies in religion help us to understand the conversations about religion, sexuality, and gender that go on around us? Find one such conversation that's been in the news recently. Learn all you can about it, then consider how it's similar to and different from the conversations discussed and analyzed in this chapter. Explore the roles of power—including colonialism, if relevant—in the conversation. What additional insights does an intersectional analysis reveal?

3. Watch B.Slade's video for "Conversation." Then do some background research by reading online comments about his gospel performance at Love Center Ministries and watching Beyoncé's video for "Formation." What's going on here? What do you think B.Slade is trying to do and say with his video? Sure, he's challenging the homophobia in the gospel industry, but what else? How does he convey these challenges? Why use "Formation" as the basis of his song? In what ways is this video a *conversation*? In what ways is it *about* conversation?

4. Using the analyses of Jakobsen, Pellegrini, and Runions as a jumping-off point, perform your own analysis of the role of religion in apparently secular spaces, whether in the United States or elsewhere. In the case you're analyzing, which religion seems to hide itself in obvious places, where it remains undetected more because it's so widespread than because it's actually hidden? Where does it appear, and in what forms? What does its presence *do*?

5. What is theodemocracy, according to Runions? What do you think of her argument that the United States is a theodemocratic country, and why? Are there countries other than the United States that you think might be theodemocratic?

RECOMMENDATIONS FOR FURTHER READING

Berlant, Lauren, and Michael Warner. "Sex in Public." *Critical Inquiry* 24, no. 2 (1998): 547–66.

Davies, Sharyn Graham. *Gender Diversity in Indonesia: Sexuality, Islam, and Queer Selves.* New York: Routledge, 2010.

Duggan, Lisa. "The New Homonormativity: The Sexual Politics of Neoliberalism." In *Materializing Democracy: Toward a Revitalized Cultural Politics*, edited by Russ Castronovo and Dana D. Nelson, 175–94. Durham, NC: Duke University Press, 2002.

Jakobsen, Janet R., and Ann Pellegrini. *Love the Sin: Sexual Regulation and the Limits of Religious Tolerance.* Boston: Beacon Press, 2004.

Jordan, Mark D. *The Silence of Sodom: Homosexuality in Modern Catholicism.* Chicago: University of Chicago Press, 2000.

Puar, Jasbir K. *Terrorist Assemblages: Homonationalism in Queer Times.* Durham, NC: Duke University Press, 2007.

Runions, Erin. *The Babylon Complex: Theopolitical Fantasies of War, Sex, and Sovereignty.* New York: Fordham University Press, 2014.

van Klinken, Adriaan. "Queer Love in a 'Christian Nation': Zambian Gay Men Negotiating Sexual and Religious Identities." *Journal of the American Academy of Religion* 83, no. 4 (2015): 947–64.

White, Heather R. *Reforming Sodom: Protestants and the Rise of Gay Rights.* Chapel Hill: University of North Carolina Press, 2015.

Young, Thelathia Nikki. *Black Queer Ethics, Family, and Philosophical Imagination.* New York: Palgrave MacMillan, 2016.

NOTES

1. Sharyn Graham Davies, *Gender Diversity in Indonesia: Sexuality, Islam, and Queer Selves* (New York: Routledge, 2010).

2. Heather R. White, *Reforming Sodom: Protestants and the Rise of Gay Rights* (Chapel Hill: University of North Carolina Press, 2015), 1. The text in question is 1 Corinthians 6:9–10, and the translation is the Revised Standard Version.

3. See John Boswell, *Same-Sex Unions in Premodern Europe* (New York: Vintage Books, 1994).

4. Queer and transgender engagement with what are sometimes called the "clobber texts" in the Hebrew Bible and the Christian New Testament constitutes some of the earliest writing on religion by self-identified LGBTQ people and their allies. These analyses date back at least to Derrick Sherwin Bailey's *Homosexuality and the Western Christian Tradition* (New York: Longmann Press, 1955), and the most-referenced classic analysis is that of John J. McNeill in *The Church and the Homosexual* (Kansas City, MO: Sheed, Andrews, and McMeel, 1975).

5. Mrinalini Sinha, *Gender and Nation* (Washington, DC: American Historical Association, 2006).

6. Adriaan van Klinken, "Queer Love in a 'Christian Nation': Zambian Gay Men Negotiating Sexual and Religious Identities," *Journal of the American Academy of Religion* 83, no. 4 (2015): 949. See also van Klinken's excellent book *Kenyan, Christian, Queer: Religion, LGBT Activism, and Arts of Resistance in Africa* (University Park: Pennsylvania State University Press, 2019).

7. Mark D. Jordan, *The Silence of Sodom: Homosexuality in Modern Catholicism* (Chicago: University of Chicago Press, 2000).

8. Ibid., 22–23.

9. Ibid., 49.

10. Ibid., 49–50.

11. See Gustavo Gutiérrez, *A Theology of Liberation: History, Politics, and Salvation*, trans. Caridad Inda and John Eagleson, 2nd. ed. (Maryknoll, NY: Orbis Books, 1988).

12. Alice Walker, "Womanist," xi, from *In Search of Our Mothers' Gardens*, xi–xii (New York: Harcourt Brace Jovanovich, 1984).

13. Thelathia Nikki Young, *Black Queer Ethics, Family, and Philosophical Imagination* (New York: Palgrave MacMillan, 2016), 10.

14. Janet R. Jakobsen and Ann Pellegrini, *Love the Sin: Sexual Regulation and the Limits of Religious Tolerance* (Boston: Beacon Press, 2004).

15. Lauren Berlant and Michael Warner, "Sex in Public," *Critical Inquiry* 24, no. 2 (1998): 547–66.

16. Lisa Duggan, "The New Homonormativity: The Sexual Politics of Neoliberalism," in *Materializing Democracy: Toward a Revitalized Cultural Politics*, ed. Russ Castronovo and Dana D. Nelson (Durham, NC: Duke University Press, 2002), 175–94.

17. Jasbir K. Puar, *Terrorist Assemblages: Homonationalism in Queer Times* (Durham, NC: Duke University Press, 2007).

18. Erin Runions, *The Babylon Complex: Theopolitical Fantasies of War, Sex, and Sovereignty* (New York: Fordham University Press, 2014), 1–2.

19. Ibid, 3.

20. Ibid., 42.

Chapter Three

Practices

Because communication—what scholars sometimes call discourse—can take symbolic as well as verbal forms, religious practice can be an important way of conversing with tradition. Conversations are also a form of practice. Just think, for instance, of conversational ways of studying sacred texts in many different traditions, from Talmud study partners in Judaism to studying the Qur'an with others in a **madrassah** (a Muslim religious school), to Protestant Christian Bible study meetings. Storytelling, too, is a form of practice, and practice can be a form of storytelling—be it the recounting of a sacred story by an indigenous elder to teach children and grandchildren about a sacred place, or the storytelling about Hindu deities in Indian classical dance. As we considered in the introduction, each of these themes connects to the others, and the examples we cover for each theme could also be examples of another.

Religious practices take many forms. People often think of religious practices as specific rituals, like a Hindu puja or a Roman Catholic Mass. But scholars who focus on lived religion—religion as it's actually lived out by everyday people—tell us that religious practice is far more than that. Getting together for a potluck might be a religious practice, especially if people bring dishes that are often associated with a particular religious culture or if the potluck is celebrating a particular religious holiday. Attending a concert might be a religious practice. So might dancing or singing. There are also more individual practices, like prayer or meditation, reading, lighting candles, even how we say things in everyday life. When a Muslim person says "inshallah"—"God willing"—after making a statement about the future, that's a religious practice. Some Christian sex manuals consider sex itself, if done with the right person in the right way, to be a religious practice, and some even encourage couples to put their Bible on the bedside table during sex, in order to invite God into the room.[1]

There are also many possible frameworks for thinking about the ways that transgender and queer people engage with religious practice. Here we'll consider four: navigating queerness and transness within traditional practices, claiming traditional practices for transgender and queer people, reworking traditional practices to be more reflective of transgender and queer lives, and creating new practices. The following example demonstrates three of these four forms of practice: navigating, claiming, and reworking. From there, we'll move into separate explorations of each form.

'Yan daudu (singular: *'dan daudu*) enact a traditional gender/sexual role in Hausa-speaking areas of Nigeria. Although British colonization may have caused the meaning of the word to shift over time, anthropologist Rudolf Pell Gaudio relates that precolonial uses seem to be linked to religion as well as to sexuality; *'yan daudu* are historically known to be practitioners of **Bori**, a traditional form of communication with the spirits through possession. Although *'yan daudu* have been severely threatened by the AIDS epidemic, by growing religious conservatism in northern Nigeria, and by the ultraconservative terrorist group Boko Haram, as of Gaudio's writing their communities continued to maintain a small underground presence in the region.[2]

'Yan daudu are people who were assigned male at birth, who enact feminine gender roles, and who are sexually attracted to and sexually active with masculine men. Some who have the economic means marry women and have children; others live in households headed by older *'yan daudu* or independent women—adult women who are not under the authority of a man—or they live alone. They pursue many different forms of work, but the discrimination they face means that sometimes that work is part of the underground economy, and *'yan daudu* are known for being available for hire by men as sex workers. While it's possible that their gender variance at one time qualified them especially or uniquely for communication with the spirit world, by the late twentieth century when Gaudio began spending time with *'dan daudu* communities they had no formal religious role. Most, like most of their fellow Hausas, were Muslims, and many also practiced *Bori*.

Here we have, then, another case in which a traditional gender/sexual role associated with spirit possession exists intertwined with Islam. Unlike *bissu*, *'yan daudu* are not currently—and perhaps never were—understood as *uniquely* chosen by the spirits for possession. At least since British occupation, though, and possibly before, *'yan daudu* have been associated with *Bori* and with independent women because all three are socially stigmatized. In addition, because *Bori* spirits sometimes possess people across gender lines, a man who is not a *'dan daudu* may put on women's clothes and act in feminine ways during possession. In these traditions of spirit possession, it's understood that this happens because a feminine spirit takes over his body—

that is, during this time it's not he but the spirit who's moving and talking. Of course, then, the spirit would dress and act in line with her gender. British colonists, however, might have brought their own ideas about the connections between gender, sexuality, and practice to their interpretations of *Bori*, and concluded that most of the men involved in spirit possession were *'yan daudu*. These are the challenges of studying history among peoples impacted by colonialism.

The religious practices of many *'yan daudu* in the late twentieth and early twenty-first centuries, like those of a fair number of other Hausas, combine Islam and *Bori*. Often relying on the spirits for help with mundane matters in everyday life, *'yan daudu* also pray regularly and strive to find the ability to go on hajj. Like *bissu* and *calabai*, *'yan daudu* who go on hajj must go as men; while this denies their gender identity, it also carries the significant advantage of not having to travel with a male escort, as women must do. In these regards, then, *'yan daudu* are *navigating* practices within their traditions—one form of engagement with practice that we'll be discussing in this chapter.

Claiming is another form of engagement with religious practice. *Bori*, it seems, has already been claimed for *'yan daudu* and other gender-variant people—including independent women, who challenge traditional femininity in Northern Nigeria by living outside of a male-headed household. Claiming Islam is currently a less widespread practice, even though historically that religion has had space for at least some gender-variant and same-sex-attracted people. But when a *'dan daudu* comes back from the hajj and begins to use the Hausa honorific title *Alhaji* (or, more often, the feminine form *Hajiya*), and when he then regales his friends with stories not only of the religious sights of Mecca but also of the sexual prowess of Saudi men, he's doing more than simply navigating Islam *as* a *'dan daudu*; he's *claiming* Islam *for* *'yan daudu*.

Reworking is our third mode of engagement with practice; *'yan daudu* also *rework* Islam in ways that make it their own. Many of the examples of such reworking that Gaudio offers are connected with *'yan daudu*'s cultural linkage to women's forms of humor and speech, and with their cultural association with the bawdiness of sex workers and independent women. In one conversation, for instance, one of Gaudio's *'dan daudu* friends said goodbye when Gaudio was about to leave for the United States by reciting a traditional set of Hausa Muslim prayers. Gaudio responded in similarly traditional fashion by saying "Amen" after each one. But his friend cleverly threw in a less traditional final prayer, and the whole sequence moved so fast that Gaudio automatically responded with "Amen" before he realized what his friend had said. Everyone erupted in laughter. Here's how Gaudio relates the conversation:

"Well then," Dan Zaria said, "may God deliver you [home] safely."
"Amen," I replied.
"And may God bring you back [to Nigeria] safely."
"Amen."
"May God cause you to find your parents in good health."
"Amen."
"May God cause you to make progress in your work."
"Amen."
"And may God make it that, when you come back, my breasts have come out fully."
"Amen."[3]

The final prayer is not a traditional one, and it's certainly not a traditional prayer for a man to say. Even for a woman, it's far too explicit to be considered appropriate as a public prayer by most Muslims. With this joke that was very much in line with *'dan daudu* culture, Dan Zaria reworked Islam to make the experience of *'yan daudu* central to his religious practice.

An even clearer example comes from another conversation that Gaudio relates. His friend Mansur, who was a dedicated Muslim, once started describing a well-endowed man he'd had sex with. As Gaudio tells it, "Mansur declared, 'Promise of God! Despite the size of that dick, I grabbed that dick with my hand. . . . The dick went in, whoosh! I invoked blessings on the Prophet Muhammad and informed God [of my faith] in my heart."[4] While many Muslims do not consider humor, gender variance, and sexual explicitness to be appropriate in prayer, all three are part of *'dan daudu* culture. For *'yan daudu* to include them in prayer, then, is to make Islam their own and to underscore that God accepts them even when many of their fellow Muslims do not. "God made us," said another one of Gaudio's *'dan daudu* friends.[5] If God made them, these *'yan daudu* argue, why should they pretend before God to be something they're not? Wouldn't that deny God's creation? In their practices, then, *'yan daudu navigate* between history and present, between traditional and newer practices, by engaging in *Bori* as part of their history and their present reality. They *navigate* Islam through going on the hajj as masculine men, and they *claim* Islam as their own through telling stories of the hajj that include trysts with Saudi men in Jiddah on the way to and from Mecca, and by claiming publicly the honorific title for a woman who's been on the hajj. Lastly, they *rework* Islam to include their own realities and cultures by weaving gender variance and same-sex desire into traditional Islamic practices. Now let's look in more depth at each of these forms of queer and transgender religious practice.

NAVIGATING PRACTICE

Is celibacy queer? Some people who practice it think so; some people who study celibacy think so too. And consider this: is there a difference between being celibate and being ace (asexual)? Many ace people identify within the larger queer community, but they wouldn't necessarily use the word *celibate* for themselves. Is that because celibacy has religious overtones? Because it may be more of a practice than an identity? What about ace people who are religious? Sometimes queer communities and religious communities have similar practices but call them by different names; neither would necessarily want to be associated with the other.

Too often, many queer people have heard from religious organizations that celibacy is the only way for them to be both queer and religious. Some conservative churches have even explained same-sex desire as God's way of calling someone to celibacy. As a result, queer folks tend to have a pretty negative view of celibacy, even as they may respect or claim ace identities. But what about people who accept themselves as queer *and* have a religious call to celibacy? In one chapter of an edited book called *Queer Christianities*, Episcopalian (US Anglican) nun Sister Carol Bernice brings a personal perspective to these questions. "I am queer and celibate," she introduces herself, "and I've often been asked, by those whom I presume are well-meaning folks, which of these states of life caused the other. The truth of the matter is that I became a lesbian and a Christian on the selfsame day—it was in September—fifteen years ago, and from that point on they both together led quite naturally and eventually to the consecrated celibate life I lead today."[6] She first fell in love and lived with another woman, but when her partner died seven years later she found herself drawn to focus her time and her energies on the sacred in the company of other women. "If queer is queer because of its stance in relation to normal," Sister Carol writes, "then . . . celibate, for me, is mighty queer."[7]

In the same volume, religious studies scholar Lynne Gerber offers a very different approach to queer celibacy from the perspective of the evangelical Protestant ex-gay movement, arguing that in certain circumstances even sexual activity might be what she calls a "queerish" form of celibacy. With the exception of the Anglican Communion, which in the US welcomes queer members, Protestant churches in general have little room for the religious renunciation of sexual activity. Consequently, Protestants who believe that same-sex eroticism is forbidden have little recourse to offer same-sex-attracted people other than heterosexual marriage. While the ex-gay movement has come in the twenty-first century to question its commitment to the idea that all human beings are naturally heterosexual and that people who experience same-sex desire can "convert" to desiring different-sex people, still both leaders and members of this movement believe that God condemns same-sex eroticism and that those with same-sex desire should resist fulfilling that desire in any way. They have even gone so far as to recommend not only different-sex marriage but sexuality within that marriage, even if the same-sex-attracted partner or partners have no desire for such sexual contact.

Why is this celibacy? Gerber argues that ex-gays engage in an unusual, "queerish" sexual practice because they must stifle the expression of their sexual desires while engaging in sexual practices that they don't desire, or that they desire only slightly or only in theory. "The queerish twist of ex-gay celibacy," Gerber argues, is that it "is a celibacy in which sexual abstinence is required in the face of one's most deeply felt erotic desires but sexual expression is encouraged and affirmed in relation to tepid desires."[8] In fact, she goes on to suggest, the ex-gay movement may be drawing on some deeply historic trends in Christian understandings of marriage. Early Jesus followers, after all, expected him to return within their lifetime. They saw little purpose in marriage or sexual activity, given that they thought the world as they knew it was coming to an end. Paul, the author of some of the most influential letters in the Christian New Testament, reluctantly recommended marriage only to those who couldn't control their lust. Marriage, Gerber points out, "was intended to contain sex and to help spouses get beyond it";[9] in fact, spouses were encouraged to work toward a celibate marriage. If celibacy is about not expressing lust sexually, Gerber explains, then ex-gays in heterosexual marriages are celibate in that sense, even if they are sexual with their spouses. In this, they are breaking with the modern emphasis on lustfully sexual companionate marriages and returning to the older Christian model—perhaps only partially, though, since sex within a different-sex marriage, and sometimes also procreation, are expected and valued in the ex-gay movement.

Navigating practices can take the form of finding one's place as a queer (or queerish) person within traditional practices like Christian celibacy and Christian heterosexual marriage. It can also mean navigating between honoring one's adherence to a traditional but now disregarded gender/sexual practice and honoring one's commitment to revitalizing other ancestral traditions. Many of the Two-Spirit men whom anthropologist Brian Joseph Gilley worked with engaged actively in such navigation.[10] Largely from the US Midwest, they belonged to tribes that once recognized gender-variant and same-sex-attracted people but no longer do. The influence of particular forms of Christianity, along with other effects of colonization, had led their tribes to reject gender variance and same-sex desire; like many of the peoples colonized by Europe, those involved in such rejection typically argue that same-sex eroticism and gender variance are European imports and are therefore fundamentally "un-Indian."

As a result of these perspectives, some of the Two-Spirit men that Gilley worked with avoided their tribal communities, while others continued to take part in non-Two-Spirit tribal and pan-tribal gatherings. Most felt strongly about participating in some way in traditional practices such as dancing, drumming, singing, and basket weaving because they were committed to fighting against the impact of colonization on Native people of all sexes, genders, and sexualities. In fact, many of the men Gilley worked with told him that they used the term *Two-Spirit* specifically for Native Americans who were same-sex attracted or gender variant and also deeply committed to Native traditions. Being Indian was not enough by itself; the Two-Spirit men Gilley knew referred to people who were out of touch with or uninterested in their ancestral traditions as "gay Indians" and distinguished them from Two-Spirit people. But how could they live out this dual commitment in their practices when many of them were members of tribes that rejected Two-Spirit people?

One approach is through what sociologists call **identity compartmentalization,** or the practice of keeping identities separate from one another. In non-Two-Spirit Native spaces, Two-Spirit people who practice identity compartmentalization focus on their Native identity and set their gender and sexual identities aside. Staying closeted, or in what some people call the "glass closet"—where everyone knows you're gay but no one talks about it—allows such people to participate fairly fully in the lives of their tribes, and in pan-Indian events like powwows. Such participation often comes at a significant price, however. Two-Spirit people in long-term relationships may be seen by their tribal communities as single, and whether partnered or dating they may have to keep a physical distance from the person they're with during these events—or go without them. Those whose Two-Spirit identity includes gender variance, as was true for many of the men Gilley knew, also had to participate in men's roles at tribal events even though they felt that women's roles were more appropriate for them. And since many of these men—and many other Two-Spirit people—see their Two-Spirit identity as a reclaiming of a traditional role that gives life and healing to the community, many who practiced identity compartmentalization felt that the homophobia and transphobia they faced limited their ability to live out this role and to heal their communities.

Identity compartmentalization isn't always necessary, and the experiences that Gilley describes among the men he worked with are specific to the Colorado and Oklahoma settings of the Two-Spirit organizations he studied. In the Pacific Northwest region of the United States, for instance, two tribes legalized same-sex marriage before either the federal government or the states surrounding them did so—the Coquille Tribe in 2009 and the Suquamish Tribe in 2011. And regardless of tribal or familial attitudes, Two-Spirit people often find space and support for their full selves in Two-Spirit spaces. Many Two-Spirit organizations sponsor and teach traditional practices, including holding ceremonies for their members. And at Two-Spirit gatherings there are no expectations about the connections between genitalia and cere-monial roles. If a person assigned male at birth wants to take a role tradition-ally performed by women, they are welcome to do so, and likewise for people assigned female taking traditional men's roles. For people who've repeatedly experienced homophobia and transphobia in traditional Native spaces, these Two-Spirit-oriented practices can break down barriers between their identities, or between their senses of self and their Native identity. Some who've avoided learning their ancestral traditions because of rejection from their communities learn those traditions from other Two-Spirit people and thereby reclaim their heritage from the complex forms of destruction wreaked by ongoing settler colonialism. In so doing, they aren't only navi-gating their traditional practices; they're claiming them specifically for Two-Spirit people.

CLAIMING PRACTICE

In addition to Two-Spirit people, others whose ancestral traditions recognize and have special roles for gender-variant and same-sex-attracted people also see engagement in those roles as an important way to combat the effects of colonialism. This is especially true for the many people who, like Native Americans and First Nations people, continue to live under the colonial rule of European settlers. Whereas **franchise colonialism** involves colonizing a people primarily for the purposes of resource extraction and importation to the colonizing country, whether the resources in question are minerals or human bodies, settler colonialism involves the mass relocation of citizens of the colonizing country to the colony, with no intent that those settlers will ever leave. Settler colonialism, then, has a much longer timeline than fran-chise colonialism; whereas franchise colonialism ends when the resources are exhausted or when the cost of exporting them outweighs the benefit, settler colonialism lasts for many generations and eventually becomes unde-tectable to the settlers.

Native Hawaiians have lived under settler colonialism for well over a century. As with a number of cultures in Southeast Asia and the Pacific Islands, Hawaiian culture has traditional roles for gender-variant and same-sex-attracted people. Referred to collectively as *māhū*—a term that also in-cludes intersex people—they are understood to be "special, compassionate, and creative," as ethnomusicologist Carolina Robertson puts it.[11] Although European colonialism and its companion, Christian missionization, created significant changes in Hawaiian gender roles, the tradition of *māhū* survived what some refer to as extensive attempts at **cultural genocide**. For male-bodied *māhū*, one area where traditional gender roles could be protected was in hula dancing. Though Hawaiians of all genders once danced the hula, and since the anticolonial movements that started in the 1970s they are doing so again, for a century and a half the influence of missionaries prevented men from dancing—something Europeans saw as a feminine activity, and certainly religiously inappropriate. Feminine *māhū*, though, continued to dance, and some say that the deity who presides over the hula is also gender variant. In coming back into their own as hula dancers and teachers, caregivers for the children of the community, and respected community members, *māhū* of all sexes and genders are claiming their ancestral traditions for themselves and reclaiming them from the clutches of settler colonialism.

Claiming practices often involves insisting on practicing one's religious traditions openly while also being open about gender variance and same-sex desire. It means saying to those who would deny that right, "This tradition is my heritage, it deserves to be practiced, and I deserve to practice it." In some cases, as with Two-Spirit ceremonies, it means creating spaces for such practice when one is denied access to other spaces. Another example of this claiming of both practices and spaces arises in anthropologist Tom Boellstorff's writings about communities of same-sex-attracted and gender-variant people in Indonesia. [12] Unlike Sharyn Graham Davies, who was working in a more rural area and in a specific ethnic context when she wrote about *bissu*, *calalai*, and *calabai*, Boellstorff learned from more urban, multiethnic communities who used the terms *gay*, *lesbi*, and *waria* for themselves. (Boellstorff italicizes *gay* and *lesbi* to indicate that, although these words are borrowed from English, they don't have quite the same meaning—that is, sexual identities are structured somewhat differently among the people he knew in Indonesia than they are, say, in Europe.) Like *gay* and *lesbi*, *waria* is a less ethnically specific term; it refers to male-bodied people who live as women.

As we've already discussed, the majority of Indonesians are Muslim. Boellstorff's discussion of religion, therefore, also focuses on Islam. But he spends some time discussing a meeting of a *gay* Christian group by way of contrast. He notes that most of the people in attendance at the worship service were *gay*, along with a few *lesbi* women and *warias*. (Interestingly, this is an extremely common pattern for queer and transgender churches around the world, as well as for many queer and transgender religious gatherings in other large religious traditions such as Judaism. It may be related to a number of different factors, including the combined impact of sexism and homophobia, or transphobia and homophobia; the tendency for religious leaders to be cisgender men; and the different ages at which queer women, queer men, and transgender people tend to navigate the relationship between their sexuality, gender, and religion.) Held upstairs above a beauty school, this gathering of around thirty people involved prayer, singing, and testimonies about God's actions in people's lives. Why, Boellstorff asks, were there not similar groups for Muslims in Indonesia at that time, especially since both Christianity and Islam in that country are represented by a wide range of social perspectives, from starkly conservative to strongly progressive? Although he spends little time on the answer, and offers it somewhat tentatively, he suggests that perhaps it's related to the idea in Indonesia that "proper" Muslim practice is done out in the open.

Yet, as Boellstorff himself notes, Muslim study groups and prayer groups aren't uncommon in Indonesia. The Christian group he attended, which specifically called itself a prayer group and not a church, would be similar to such Muslim groups. So why were there no *gay* ones? As we've seen, there are now a small handful of mosques around the world that openly welcome same-sex-attracted and gender-variant people—in Cape Town, South Africa; Toronto, Ontario, Canada; and Washington, DC, in the United States, for example. Each is led by an openly gay imam. Perhaps at the time when Boellstorff was conducting his research, there simply wasn't yet space in Indonesia for an openly gay imam. Perhaps one simply hadn't come along. Perhaps there was a gay Muslim prayer group, but it was kept quieter than the Christian ones. It's hard to say, but what Boellstorff does offer us is a snapshot of a particular time and place in which *gay*, *lesbi*, and *waria* Christians were claiming their religion publicly while *gay*, *lesbi*, and *waria* Muslims were only doing so in private.

REWORKING PRACTICE

In some ways, a prayer service led by an openly gay imam and proudly attended by openly queer and transgender people is in itself a reworked practice (though it's also worth noting that reworking always has its limits; for instance, these imams are still all men). Many transgender and queer people engage in even more profound reworking of their religious traditions, however, and these three types of engaging with the practices of existing traditions actually represent a spectrum of increasing depth of change. Navigating practices usually takes the form of figuring out where one fits within existing practices; claiming practices means finding or creating space in which one can be openly queer or transgender and engaged in religious practices. Reworking practices means making traditional practices directly relevant to and reflective of one's own life as a transgender and/or queer person. Reworked practices, therefore, are a lot like the reframed stories we talked about in chapter 1.

In Filipinx cultures, the line may at times be fine between reclaiming traditional roles and reworking them into new practices for the feminine gay men and transgender women who identify with the traditional gender-variant role of the **baklâ**. As Michael Sepidoza Campos writes, even in the strongly Roman Catholic culture of the Philippines *baklâ* are known and appreciated—if sometimes quietly—for their artistic abilities and their fashion sense.

In fact, he explains that in his own hometown many of the *santos*, or figures of the saints, "particularly those renowned for their beauty, were actually maintained by wealthy baklâ patrons. If they belonged to society matrons, such images would often be placed in the care of a talented baklâ celebrated for his taste. . . . For a brief moment in the town's collective spirituality," Campos reflects, "it is the baklâ who acts as priest, who dresses the santo and so reimages God before the people." [13]

If the *baklâ* in Campos's hometown reimaged God by dressing santos, the gay men that Martin Manalansan came to know in New York, many of whom drew on or reclaimed the figure of the *baklâ*, went a step further when they presented a queer Santacruzan as a fund-raiser in the early 1990s. [14] The Santacruzan is a well-known Filipinx festival that blends the celebration of sacred story—Queen Helena, the mother of Emperor Constantine, discovering the cross on which Jesus was crucified—with the celebration of key events in Philippine history. The Santacruzan is a procession, a parade through a town or neighborhood, and is presided over primarily by women, selected as the Santacruzan queens to represent various figures in the stories being told and dressed in beautiful clothes accordingly. While there is some established (though somewhat scandalous) tradition of cross-dressed Santacruzans in the metropolitan area around Manila, the New York Santacruzan queered the ritual not only through having gay men as the Santacruzan "queens" (with the pun on the slang word for feminine gay men absolutely intended) but also through putting a particularly queer spin on the characters involved during the Santacruzan fashion show fund-raiser. Some were dressed as dominatrices, for example, and the biblical figure of Judith, who saved her people by cutting off the head of a general who'd laid siege to her city, carried instead the head of conservative US president George H. W. Bush. Emperor Constantine was played by a man dressed only in a sleek, tight Speedo swimsuit, and of the three women on stage—all lesbians—one wore the standard "butch lesbian" attire for the era while another sported traditional Filipinx men's formalwear. The Queen of the Flag, Reyna Banderada, even queered the national flag of the Philippines by wearing elements of it strategically placed over his nipples and crotch. More than even the cross-dressed Santacruzans in the Phillippines, the New York version reworked the ritual procession into a practice that not only included but celebrated queer cultures and especially queer Filipinx cultures.

In a different way, transgender Jews have found reworked practices central to their full inclusion in their religion. In part this is because many traditional Jewish practices are binary gendered, open to or expected of only men or only women, or expected to be conducted somewhat differently (including in different spaces) by men and women. In part, too, it's because restrictions on body modification, especially the damaging or removal of testicles, are a part of traditional Jewish approaches to human bodies. And in part it's because transitioning in whatever form—to living as one's true or newfound gender, to taking hormones, to having surgery, and so on—is a significant rite of passage in many transgender people's lives, and they often seek out meaningful ways to ritualize those rites of passage.

Balancing on the Mechitza, a book named after the divider that separates men and women in Orthodox synagogues, contains a number of personal stories about reworking Jewish practices to provide important rituals for transgender people, from Aaron Devor's ritual of crossing a bridge between the women in his community and the men, to Catherine Madsen and Joy Ladin's ritual for gender transition that draws on Jewish traditions of burial and cleansing, to Martin Rawlings-Fein's creative approach to the ritual of conversion for an adult man.[15] Drawing on those and other resources, as well as their own ingenuity, the transgender Jews whom S. J. Crasnow interviewed focused their own reworked practices on an ancient tradition: the *mikveh*, or ritual bath.[16]

A *mikveh* is traditionally a gender/sex-segregated space, guided by **cisnormative** assumptions that biology and gender go together only in certain ways. Although *mikvaot* (the plural of *mikveh*) are usually specially designed spaces used only for that purpose, they may also be natural bodies of flowing water—and this fact has proven useful to some transgender people seeking to perform a *mikveh* ritual. The *mikveh* is traditionally used for purification of the body, and as Crasnow explains, although it historically has been used by men as well as women, it came long ago to be largely a women's space and a women's practice, used especially for purifying the body after menstruation. Because of this focus on the implied impurity of women's bodies, Crasnow writes, "some have read . . . mikveh as sexist or outside the realm of egalitarian Jewish practice. . . . More recently, however," they add, "some feminist and LGBTQ Jews have reevaluated and reclaimed mikveh practice,"[17] and as Jewish feminists have reworked the *mikveh* into a women-affirming space, transgender and queer Jews have followed suit.

Because of increasing feminist, queer, and transgender reliance on the *mikveh*, demand has arisen for more inclusive *mikveh* spaces. Crasnow studied one in Boston named Mayyim Hayyim, or Living Waters. In this space the baths aren't gender divided, and there are no restrictions on who can go into them. Preparation rooms include wheelchair accessibility and facilities for a baby. *Mikveh* attendants, a traditional role, are volunteers who've been trained in welcoming visitors, including transgender and queer people. In this inclusive space, the *mikveh* itself reflects the nonbinary life experiences of transgender Jews; furthermore, it becomes a space where reworked practices can take place, especially because it provides **liturgies**, or ritual scripts, for such practices. These liturgies draw on traditional Jewish rituals and prayers, recasting them in ways that directly address the experience of transgender Jews. Some are reworded while others, such as Emily Aviva Kapor's use of the blessing known as the *Shehecheyanu*, are given new meaning by their inclusion in the ritual. The traditional wording of the *Shehecheyanu*— "Blessed are You, Eternal One, our God Ruler of Time and Space who has kept us alive and sustained us and helped us to arrive at this moment"—takes on new meaning when spoken by transgender people who have lived through denials of and persecution for their gender but have come through those challenges and arrived at the ritual moment of transition.

NEW PRACTICES

Finding and creating religious practices that celebrate transgender and queer cultures can be challenging in religions that have not traditionally—or at least, not recently—done so. People trying to create these innovations face challenges from other members of the religion, sometimes even other transgender and queer members. Furthermore, some people feel that traditional religions aren't worth innovating anyway. For these people, traditional religions have too many problems—often they include not only homophobia and transphobia but sexism, social conservatism, and similar concerns—and can't be salvaged. Those who hold such positions typically either look elsewhere, to another religion, or walk away from religion entirely. Some, though, start something new. We could say that new practices arise from a combination of new needs and new opportunities. A need may exist, but without the opportunity to fill it, it goes unresolved. Likewise, an opportunity won't be taken advantage of in the absence of any significant need for it. The development of the Radical Faeries, though, stemmed from a case where both need and opportunity were in ample supply

"A Call to Gay Brothers," proclaimed the flyer that spread out from the Los Angeles area in 1979. "A Spiritual Conference for Radical Fairies." The advertised gathering was to take place at a spiritual retreat center in Arizona over the US Labor Day holiday weekend at the beginning of September. The brainchild of three gay thinkers and activists—Harry Hay, Don Kilhefner, and Mitch Walker—this gathering turned into the founding event for a new religious movement known as the Radical Faeries (the spelling of the name was eventually changed from the original spelling on the flyer). The goals of the first gathering, as described on the flyer, were "exploring breakthroughs in gay consciousness," "sharing gay visions," and discovering "the spiritual dimensions of gayness." Hay, in particular, had by that time spent decades studying scholarship on gender variance and same-sex attraction, convinced that gayness was innate and that gay people had a special purpose in the world. He was especially inspired by accounts that linked gender variance and same-sex desire in the figure of a feminine man who was attracted to other men and who served an important spiritual function in his community by virtue of his gender/sexuality. Importantly, for Hay this figure did not necessarily experience solely cross-gender attraction; Faeries could (and did!) have sex with one another.

In an influential essay written early on in the development of the Radical Faeries, Hay relates that he had exhorted those attending the first gathering "to tear off the ugly green frog-skin of Heteromale imitation . . . to reveal the beautiful Fairy Prince hidden beneath."[18] You can sense a few important aspects of Hay's thought in this quotation. First, each gay man *has* a "beautiful Fairy Prince" inside who doesn't look or act like a "Heteromale." Second, being gay is just as much about gender as it is about sexuality—Hay is concerned, after all, not just with "Hetero" imitation but with "Heteromale imitation." Third, gay men who act like straight men are being untrue to their nature. Fourth, it seems that Hay thought Heteromales were ugly! Or, at the very least, he seems to have believed that imitating Heteromales made gay men ugly.

The religious movement that developed from that first gathering, and from Hay's writings in particular, is a part of the larger earth-focused neo-pagan movement just as much as it is a part of the queer religious movements that had been in full swing for more than a decade at that point. Like much of neo-paganism, it's eclectic, drawing from what it understands to be ancient, earth-based religions around the world. It reveres the Great Goddess and God of neo-paganism, and also (because those deities are understood to take many forms around the world) focuses on gay deities. The original practitioners were only gay and bisexual men, although more recently some Faerie circles have opened to women and to transgender people.[19] With their focus on gender variance as part of gayness, many Faeries present as feminine, at least in ritual contexts. Most are not transgender women, although a sizeable number identify as genderqueer or nonbinary. Faerie practices focus on honoring and healing the earth, honoring and healing queer folk and especially gay men, and exploring the sacred aspects of gayness and queerness. While their practices draw to a certain extent on borrowed (some would say appropriated, since many Faeries are non-Native and white) Native traditions and on the larger world of neo-pagan practices, many are original innovations designed to create a nurturing and celebratory religious space for gay men and other queer and trans folks.

Another queer religious space—or perhaps, in this case, a queer space in which religious exploration also takes place—stemmed in part from the Radical Faeries. The Black Leather Wings were originally an offshoot of the Radical Faeries in San Francisco. Open to people of all genders and sexualities, they focus on the spirituality of BDSM practices. But while they may be among the best-known organizations to connect BDSM and religious or spiritual practice, many other practitioners have made similar links, and to many different religious traditions. Perhaps among the most famous is Troy

Perry, the founder of MCC, who has been open for many years about being a part of the gay leather culture. The leather spirituality group known as the Defenders started as an offshoot of the LGBTQ Catholic organization Dignity in 1981, and Zen Buddhist priest Vajra Karuna wrote in the late 1990s about "Zen in Black Leather," arguing that "the concepts found in the highest forms of spirituality are also to be found in the best of S&M practices" and enumerating these concepts as faith, tolerance, compassion, self-worth, courage, belonging, liberation, joy, power, and peaking.[20] Around the same time, Jill Nagle wrote in a collection of queer Jewish narratives about a "queer naked Seder" that she'd attended at a Radical Faerie house in San Francisco. Since the seder tells the story of the ancient Israelites' escape from bondage, as you might imagine this "Seder sex party" included BDSM.[21]

QUEERING RELIGION/RELIGIONING QUEER

Queer religious practices, especially the reworked and new ones—the ones that are queer in the sense of disrupting the normal, taken-for-granted way of doing things—disturb some people. While a *Verstehen*, lived-religion approach to the study of religion encourages us to approach those disturbed reactions with empathetic understanding, whether we share such perspectives or not, an analytical approach also challenges us to ask why queered religious rituals are so disturbing to some people. Our strongest emotional reactions can tell us a lot about how we understand the world, especially those parts of our understanding that we take so much for granted that we don't even really notice them.

Many years ago, I taught the course this book is based on for the second time. *Queer Jews*, the collection containing Nagle's article, had just been published. I'd already been working in the area of queer studies in religion for some time, so I didn't think twice about assigning the article. I thought it was an interestingly queer approach to Judaism; I thought my students would be intrigued too. But the day they read the article, I walked in to find my usually excited and enthusiastic students uncharacteristically subdued and uncomfortable. These folks, many of them queer and the rest staunch queer allies, had been fine with (if somewhat surprised at) the idea that religion can be sex positive. They had fun with the Jewish idea that sex on Shabbat is a good deed, and with a film that mentioned two lesbians' reclaiming of that idea to have sex with each other on Shabbat in order to celebrate the God who'd made them lesbian. But sex during a ritual, it seemed, was different. My students thought it was disrespectful, sacrilegious somehow. Underlying their discomfort was a widespread assumption that sexual practices and (proper) religious practices don't go together. Here's the catch, though: for some people, and for some religions—not just queer ones—they do. Isn't putting a Bible on your bedside table and inviting God into your sex life a religious act? Isn't having sex on Shabbat a religious act? Where exactly is the line between religious sex acts and sexual religious acts that are acceptable and those that make us uncomfortable?

Maybe the line is the problem, though. From a *Verstehen*, lived-religion perspective, people like Jill Nagle and Vajra Karuna are describing religious practices. Radical Faeries who have ecstatic sex in the middle of a Faerie ritual are engaging in religious practices. How can we accept that some practices are "genuinely" religious and others aren't? Such judgments violate the very tenets of this approach to the study of religion; they also underlie the conviction many people have that religion, queerness, and transness don't mix. But maybe we aren't thinking *queerly* enough about religious practices, or *transing* them enough, as Max Strassfeld encourages us to do; maybe we aren't thinking *religiously* enough about queer and trans practices. [22]

What can we learn from studying practices at the intersection of queer studies, transgender studies, and religious studies? From this chapter, we've learned that religious practices involve far more than prayer services where everyone has to act straight and cisgender. We've thought about celibacy as queer, reclaiming traditional roles as not only a queer and transgender affirming act but a profound act of decolonization, traditional practices like the Santacruzan and the *mikveh* as spaces for the affirmation of transgender, queer, religious, and ethnic identities together. But in this section, we've started to ask exactly what all three of these fields of study mean when they say "religion," and why.

Think for a moment about how people use religious language in everyday life. They may say they do something "religiously" when it (seemingly) isn't a religion—like going to the gym, for instance. They may say that something is their religion when it (seemingly) isn't any such thing—like a sports team or a famous singer or a film. Some cultural phenomena are referred to as "cult classics" or "cult sensations," using a word that originally meant the worship of a specific figure within a larger religion, like the cult of Saint Sebastian, but now is used more commonly as a derogatory and discriminatory word for new religious movements. People talk about rituals—another term for religious practice—even when they don't (seemingly) mean that their practice is religious. They talk about worship in (seemingly) nonreligious contexts too. Wouldn't it be logical within the *Verstehen*/lived-religion approach we've been following in this book to take these things seriously as forms of religion? The difference, of course, is that the people who use such turns of phrase don't think the things they're talking about are actually religion—so this is different from, for instance, taking Jill Nagle seriously in her claim that the queer naked seder was a religious practice. But here's an easier example: queer nuns.

Sometimes when I tell people that I wrote a book on queer nuns, they say something like, "Oh, I know some queer nuns! I'm positive that Sister Mary Joseph, my biology teacher, was gay." Sister Mary Joseph, in this story, is usually a Roman Catholic nun, and while she could certainly have been gay, she's not the kind of queer nun we're talking about here. The book called *Queer Nuns* is about a worldwide order of nuns that actually calls their members queer nuns.[23] They're religiously unaffiliated, although quite a few of them consider themselves religious or spiritual and experience their ministry with the order as a part of their spiritual practice. They aren't celibate—in fact, the Sisters of Perpetual Indulgence do a lot of work on safer sex education and HIV prevention and treatment. They're a volunteer order; the nuns manifest when they have the time to put on their makeup and drag. Yes, makeup and drag. These are queer nuns indeed. But just as they're serious about being queer, the Sisters of Perpetual Indulgence are also very serious about being nuns. They do what other orders of nuns—Roman Catholic, Buddhist, Episcopalian, Jain—do, they say, but for communities that other orders of nuns rarely serve. They aren't just queer (and transgender) nuns, then; they're nuns for queer and transgender communities.

What would happen if we took the Sisters of Perpetual Indulgence at their word that they're nuns? First, we'd have to redefine what it means to be a nun. How do we typically define words that we already know? If it's a word we don't know, we go to the dictionary, but if we do know it and someone else asks us what it means, what do we do? Think about it for a minute—what do *you* do? Often, we think of different examples of that word and try to describe what they all have in common. What's a tree? It's a very tall plant, with lots of branches and leaves, or needles, and sometimes flowers or fruits. There are some exceptions to this explanation—palm trees don't really have branches, for instance, just fronds at the top, and some trees are pretty short—but it describes most of the trees that a lot of us are familiar with.

So, what's a nun? Seriously. Try to define the word.

What examples did you think of? The nuns you know in your own life? The nuns in popular culture, like in the movie *The Sound of Music* or Tilda Swinton's character in the 2016 film *Doctor Strange*? The nuns you hear about from friends? Does your definition include Christianity? (Remember, there are nuns who aren't Christian.) Does it include seclusion? (Some nuns are cloistered, or separated from the world, and some aren't.) What about celibacy? Femaleness? Nuns' orders other than the Sisters of Perpetual Indulgence are open only to women (including, for a few, transgender women), and they require celibacy. But the Sisters of Perpetual Indulgence have members of all genders, and although some of their members are ace, the order doesn't require celibacy and is in fact very sex positive. Can your definition of nun include the Sisters? Should it? If it doesn't, aren't we saying that queer people's religious experiences don't count as much as other people's religious experiences?

Here's another, more provocative example. A now-classic article by religious studies scholar Paul Gorrell argues that circuit parties are a religious experience for the gay men who attend them. Circuit parties are massive dance parties that take place in different cities at the same time every year. Each party has a name, they're scheduled not to overlap whenever possible, and some men with the means and the freedom to do so travel each year to as many of the different parties as they can. That's why they're called circuit parties—there's a "circuit" you can travel on to go to them. The gay party circuit, Gorrell explains, has its own culture and its own rituals, such as fan dancing with flags "to release the spirits of those who have died into the life of the party."[24] Moreover, he argues that circuit parties *are* a form of religion, "a more transgressive approach to worship, human desire for the divine, and religious ritual, than the current 'gay take' on theology and the admirable search for a place at the table that many gays and lesbians are fighting for in traditional religious communities."[25] Insightfully applying some of the classic theories about religion to his topic, Gorrell insists that circuit parties fit these theories just as much as other religious rituals do. In a gay culture under fire from both homophobia and erotophobia (fear of eroticism) in the aftermath of the AIDS epidemic, Gorrell notes, religious ritual for some gay men involves creating a safe space for the worship of the erotic. "When we look to traditional church symbols, rites, and books to identify the religious sensibilities of the gay community," he explains, "we miss how the sacrament of male beauty is a core belief of gay men that not only inspires them to devotion but also, like any sacrament, instructs them about how to live their lives."[26]

When we consider the ways in which many people are willing to accept a connection between sex and religion and the ways in which they draw the line, we discover that even for queer and transgender folks and their allies, those lines all too often delineate a boundary between "normal," acceptable erotic and religious practices and "offensive," "going-too-far" erotic and religious practices. This line leaves mostly queer and transgender people— and, often, other nondominant groups—on the wrong side of the tracks yet again. What if we took circuit parties seriously as real ritual, the beauty of gay male bodies as an actual sacrament, the Sisters of Perpetual Indulgence as true nuns, gender transition rituals as an integral part of Jewish tradition? Religious studies scholars would be forced to change their definitions of all these classic elements of religion to reflect the full inclusion of transgender and queer people. Queer and transgender studies scholars, for their part, would have to acknowledge what scholars of queer and trans studies in religion have known all along: Religion is one of the queerest things about being human.

STUDY QUESTIONS

1. *'Yan daudu* relate to religious practices in a number of ways. What are these?
2. What are the three ways of relating to traditional practices (remember, the fourth type of engagement with practice in this chapter is creating new practices)? How are they different from each other, since all of them involve transgender and queer people engaging with traditional practices?
3. In what ways is claiming practices also a form of decolonization for some gender-variant and same-sex-attracted people?
4. Why does Lynne Gerber suggest that ex-gays practice a "queerish" form of celibacy? Since they're expected to be sexually active, how can this be celibacy? How, for Gerber, is it like earlier Christian understandings of marriage?
5. What is a Santacruzan, and how did the people Manalansan worked with create a gay one? How did the gay Santacruzan create a queer Filipinx religious space?
6. How have transgender Jews reworked Jewish tradition to reflect their own lives and spiritual needs?
7. How did Harry Hay understand gayness? Based on the discussion in this chapter about the Radical Faeries, what kind of community do you think their founders were trying to create? Why? How does this goal relate to Hay's ideas?

FOR FURTHER THOUGHT

1. How do practices, stories, and conversations relate to one another in the religions around you? How do they relate to queer and transgender, or same-sex-attracted and gender-variant, people? How do those people navigate those religions? If you don't know, find out! Ask people you know, search online, ask religious leaders—there are many possible sources of information to draw upon.
2. Think back to what we've learned in previous chapters about the potential inaccuracies and complicated power dynamics involved in assigning originally Global North/Global West sexual and gender identities to people in the Global South/Global East who don't claim those identities. In light of these ideas, would it be useful to call *'yan daudu* transgender? Gay? Given the increasingly conservative nature

of Northern Nigeria and the threat from Boko Haram at the time of Rudolf Pell Gaudio's writing, what possible outcomes (positive and negative) might there be of *'yan daudu* beginning to identify themselves as trans or gay?

3. Do you think there's a difference between being ace and being called to celibacy? What about between polygamy and polyamory? If there are differences here, what exactly are they? If there aren't, why do you think so many people feel like there are?

4. Find some Jewish gender transition rituals, either online or in printed sources like *Balancing on the Mechitza*, and read through them. Or, if you're more interested in another tradition, see whether you can find gender transition rituals for that tradition. What different approaches do you see to the process of creating a fully trans-inclusive religion through such rituals? What do those who have crafted these rituals retain from the existing tradition? What do they add or change? Why?

5. Some scholars of performance and ritual like to ask what actions *do*, rather than what they *say*. The question above asks you to analyze what gender transition liturgies *say*; now try analyzing what they *do*. In what ways do these liturgies change or maintain the world, the participants, the space of the ritual, and so on? How might the concept of performativity, as discussed in the Introduction, help with this analysis?

6. How did you react to the idea of a "queer naked Seder," as described by Jill Nagle? What ideas do you hold about sex and religion that might have influenced your reaction, whether it was positive, negative, or neutral? Did you have a similar reaction to the idea of "queer nuns" who aren't celibate and who dress in makeup and drag, or a different one? Why do you think this is?

7. What do you think of the argument that refusing to consider the Sisters of Perpetual Indulgence as nuns, or circuit parties and gay men's veneration of beautiful male bodies as ritual and worship, means marginalizing the experiences of queer and transgender people in the study of religion? Why? Develop an argument (a point made with evidence and reasoning) to support your position on this claim.

RECOMMENDATIONS FOR FURTHER READING

Boellstorff, Tom. *A Coincidence of Desires: Anthropology, Queer Studies, Indonesia*. Durham, NC: Duke University Press, 2007.

Campos, Michael Sepidoza. "The Baklâ: Gendered Religious Performance in Filipino Cultural Spaces." In *Queer Religion*, Vol. 2: LGBT Movements and Queering Religion, edited by Donald L. Boisvert and Jay Emerson Johnson, 167–91. Santa Barbara, CA: Praeger, 2012.

Crasnow, S. J. "On Transition: Normative Judaism and Trans Innovation." *Journal of Contemporary Religion* 32, no. 3 (2017): 403–15.

Derogatis, Amy. *Saving Sex: Sexuality and Salvation in American Evangelicalism*. New York: Oxford University Press, 2015.

Dzmura, Noach, ed. *Balancing on the Mechitza: Transgender in Jewish Community*. Berkeley, CA: North Atlantic Books, 2010.

Gaudio, Rudolf Pell. *Allah Made Us: Sexual Outlaws in an Islamic African City*. Malden, MA: Wiley-Blackwell, 2009.

Gilley, Brian Joseph. *Becoming Two-Spirit: Gay Identity and Social Acceptance in Indian Country*. Lincoln: University of Nebraska Press, 2006.

Gorrell, Paul J. "Rite to Party: Circuit Parties and Religious Experience." In *Gay Religion*, edited by Scott Thumma and Edward R. Gray, 313–26. Walnut Creek, CA: AltaMira Press, 2005.

Hay, Harry. *Radically Gay: Gay Liberation in the Words of Its Founder*, edited by Will Roscoe. Boston: Beacon Press, 1996.

Karuna, Vajra. "Zen in Black Leather." In *Queer Dharma: Voices of Gay Buddhists*, Vol. 1, edited by Winston Leyland, 247–52. San Francisco: Gay Sunshine Press, 1998.

Manalansan, Martin F. IV. *Global Divas: Filipino Gay Men in the Diaspora*. Durham, NC: Duke University Press, 2003.

Nagle, Jill. "Queer Naked Seder and Other Newish Jewish Traditions." In *Queer Jews*, edited by David Shneer and Caryn Aviv, 70–83. New York: Routledge, 2002.

Robertson, Carolina E. "The Māhū of Hawai'i." *Feminist Studies* 15, no. 2 (1989): 312–22.

Strassfeld, Max. "Transing Religious Studies." *Journal of Feminist Studies in Religion* 34, no. 1 (2018): 37–53.

Stover, John A. III. "When Pan Met Wendy: Gendered Membership Debates among the Radical Faeries." *Nova Religio* 11, no. 4 (2008): 31–55.

Talvacchia, Kathleen T., Michael F. Pettinger, and Mark Larrimore, eds. *Queer Christianities: Lived Religion in Transgressive Forms*. New York: New York University Press, 2015.

Wilcox, Melissa M. *Queer Nuns: Religion, Activism, and Serious Parody*. New York: New York University Press, 2018.

NOTES

1. See Amy Derogatis, *Saving Sex: Sexuality and Salvation in American Evangelicalism* (New York: Oxford University Press, 2015).

2. Rudolf Pell Gaudio, *Allah Made Us: Sexual Outlaws in an Islamic African City* (Malden, MA: Wiley-Blackwell, 2009).

3. Ibid., 120.

4. Ibid., 121.

5. Ibid.

6. Sister Carol Bernice, CHS, "How Queer Is Celibacy? A Queer Nun's Story," in *Queer Christianities: Lived Religion in Transgressive Forms*, ed. Kathleen T. Talvacchia, Michael F. Pettinger, and Mark Larrimore (New York: New York University Press, 2015), 49.

7. Ibid., 52.

8. Lynne Gerber, "'Queerish' Celibacy: Reorienting Marriage in the Ex-Gay Movement," in *Queer Christianities: Lived Religion in Transgressive Forms*, ed. Kathleen T. Talvacchia, Michael F. Pettinger, and Mark Larrimore (New York: New York University Press, 2015), 32.

9. Ibid.

10. Brian Joseph Gilley, *Becoming Two-Spirit: Gay Identity and Social Acceptance in Indian Country* (Lincoln: University of Nebraska Press, 2006).

11. Carolina E. Robertson, "The Māhū of Hawai'i," *Feminist Studies* 15, no. 2 (1989): 312–22.

12. Tom Boellstorff, *A Coincidence of Desires: Anthropology, Queer Studies, Indonesia* (Durham, NC: Duke University Press, 2007).

13. Michael Sepidoza Campos, "The Baklâ: Gendered Religious Performance in Filipino Cultural Spaces," in *Queer Religion*, Vol. 2: *LGBT Movements and Queering Religion*, ed. Donald L. Boisvert and Jay Emerson Johnson (Santa Barbara, CA: Praeger, 2012), 178.

14. Martin F. Manalansan IV, *Global Divas: Filipino Gay Men in the Diaspora* (Durham, NC: Duke University Press, 2003); see especially 128–36.

15. Noach Dzmura, ed., *Balancing on the Mechitza: Transgender in Jewish Community* (Berkeley, CA: North Atlantic Books, 2010).

16. S. J. Crasnow, "On Transition: Normative Judaism and Trans Innovation," *Journal of Contemporary Religion* 32, no. 3 (2017), 403–15.

17. Ibid., 406.

18. Harry Hay, "Toward the New Frontiers of Fairy Vision . . . Subject-SUBJECT Consciousness," in *Radically Gay: Gay Liberation in the Words of Its Founder*, ed. Will Roscoe (Boston: Beacon Press, 1996), 254.

19. See John A. Stover III, "When Pan Met Wendy: Gendered Membership Debates among the Radical Faeries," *Nova Religio* 11, no. 4 (2008): 31–55.

20. Vajra Karuna, "Zen in Black Leather," in *Queer Dharma: Voices of Gay Buddhists*, Vol. 1, ed. Winston Leyland (San Francisco: Gay Sunshine Press, 1998), 247–52.

21. Jill Nagle, "Queer Naked Seder and Other Newish Jewish Traditions," in *Queer Jews*, ed. David Shneer and Caryn Aviv (New York: Routledge, 2002), 70–83.

22. Max Strassfeld, "Transing Religious Studies," *Journal of Feminist Studies in Religion* 34, no. 1 (2018): 37–53.

23. Melissa M. Wilcox, *Queer Nuns: Religion, Activism, and Serious Parody* (New York: New York University Press, 2018).

24. Paul J. Gorrell, "Rite to Party: Circuit Parties and Religious Experience," in *Gay Religion*, ed. Scott Thumma and Edward R. Gray (Walnut Creek, CA: AltaMira Press, 2005), 314. See also Donald Boisvert, "The Spirit Within: Gay Male Culture as a Spiritual Venue," pp. 351–66 in the same volume.

25. Ibid., 315.

26. Ibid., 325.

Chapter Four

Identities

What is identity? How do we come to have one—or many? Take a minute to think about these questions, and maybe even write down some answers:

- What parts of you make up your identity?
- What things about you aren't part of your identity?
- What differentiates these two categories—what's different about the things that are part of your identity and the things that aren't?
- How did you come to have your identity?
- Do you consider your identity intrinsic to you? Is it permanent, or something that changes over time? Is it inborn?

These are all questions that many queer and transgender people consider when thinking about the sexual and gendered aspects of their identities. Interestingly, heterosexuals and cisgender people rarely ask the same questions, because these aspects of their self-understanding are dominant categories; as we covered in the introduction, dominant categories are unmarked and often treated as simply "normal." If your identity is normal and unremarkable, there isn't really much reason to wonder how it came about! Religious people also consider these questions, especially if they aren't part of a dominant religion. Was religion one of the categories you included in your answers to the questions above? Was sexuality? What about gender? Why do you think this is?

THINKING ABOUT IDENTITIES

Often, we think about sexual and gender identities differently from how we think about religious identities. Many people in the Global North/Global

West think of religious identities as chosen, and sexual and gender identities as innate. Why? In terms of religious identities, the main reason is the cultural dominance of Christianity in these regions. Christianity is a conversion-focused religion that values teaching the religion to others. Plus, many branches of Protestant Christianity hold that people aren't truly Christian until they've freely chosen to be. That's why some Protestant groups don't baptize children into the faith—they don't believe people are ready to make a valid choice about following Jesus until they're grown up. In fact, the First Amendment to the US Constitution, which attempts in part to prevent the government from influencing people's religious decisions, comes out of exactly this perspective that true religion must be freely chosen—the famed "separation of church and state" in the United States is a Protestant policy! Gender and sexual identities, on the other hand, are more often thought about in such cultures through the model of the invert—a medical designation for a state of being that even the early sexologists thought was at least deeply rooted if not innate. Since the medicalization of gender variance and same-sex desire began in the nineteenth century, there have been debates over whether these "conditions" are curable or preventable. No such debates have taken place around heterosexuality or cisgender identities.

Although nondominant religions and nondominant sexualities and genders are often treated differently from the dominant groups—usually to the detriment of the nondominant groups—they're also treated differently from each other. People from nondominant religions are often treated as having made the wrong choice, and under some circumstances are forced to convert to the "right" religion. Though dominant groups sometimes "racialize" religions, treating religious identity as indistinguishable from racial identity (this is especially true for stereotypes of Islam and Judaism), at the same time practicing that religion is often still considered a choice. The most infamous example of such assumptions is the 1492 Spanish edict that required all Jews and Muslims—of whom there were quite a few in Spain at the time—to convert to Christianity, leave the country, or be executed. While Spanish Christians stereotyped Jews and Muslims as people, and certainly didn't believe those characteristics would change when they converted, at the same time they still saw Judaism and Islam as practices that could be left behind by (constrained) choice.

But some religious groups and individuals don't see their religious identities as chosen; Judaism is a prime example because of the tradition that being Jewish is inherited from one's mother. In most Orthodox Jewish circles people can't convert to the religion, and they may not be accepted even if their father was Jewish but their mother wasn't. In other branches, however, Jewishness can be either inherited or chosen, and Jews-by-choice—those who've converted to the religion—are welcomed. For some people, finally, religious identity is both inherited and chosen. People speak, for instance, of being "culturally Mormon," "culturally Muslim," or "culturally Jewish" but choosing not to practice the religion itself, whereas others were born into a religion but raised nonpracticing, and then chose as adults to practice it. Why do you suppose so few people call themselves "culturally Christian," though? Think about that for a moment.

So religious identity is complicated; people seem to think it sometimes has a heritable aspect, but ultimately it's considered by many to be chosen. Some people still make a "choice" argument about sexuality and gender, too, usually for the purposes of encouraging people to choose heterosexuality and cisgender identity, although in queer academic and political circles there are very different discussions about sexual identity and choice. But because of the medicalization of same-sex desire and gender variance, more often the discourse from all sides around such issues focuses on innateness. The argument that gender and sexual identities are innate serves to counter those who suggest that transgender and queer people should be encouraged or forced to make "better" (that is, heterosexual and cisgender) choices, but it also invites scientific and pseudoscientific investigations into what "causes" these innate identities. As scholars in critical disability studies and crip theory remind us, claims of innateness can be and have been used to justify attempts at early detection, cure, and eradication. In fact, decades of research on "homosexuality" sought to do exactly that, often by intervening in the gender identity development of children deemed "proto-homosexuals." Contemporary homophobic and transphobic versions of the "innateness" model for gender and sexual identity, many of which are religious, commonly liken these identities to inherited risk factors for health problems, often using alcoholism as an example. They argue that just as someone with many alcoholics in the family might have a genetic tendency to addiction, someone who's gender variant or attracted to the same sex (usually these two are rolled in together in such discourses, as in older, more mainstream scientific ones) has a genetic tendency to these ways of being. They go on to add that just as someone with a genetic predisposition to addiction should avoid alcohol altogether (a point that is very much debated in addiction research, but this is their approach), so too someone with same-sex desire and gender variance should avoid putting their desires and sense of self into practice.

These discussions show us that essentialist and constructivist approaches to sexuality, gender, and religion aren't inherently liberatory or oppressive. Saying that gender and sexuality are innate can provide a platform for human rights or an opportunity for treatment, genetic testing, and eradication. Saying that they're chosen can open a door to those who argue that people simply should choose differently, but it can also reflect more accurately and even honor the lived experiences of some gender-variant and same-sex-attracted people.

Theologian and religion and culture scholar Justin Tanis offers a third option for understanding identity. At least for those who believe in a deity and think about the deity in certain ways, his approach circumvents entirely the stalemate between essentialist and constructivist approaches. In his path-clearing 2003 work *Transgendered: Theology, Ministry, and Communities of Faith*, Tanis explores the relationships between transgender people and religion, especially but not solely Christianity. He looks to the experiences of transgender people who hold religious beliefs, follow religious practices, and take part in religious organizations, and he offers his own theological perspectives on being transgender. Among the latter is his chapter on gender as a calling.

Many religions have world concepts in which deities and spirits choose humans for particular roles ranging from prophecy to renunciation to spirit possession; the Protestant traditions within which Tanis works draw their understanding of the divine calling from Martin Luther, the instigator of the Protestant movement within Christianity. Part of the **populism**, or focus on everyday people, in Luther's theology was his insistence that every person was called by God to a particular way of living in the world, and that all people should therefore live each day in the service of God even if they were engaged in mundane daily tasks. Luther referred to this calling as a *vocation*. Today, the range of uses of this word reflects Luther's ideas. People still speak of a "religious vocation"—a calling to a full-time life of religious service—but the word is also used to refer to a career one feels called to or seems particularly suited to. We say someone has "found their calling" when they find a job or a career that they love, or for which they seem particularly talented, and "vocational training" is the term for education in the skills needed for a particular career. Though today these sorts of vocations or callings aren't usually treated as divine, for Luther they were.

For Tanis, the argument that gender is a calling is a theological one. Sidestepping the essentialist-constructivist debate that chases its tail trying to determine whether trans identities come from "nature" or "nurture," Tanis argues instead that they come from God. "Rather than seeing transgenderism as a medical problem to be corrected, a psychological incongruence between body and spirit, or even a quirk of societal organization," he writes, "I look at my experiences of gender as the following of an invitation from God to participate in a new, whole, and healthy way of living in the world—a holy invitation to set out on a journey of body, mind, and spirit."[1] How long he's been transgender, how he became transgender, even whether being transgender is permanent—these no longer matter when gender identity is reframed as a calling. Such an understanding also avoids the dangers of essentialist and constructivist approaches, which can both be turned into arguments for the eradication of transgender identities and transgender people. It seems that it's not the *explanation* for an identity that drives oppressive or liberatory approaches to it; it's the *value* placed on the identity in the first place. Considering gender identity to be a divine calling makes being transgender intrinsically good and holy; if gender identity comes from God, then it no longer matters whether it's innate or chosen, permanent or transitory. "The concept of gender as a calling," Tanis explains, "allows me to be called to live one way yesterday, another way today, and even yet another tomorrow. . . . Gender, like any other calling, is also an ongoing revelation."[2]

As several scholars have begun to argue, **Black Atlantic traditions** offer additional ways of understanding identity and the self.[3] The term *Black Atlantic* refers to the black communities and cultures that are connected by the Atlantic Ocean, in particular those West African cultures from which people were taken into slavery during the transatlantic slave trade and the cultures they formed in the Americas and the Caribbean during and after slavery. Sometimes the latter cultures are called *African diasporic cultures*; the term *Black Atlantic* emphasizes that there remain connections between living communities and cultures on both sides of the ocean.

African diasporic communities took shape differently in different regions because of the cultural backgrounds of those who started and influenced those communities, the other cultures (including indigenous cultures of the Americas) that surrounded them, and the varying effects of slavery. For instance, the large West African spirit population had a much better chance of continued recognition by and engagement with their human relatives in communities with large numbers of African-descended people and in communities where Roman Catholicism, with its comparably well-populated world beyond the human, was the dominant religion than they did in communities where African-descended people were largely isolated from each other and where Protestant Christianity, with its comparably much smaller spirit world, predominated. In Catholic colonies and countries, new versions of traditional West African practices developed and eventually flourished, often together with Catholicism. You may know them by such names as Vodou, Candomblé, Lucumí (sometimes known as Santería), and so on. In Protestant colonies and countries—mostly the United States and Canada, with the exception of New Orleans—African cultural heritage still shaped the cultures of African-descended people but that heritage was often directed specifically into Protestant Christianity. Nevertheless, today many African Americans and Afro-Canadians are seeking out Black Atlantic traditions in an effort to reconnect with their ancestral traditions.

Black studies scholar Roberto Strongman suggests that African diasporic philosophies of the self can give queer studies and religious studies scholars new tools for thinking through religion, gender, sexuality, and embodiment. Those philosophies, he argues, turn on the idea of **transcorporeality**, which Strongman defines as "the distinctly Afrodiasporic cultural representation of the human psyche as multiple, removable, and external to the body that functions as its receptacle."[4] He uses the cashew pear as an illustration for transcorporeality, because with this fruit the seed (the cashew nut) grows not inside but down below the fruit itself. If the psyche is external to the body and is removable like the cashew is to the cashew pear, then it can travel without the body (as some people believe happens in certain kinds of dreaming or trance), it can be kept elsewhere for safe keeping (but with serious consequences if the body dies in the meantime), and it can be set aside temporarily to make room for another consciousness, which is what happens in possession. In these traditions, the spirits routinely gather with their human communities by temporarily borrowing the bodies of initiates. This fact, as Strongman and others have pointed out, has significant consequences for gender and sexuality. Strongman explains that "this unique view of the body . . . allows the regendering of the bodies of initiates, who are mounted and ridden by deities of a gender different from their own during the ritual ecstasy of trance possession."[5]

Elizabeth Pérez, building on Strongman's work, adds that the practice of possession also produces what she calls a "trans-generic body, a body able to cross between two genera: *homo sapiens* and a genus of spirits."[6] And Omise'eke Natasha Tinsley makes even clearer the recentering of gender studies that we might accomplish through these traditions when she asks "what it would sound like if scholars were to speak of [the *lwa*—Haitian Vodou deity/ spirit] Ezili the way we often speak, say, of Judith Butler—if we gave the centuries-old corpus of texts engaging this lwa a similar explanatory power in understanding gender."[7] Citing the performance artist MilDred, who has been exploring various *lwa* in her own work, Tinsley explains that "she . . . puts forth that all people have the possibility to be simultaneously man and woman . . . but not because gender is constructed, or performative, or any other queer theoretical word. No, because they're always surrounded by multiple, multiply gendered spirits and may temporarily *become* any of those spirits at any time."[8]

IDENTITY POLITICS AND MULTICULTURALISM

So far, we've discussed models of identity that understand it as *innate* or *inborn*, as individually *chosen*, as a *calling* from God, and as a removable, multiple, *transcorporeal*, and *transgeneric* feature of humans in community with beings beyond the human. It's important to notice the range in these definitions between individually constituted identities, where the self is defined in isolation from any community even though the available identities are still socially defined, and communally constituted identities, where many selves influence and define each other. These models have consequences not just for people's self-understanding but also for political movements and public policy. In many Global North/Global West cultures, for instance, individualistic interpretations of even communally based philosophies of the self have led in recent decades to what's often called **identity politics**: a narrow approach to justice that's based solely on identity, wherein all people who share a particular identity are considered to have the same or at least very similar experiences. It was this sort of understanding that led Global North/Global West feminists to claim "sisterhood" between all women, ignoring the ways that they contributed to the oppression of other women on the basis of class, race, colonialism, and the like. The problem, in other words, is that this approach to justice is neither communal nor intersectional. In a thoughtful analysis of the lives of queer Muslims in Australia, Ibrahim Abraham makes a similar argument against a concept that became a buzzword for political liberals in many Global North/Global West countries in the 1990s: *multiculturalism.*[9]

Touted in the 1990s as a way to create a "tolerant" society, multiculturalism is an approach to cultural multiplicity that relies on ideas from identity politics. While it often presents differences between groups of people as minor variances to be celebrated—ripples, you might say, on the surface of an otherwise calm body of water—by interpreting differences in this relatively shallow way multiculturalism also defines various groups of people as *being* fundamentally different from one another and, importantly, different from the norm. In this understanding, a Sikh college student from California's Central Valley whose family has been in the United States for four generations has more in common with an elderly Sikh who just immigrated from India than he does with his Latinx Catholic roommate whose family has been in Southern California since it was part of Mexico. In addition to positing similarities between people that are predictable based solely on their belonging to a particular identity group, that are shared among that entire identity group, and that nevertheless are only on the surface, multiculturalism also presupposes shared values among people in a particular country or region. As you might guess, these are the values of the dominant group.

Multiculturalism's approach to religion stems right out of some of the early roots of religious studies, claiming that all "true" religions share the same basic values and often articulating those values through the Christian Golden Rule: Treat others as you would want to be treated. The problem with this, of course, is that people *don't* all share the same values. Multiculturalism was a well-meaning approach, but its lack of intersectional analysis, its failure to consider the impact of unmarked categories like Christianity and whiteness in its conceptualization, and its tendency to draw tidy lines around (and therefore between) communities have made it into a force for injustice in the perspective of many trans, queer, feminist, and womanist scholars.

Because liberal multiculturalism claims that all people are, at base, the same, it reserves the right to judge certain perspectives as irrational or backward. In other words, multiculturalism has often become a framework in which specific sets of values come to be represented as universal, in which the image of difference as minor window dressing overlying a fundamental unity comes to support the enforcement of a particular vision of that unity. Abraham notes, for instance, in regard to Western debates (largely among non-Muslims) about women wearing the hijab, or headscarf, that

> freedom of choice is held up as a bastion of the liberal "West," yet [this principle] ran aground when it was observed that young women were making *un*western choices. The answer was to rhetorically curtail this by insisting those who acted in contrary fashion were obviously being coerced; but it is to be hoped that one day they may be liberated, at which point they will be in a position to enjoy their freedom of choice as others do. The sign of this liberation will be their choosing to conform with the norms of liberal capitalist society.[10]

Because women choosing to cover their heads for religious reasons doesn't accord with liberal Western values, in other words, this choice has not been celebrated as part of the multicultural "freedom of choice" but rather has been rejected under the presumption that no one who was truly free would make such a choice.

Similar dynamics were at work in the mid-2000s, when the Netherlands introduced a new test for citizenship that required applicants to watch a film clip of two men kissing. People who were uncomfortable with the film had their fitness for Dutch citizenship questioned. Coming in the wake of a sharp increase in Islamophobia in Europe, this citizenship test encoded assumptions that Muslim immigrants will be a danger to gay Dutch citizens—and that Muslim immigrants will be heterosexual! Like the hijab argument that Abraham analyzes, this approach to multiculturalism enforces the inclusion of some at the cost of the exclusion of others. It's not actual inclusion, in other words, but rather the creation of a sort of multicultural "charmed circle" of people who all (apparently) think the same. Included in this circle, importantly, are plenty of white Christians who would be uncomfortable with two men kissing, and who cover their heads for religious reasons. It turns out that it's not human differences that are the window dressing in liberal multiculturalism, but inclusion itself.

In the place of liberal multiculturalism and identity politics, which make identities like "queer" and "Muslim" into hostile opposites and make queer Muslim identity appear impossible, Abraham suggests an approach he calls "critical hybridity." Drawn from the work of postcolonial theorist Homi Bhabha, the concept of hybridity underlines the forcibly combined nature of colonized cultures, which are often forced to imitate the cultures of the colonizer yet also prevented from ever becoming part of those cultures, defined as always an imperfect imitation. Drawing Bhabha's ideas together with

Marxist thought, Abraham turns to the concept of *critical* hybridity, which relies on the Marxist idea of critique as an analysis of the material roots of power and oppression. *Material*, here, refers to economics in a broad sense: money, but also more tangible material resources. Marx thought that the material aspects of life determined how people thought about themselves and their world; Marxist analysis today continues to prioritize materialist analysis. Critical hybridity, then, focuses on "not an unending celebration and display of difference [such as multiculturalism promotes] but rather a critique of the conditions that constrain the complexities and exclude the totality of cultural exchange," Abraham explains, quoting thinker Nikos Papastergiadis.[11]

Critical hybridity, in fact, was exactly the approach taken by the queer Muslims that Abraham interviewed. Resistant to Australian liberal multicultural expectations of assimilation, they insisted that they were *both* queer *and* Muslim, and deserved to be respected as both—and also as women, as people from specific countries or ancestries, and so on. They insisted that non-Muslim Australian communities, and especially queer communities, needed to respect them as Muslims; that non-queer Australian communities, including Muslim communities, needed to respect them as queer people; and that all of their communities needed to respect them as Australians. In other words, justice for these Australians meant refusing a forced choice between Muslim identity politics and queer identity politics, and instead embracing, and encouraging their fellow Australians to embrace, critical hybridity.

These considerations—the questions at the beginning of the chapter, Tanis's ideas about gender as a calling, African diasporic transcorporeality and transgeneric bodies, and Abraham's argument about critical hybridity—show us that identity is pretty complicated. It can be highly individual in some cultures but it's neither fixed nor inborn, even if biology might play a role in some of the experiences that draw us to specific identities. It's profoundly cultural and in many cultures communal, since the cultures and communities around us affect not only the identity options that are even available (for instance, "gay" wasn't an available identity in seventeenth-century China, but there were other ways of understanding same-sex desire that may or may not have been identity based), but also how we and our communities navigate them (having a Jewish father but not a Jewish mother makes for different identities in Orthodox and Reform Jewish communities, for example). What counts as an identity to some people doesn't count to others, and each aspect of our identities can impact the others. The concept of performativity reminds us that how we identify makes something in the world; it helps to create us as selves, as subjects, and it helps to create or reshape that identity within the cultures and communities we engage with.

How, then, should we study identity within queer and transgender studies in religion? Many scholars who've studied religion and identity, including myself, have focused on how queer and transgender people navigate between their religious, gender, and sexual identities. Such approaches, though, rely on the assumptions that Abraham criticizes—that sexuality, gender, and religion are separable and potentially in conflict. It's true that some people do consider those identities to be in conflict, and they attempt to separate them or to eradicate one of the conflicting identities. But conflict is only one way for these identities to relate. If we begin with the assumption that gender, sexuality, and religion are separable and at odds, we have a lot of catching up to do when we encounter cases where they're not. So how do these questions actually play out in intersectional ways in the lives of everyday people? The rest of this chapter draws from postcolonial studies, settler colonial studies, and lived-religion approaches to explore the complexities of sexual, gender, and religious identities as they're actually lived out.

HIJRA OR TRANSGENDER? HINDU OR MUSLIM? *HIJRA* IDENTITY AND GLOBAL POLITICS

Anthropologist Gayatri Reddy came into her fieldwork among **hijras** in Hyderabad, India, with some assumptions about their religious identities. *Hijras* are people assigned male at birth who dedicate themselves to a goddess, live as women, are often sexually active with men, and typically undergo at least certain aspects of medical transition such as the removal of male genitalia. Because of these aspects of their identities, because they're considered auspicious in Hindu tradition, and because they dedicate themselves to a Hindu goddess, Reddy was startled to learn that the *hijras* with whom she worked considered themselves and all other *hijras* to be Muslim. Her *hijra* friends, of course, didn't find this startling at all; what they were surprised by was Reddy's puzzlement. Reddy explains that "it is practice—through the various acts that they employ, the proscriptions they are subjected to, and the festivals that they celebrate—that facilitates hijras' claims to Islamic identification."[12]

It isn't particularly unusual for practice to be central to Muslim identity. One of the first ways that someone unfamiliar with Islam is often introduced to the religion, for example, is through the Five Pillars. The first of these, the *shahada* or statement of faith that there is no god but God and Muhammad is God's messenger, appears at first glance to be belief rather than practice, but it's the *action* of affirming this belief that's at stake. The other four pillars—prayer, almsgiving, fasting during important holidays like the month of Ramadan, and making the pilgrimage to Mecca (the hajj)—are also all clearly centered on practice. Yet while some of these, especially prayer and the hajj, are important to the hijras that Reddy worked with, they also affirm their Muslim identities in a number of other ways just as most Muslims do. One of them, Munira, told Reddy that "once you become a hijra . . . then you become a Musalman [Muslim—MW]. [You] say *salam aleikum* [an Arabic greeting traditionally used by Muslims—MW] when you meet other hijras, wear a green sari for special occasions, do not wear a *bindi* [facial jewelry worn by some Hindu women—MW], eat *halal* [Islamically prepared—MW] meat, have the *khatna* [circumcision], you say *namaz* [prayers—MW], older people go on the *hajj*. It is like that. That is why we say 'now we are Musalmans.'"[13] In addition to prayer and pilgrimage, Munira marked her and other *hijras'* identities as Muslim through more mundane practices like greetings, attire, embodiment, and food. She even once remarked to Reddy, "only half-joking, 'We are even more Muslim than Muslims. They cut off only so much [the foreskin of the penis, during circumcision], and we cut off the whole thing.'"[14]

The Muslim identities of Hyderabadi *hijras* coexist with their traditional Hindu practices. Their origin story involves a goddess, to whom they make offerings—do puja—on important occasions, and in observance of those special occasions they follow a local Muslim tradition of wearing green. When goats are given to the goddess, they are slaughtered by a Muslim butcher so the meat and the blood will be halal. *Hijras* even risk discipline and often a fine from their superiors by wearing a bindi because it looks pretty, but when they go out alone in public many don a burqa that fully covers them over their saris for the sake of modesty. Here, then, is another case where an outsider might be tempted to accuse the people in question of trying to have it all—to be both Hindu and Muslim at the same time. In a country where violence against Muslims has been a constant presence since its partition along religious lines in 1947, though, openly enacting a Muslim identity doesn't always benefit people—this is hardly about self-interest or self-indulgence. Furthermore, given the discrimination that *hijras* already face despite being considered an auspicious presence at certain special events, adding the risk of Islamophobia to the mix isn't exactly a self-serving gesture. While the origins of Hyderabadi *hijras'* Muslim identification are unclear, at least as of Reddy's writing, the fact that they do identify as Muslim while also living out identities based in Hindu tradition and honoring a Hindu goddess (using halal meat!) is indisputable. Perhaps we can learn just as much from Reddy's and our own surprise at their identities as we can from the identities themselves.

Another aspect of *hijras'* complex identities is their shifting use of the term *transgender*. As we've already discussed, this term is a complex part of the workings of global power. Used by some to describe an innate identity that's shared by all gender-variant people across time and space, *transgender* is a recently invented term that came into use around the late 1980s. Pushing back against the inversion model of sexuality that combined gender variance and same-sex desire into a single identity or medical diagnosis, transgender activists have argued instead for separating gender and sexuality as concepts and identities. The concept of transgender rights, then, refers to the rights of all gender-variant people to dignity, equality, and justice, often on the basis of an argument that gender identity is an innate human quality. This concept works well for some transgender people, and certainly there's a lot to be said for efforts to bring dignity, equality, and justice to all people. But as we've also discussed, when those efforts come in a one-size-fits-all package, they sometimes do more harm than good. Political and economic elites in Global North/Global West countries who are committed to the idea of gender as a permanent and innate aspect of human identity that's separate from desire and sexuality may bring that commitment into Global South/Global East spaces where gender variance is structured differently, and attempt to "educate" gender-variant and same-sex-attracted activists there so that they understand the "true nature" of being transgender. While such approaches are blatantly insulting to the audience's intelligence, often political and economic support are affected by activists' and organizations' willingness to adopt the Global North/Global West language and priorities. Gaining much-needed support and funding through claiming the language of "LGBT," at least in public, they may also become more vulnerable to nationalist attacks for having "sold out to the West."

But this also isn't a simple story of naive people in the Global South/ Global East being taken in by the ignorant, arrogant universalizing of Global North/Global West elites. Same-sex-attracted and gender-variant people in the Global South/Global East are thoughtful and strategic in their adoption of Western gender and sexuality terms. The *hijra* activists who successfully brought an antidiscrimination lawsuit against the Indian government in 2014 were identified in Indian media reports as both *hijra* and transgender, with reporters using the terms interchangeably.[15] In 2015 the city of Raigarh elected India's first *hijra* mayor; media coverage and activists celebrated her election as a milestone for the transgender community.[16] Like the Hyderabadi *hijras*' Muslim identities and Hindu practices, Indian activists' use of local terms and their strategic engagement of Global North/Global West terms coexist, not just in compartmentalized spaces but freely intertwined. At one moment telling the story that *hijras* began when a goddess discovered that her husband was going out every night to have sex with other men, and in rage she cut off his penis (thus linking same-sex attraction and gender variance), in the next moment these same communities insist that "transgender" and "gay" are separate categories that shouldn't be confused with one another. We shouldn't see this complexity as confusion or scheming, but as an effective way to navigate multiple structures of gender and sexuality that are swirling together where local, colonial, postcolonial, and global forces meet.

TRANSGENDER OR GAY?
IDENTITY, SCIENCE, POWER, AND MODERNITY IN IRAN

Other kinds of complexity—and other opportunities for misinterpretation from the outside—exist with regard to gender and sexual identities in the Islamic Republic of Iran, where same-sex sexual activity is illegal and carries penalties up to and including death, while medical transition for transgender people is not only permitted but even supported by the government for people with limited financial resources. This situation puzzles some people in the Global North/Global West, who look to their own countries and regions of the world as the model for other countries to follow. Since it took some time for such countries to separate transgender people from the inversion model and to accept the idea of transgender rights (an idea that still isn't widely accepted in most places), using these countries as a model or a guiding light for all so-called LGBT activism around the world suggests that gay rights happen first, transgender rights follow, and bisexual rights sort of come in the side door almost by accident—if they come in at all. The vision in this model is that eventually all countries around the world will have followed this path and LGBT rights will have been established everywhere. These expectations make it difficult to understand the Iranian situation. So how did it come about?

Historian Afsaneh Najmabadi reminds us that up until the Islamic Revolution in 1979, Iran had spent much of the twentieth century focused on the idea of modernization. Today often considered a synonym for *Westernization*, as we discussed in chapter 1, the term *modernization* at the time was a positive word to many people.[17] It meant being scientifically and technologically advanced, and culturally current. It was very much Global North/Global West countries like Western Europe and the United States that set the standards for modernization, though, so although the term wasn't considered negative by most people at the time, those who did see it as a form of Westernization were also correct.

Part of being considered "modern" in the twentieth century, and still today, is being up to date on the latest scientific and technological innovations. Like the liberal Christians in the United States who added the word *homosexuality* to the Bible in 1946 based on their knowledge of modern psychology, up-to-date Iranians at the time were also paying attention to new developments in the scientific structuring of gender and sexuality. Unlike their North American counterparts, though, they saw gender expression as different from same-sex desire until the middle of the twentieth century. Since some intersex people experience significant changes in external sexual characteristics during puberty, appearing to spontaneously change sex, in the first half of the twentieth century, gender affirmation surgery was understood by both scientists and the general public in Iran as a way to help intersex people; intersex people and transgender people were conceived of as fairly interchangeable and were treated as unusual in a largely positive sense. Of course, being treated as positively unusual isn't always a positive experience for the "unusual" person, but reactions to gender-variant people during this time in Iran were quite different from reactions to people who were sexually active with the same sex. Same-sex eroticism, Najmabadi explains, was approached as an illness and was religiously condemned as well in this majority Muslim country, just as it was in many Christian countries at the time. Modernity in Iran in the first part of the twentieth century included revulsion toward same-sex eroticism and fascination with gender variance.

Iranians began increasingly conflating same-sex desire and gender variance through the inversion model in the mid-twentieth century, in part through shifting scientific focuses and in part because of a high-profile murder case in which a female-born, masculine-presenting person murdered a young woman who was a love interest. What exactly was the pathology that led to this murder? the popular press wondered. Scientists weighed in, as did the general public. Was the murderer already depraved because of being same-sex attracted or gender variant? Was the person made ill by severe discrimination from family and friends? Did the murder happen because the killer was a homosexual, and homosexuals are mentally deranged, or because the person was a transsexual (the word that was used at the time) and was denied the opportunity to live as a man and therefore became deranged? It's also worth noting that there seems to have been no consideration of intimate partner violence in this case, even though that's in many ways the most plausible description of what happened. But even here, although the discussion of the case came close to conflating gender variance and same-sex desire, the possibility remained for gender-variant people to be understood as the victims of illness and prejudice, both of which could be alleviated.

The Islamic Revolution took Iran from a religiously neutral form of government to a theocratic one in which specific and highly socially conservative interpretations of Islam were written into national law. At the time of the revolution, numerous sources indicate the presence of a growing underground "gay" culture in Tehran, consisting of both same-sex-attracted and gender-variant people, including people who were both. Yet in the same decade, gender affirmation surgeries came to be banned in Iran on the basis that sex change was not truly possible—an argument still made by social conservatives and certain feminists, too, in many places today. Whereas the underground culture thrived despite unfavorable medical and political opinions, the revolution brought severe violence to gender-variant and same-sex-desiring people. In the eyes of the religious conservatives who ended up in control, same-sex eroticism and gender variance came to represent not only un-Islamic conduct but also the corruption of the now-overthrown (and in fact quite corrupt) government of the shah. Conservative gender norms, structured around a clear-cut and strictly separated binary, were literally policed, and those who were arrested were subjected to terrifying violence. Same-sex-desiring and gender-variant people were publicly executed, and even medical providers sometimes threatened their lives.[18] Just a few years after the revolution, though, a transgender woman activist named Maryam Mulk-ara went directly to Ayatollah Khomeini, the top religious leader in the new Iranian government. After a conversation with the activist, the ayatollah issued a formal legal opinion or fatwa indicating that, as Mulk-ara put it in an interview with Najmabadi, "changing sex with a doctor's approval is not prohibited."[19] She left the ayatollah's house in a chador—a women's outer garment that was commonly worn in Iran after the revolution—that was made for her by the ayatollah's female relatives.

With a supportive fatwa issued by the highest religious authority in the country, the position of transgender people in Iran began to shift. Today those with a medical diagnosis can change their national identity cards and can even receive government assistance in paying for medical treatment as they transition. But there has been no such fatwa with regard to same-sex eroticism. In a context where same-sex desire and gender variance were often connected by both popular culture and medical discourse during the twentieth century but were then strictly separated, first by science and then by religious rulings, this state of affairs sometimes leaves same-sex-attracted people wondering whether they're actually trans. Why?

To explain this situational blurring of the lines between same-sex attraction and gender variance in contemporary Iran, let's return to one of the questions we considered at the start of the chapter: How do people know their identities? In cissexist and heterosexist societies, where people are presumed to be cisgender and heterosexual until proven otherwise, most cis and straight people can't tell you how or when they knew they were cis or straight. They simply always have been, because that's what society told them they were. But some people have the sense that they're different; when at some point that difference solidifies in their experience around sexuality and/or gender, they and others around them often look back into their earlier life and discover clues. This process is a common part of identity negotiation; it happens with religious conversion, too. In Iran, a certain amount of gender variance prior to puberty is considered acceptable, even cute. But for someone who continues to express gender variance after puberty or who develops same-sex attraction, those early childhood experiences suddenly become meaningful in a way they don't for the person's straight, cisgender sisters and brothers.

By definition in Iran, thanks largely to the European scientific legacy of the invert, transgender people are understood to be same-sex attracted until they transition and become "properly" heterosexual. So, for instance, if you were raised as a girl but liked to play ball with the boys, if you prefer as an adult not to wear makeup and you're sexually attracted to women, how should you understand your identity, especially when most of the lesbian, gay, and transgender people you meet are convinced they know "what" you are but they don't agree with each other? This was the dilemma of some of the Iranians whom Najmabadi interviewed, but it's also a common dilemma in many cultures influenced by the inversion model. And it's one thing to explore one's sexuality and gender in a family and a cultural and political setting where there are no positive or negative consequences for choosing one identity over the others, but very few people live in such a setting today. If you aren't certain you're trans, and you don't really want surgery, but you also don't fit well with your culture's expectations for your assigned gender, then if you're attracted to a different sex you might simply understand yourself as a "gentle man" or a "strong woman." If you're attracted to the same sex, though, and you live in Iran, you'd have to choose between transitioning, which would give you legal rights and place you in good standing with God, and living with a same-sex partner, which might (or might not) feel more true to who you are but would come with significant discrimination, risk, and a sense that you were sinning against God. Which would you choose?

As Elizabeth Bucar and Faegheh Shirazi point out, some Westerners interpret the current political situation in Iran as one where the government is attempting to eradicate gays and lesbians by forcing them all into sex reassignment surgery. They argue, though, that this interpretation "does not do justice to the complicated manner in which Islamic epistemologies and ethics have influenced contemporary views of sexuality in Iran."[20] Rather than impose on Iran a Western model in which "LGBT . . . has become more than just an acronym . . . but also a waiting line with 'T' (trans) as the last sexual dissent to gain rights because it is presumably the least normative and the most queer,"[21] we can instead ask about the ways in which understandings of sexuality, gender, religion, science, and the self in contemporary Iran have made it difficult for some people to decide whether they're butch lesbians and femme gay men, or whether they're trans. When the final arbiters are not queer and trans folks themselves but medical professionals—when it takes a doctor to tell you who you are—and when those professionals control not just access to medical treatment but to legalization, then the stakes become even higher and the decision more difficult and more dangerous.

WHO OWNS TWO-SPIRIT IDENTITY?
SETTLER COLONIALISM AND CULTURAL APPROPRIATION

Another way that outsiders can complicate religious, sexual, and gender identities is through claiming identities that don't belong to them. But wait—

how can an identity belong or not belong to someone? Well, we've just talked about outsiders, in this case meaning cisgender and straight medical professionals, determining whether the identity "transgender" belongs to someone else. Outsiders also sometimes decide that someone else's identity belongs to them. Different cultures have different ideas about how ownership is determined, or whether something even can be owned at all. We've already seen how different religious groups have different ideas about the ownership and accessibility of religious identity—whether it's possible to convert to Judaism, for example, or whether you have to be born to a Jewish mother in order to be Jewish. Even within religious groups there's sometimes disagreement over who owns an identity: Are queer and transgender people who live out their identities through being sexually active or living as the appropriate gender, but who also go to Mass, Catholics in good standing? They say so, and in the next chapter we'll consider one of the organizations that supports them in that, but the Roman Catholic hierarchy disagrees. Likewise, are trans and queer Mormons who've been disfellowshipped—kicked out of the LDS church—still Mormon? Many of them consider themselves to be, but the LDS church has a different opinion.

These examples are ones in which the power dynamic is tilted in favor of the religious organization, where transgender and queer folks are claiming identities in a religion that would deny them simply because they're transgender and queer. In other cases, though, it's the queer and trans folks claiming a religious identity who are the ones wielding the greater social and cultural power, and those trying to protect that identity are the disempowered ones. This is the case with non-Native appropriation of traditional Native practices and identities. Analyzing the power dynamics of appropriation in the context of a chapter on gender, sexual, and religious identities will take us through questions of cultural ownership, issues of cultural genocide, and definitions of religion; as we traverse these topics, remember that our central question has to do with how claims to identity by one group of same-sex-attracted and gender-variant people may be seen as causing harm to another group of same-sex-attracted and gender-variant people.

In Global North/Global West cultures, religious practices are typically like air; they can't be owned. These cultures do tend, *sometimes*, to respect religions' ideas about proper preparation—that one shouldn't engage in particular religious practices without respecting the proper preparatory steps, for instance, or without following the proper procedures—but there's often very strong resistance to the idea that some religious practices are simply off limits. If you live in a culture like this, test out this idea: Ask a bunch of your friends whether they think a person should be prevented from practicing a religion, even with the proper preparation, simply because of who they are or aren't. Most people will probably answer "no." Religious practices—"spirituality," to many people—are often considered something that should be freely available to all people, and literally *for* free, as in free of charge.

In some ways, this perspective is one of the legacies of the world-religions model; if all religions are comparable expressions of a universal human experience of the sacred, then they must in some ways be interchangeable, and universal to humanity. So this view is socially constructed, one way to structure the relationship between religion, culture, and individuals. Remember, too, that the world-religions model at its origins was one of the structural supports for colonialism. We have reason, then, to be suspicious of the power dynamics involved in its descendants. Add to this fact the history of cultural genocide that's been an important tool of settler colonialism in particular, and you may start to see another perspective on the claim that religion is a resource for all human cultures and should be openly shared with all.

Cultural genocide is the process of killing off the culture of a group of people. In the United States, Captain Richard H. Pratt called this a strategy of "kill the Indian, and save the man."[22] Pratt was the founder of the Carlisle Indian Industrial School in Pennsylvania, part of the infamous boarding school system in which hundreds of thousands of Native children from lands the United States had colonized were forced to shed their own culture and adopt European ways. Canada maintained a similar boarding school system for First Nations and Métis children. These schools, which ran for well over one hundred years in both countries, were mandatory for much of their history. In the United States, it wasn't until 1978 that Native parents gained the legal right to refuse to allow their children to be taken away to boarding schools. In Canada, the last Indian boarding school didn't close until 1996. In these schools, which were commonly the site of physical, sexual, and emotional abuse, children were punished—often severely—for speaking their own language. They were forced to adopt Western clothing and hairstyles, eat Western food in Western ways, and practice Christianity. Practicing their own religious traditions, like speaking their own languages, was strictly forbidden, under the threat of severe punishment. Many Native traditions and Native languages fell into disuse as a result of the boarding school system, and even those who remembered the old ways sometimes refused to teach them. Some Native people moved away from their homelands, sometimes even changing their children's ethnic identities when they could, to try to protect them from the harm that had come to their parents.

Other systems also contributed to cultural genocide among colonized peoples. Early anthropologists and archaeologists, among other scholars, considered indigenous cultural heritage to be artifacts. Robbing graves, stealing sacred ritual objects, and sneaking in to take pictures and record films of sacred practices without permission or when they'd been actively banned from doing so, they ignored indigenous property rights and denied indigenous people's rights to control access to their own cultural traditions. With the excuse that they thought indigenous cultures were dying anyway—after all, their governments were actively trying to kill those cultures off, and the United States even banned the practice of Native traditions for several decades—these Western scholars competed against each other to "preserve" cultural "artifacts" so that their own children and grandchildren could gaze in awe at long-lost (because intentionally destroyed) cultures that Native people's children and grandchildren had been deprived of. Given this history, is it any surprise that many Native and First Nations people are profoundly suspicious of non-Native attempts to learn and practice their traditions?

Furthermore, most indigenous traditions are closely tied to the land and the people; it simply makes no sense for someone who's not part of a particular tribe, with a particular homeland, to practice those traditions. Unlike religions that were intended for people to convert to, like Christianity, Islam, and Buddhism, many indigenous traditions are rooted both in the land and in the ancestry of the people from which they grew. Even when a religion remains rooted in specific geographical areas—Jerusalem for Jews or the Ganges River for Hindus, for example—when the religions move locations through exile or conversion they often become portable. Their rituals can be practiced anywhere in the world, provided that the appropriate preparations are made. The same isn't true for many indigenous traditions. Finally, Native cultures often understand cultural ownership differently from the colonizing cultures around them. Global North/Global West cultures understand ownership of a song, for instance, to mean that the person who wrote it (or their descendants, but only within a specific period of time after the song was written) should give you permission to perform it, and probably receive royalties from you, if you're going to be paid for the performance. But you can sing the song in the shower, or walking down the street, any time you want. This is even true for sacred songs—it's okay to hum a Christian hymn or a Christian rock song while you're on the train to work, even if the composer is still alive and even if you aren't Christian. In many Native North American traditions, though, sacred songs are owned by particular people and particular families, and other people can't simply get up and perform those songs anywhere, or without permission.

These factors—the history of cultural genocide, the geographic and cultural locatedness of indigenous traditions, and indigenous structures of cultural ownership—make non-Native practice of indigenous traditions inappropriate and disrespectful in many cases. But two factors—a history of rejection by their own families' religions and the romanticization of Two-Spirit histories—have led some non-Native queer and transgender people in settler colonial countries like the United States and Canada to be intensely drawn to Native traditions. Using the familiar argument that spirituality is for everyone and that no one should be denied access to spiritual resources, non-

Native queer and trans people perpetuate settler colonialism in their quest for religious traditions and identities that honor instead of condemn them.

Brian Gilley writes about the challenge this non-Native fascination posed for the Two-Spirit people he worked with.[23] One of the organizations he studied held an annual retreat in the mountains in order to provide a space for spiritual practice and development for Two-Spirit people. Often denied full access to their traditional practices at tribal and pan-tribal gatherings that aren't designed specifically for Two-Spirit people, the people who attended the retreat appreciated the opportunity to learn and practice in the company of other Two-Spirit people. While tensions still arose over what traditions they would practice, and precisely how Two-Spirit identity could and couldn't change traditional gendered rules of participation in various events, the biggest challenge arose from the presence of what came to be called "New Age lesbigays."[24] Since many Two-Spirit people are alienated from their tribes because of homophobia and transphobia, and because colonial control of Native identity has led to many Native people not being officially enrolled in tribes (in the United States, Native people are the only people who have to carry an ethnic identity card and the only ones whose ethnic identity is determined by the government), Two-Spirit organizations are reluctant to exclude anyone claiming Native identity. At the same time, the increasing romanticization of Native identity among many Global North/ Global West people over the course of the last few decades of the twentieth century has led non-Native people to adopt Native identities as though they believe that both spirituality and ancestry should be freely available to anyone. Nearly everyone these days, it seems, has a legend of an "Indian princess" in their family tree.

These non-Native, queer, and probably also trans folks who attended the Two-Spirit gatherings that Gilley attended longed for entry into cultures that they believed—based on Orientalist writings by non-Native people about the celebration of Two-Spirit people in Native cultures—would embrace and value them for their queerness and transness. They were wrong, of course; Two-Spirit people often have to struggle for the acceptance of their tribes. They were also ignorant of Native cultures, having learned only romanticized popular cultural representations of "Indians." At one gathering, Gilley relates, jokes circulated among the Two-Spirit people present about the "New Age lesbigay" who had clutched her heart in agony when someone uprooted a small sapling to make room for a tent, and about another who had suddenly declared his hand drum possessed and thrown it into the fire. All joking aside, though, the non-Native people who attended these gatherings claiming some vague family secret about an Indian ancestor or a personal feeling that they must be Native wanted to take on an identity without dealing with the colonial heritage that the Two-Spirit people at the gatherings suffered from: poverty, intergenerational trauma, and colonially imposed homophobia and transphobia, among others. They wanted the cultural practices without the cultural commitment, so although they were responded to with humor, they were really not all that different from the anthropologists who stole sacred objects. Religious appropriation is, after all, a form of cultural theft and cultural genocide. Identity is often inextricable from power.

Anthropologist Scott Lauria Morgensen's book, *Spaces between Us*, focuses on the non-Native side of this equation, exploring non-Native queer fascination with Native traditions and Native identities in the context of US settler colonialism.[25] One of his chapters focuses on fantasies of indigeneity and engagement with Native communities among the Radical Faeries. As we learned in chapter 3, the Radical Faeries are a largely white religious movement founded in the late 1970s that has traditionally focused on developing and affirming what Faeries believe to be the unique spiritual qualities of gay men. Drawing heavily on the writings of Harry Hay, Radical Faerie philosophy presumes that gay men have an innately feminine nature, or at least a feminine side, and it often associates that perspective with Native Two-Spirit people. As a consequence, Faerie culture is among those non-Native cultures that romanticize and appropriate Native traditions, even when individual Faeries may be more aware of or sensitive to their settler colonial context. Morgensen describes this starkly; after noting the Faeries' traditional openness to people across class backgrounds, across genders and sexualities, across race, and across the common urban-rural divide in gay cultures, he remarks that "on joining, all were promised a global and transhistorical gay nature by addressing non-Natives as inheritors of Native culture on Native land."[26]

Morgensen reminds us that one of the tools with which settler colonialism maintains its power in places like the United States is erasure. Colonialism is placed safely in the past, and contemporary citizens of settler colonial countries are absolved of their responsibility for perpetuating settler colonialism through placing all colonized people safely in the past as well. In the United States, many schools continue to teach their students about Native people solely in the past tense, with no discussion whatsoever of contemporary Native American lives. Likewise, most non-Native queer and transgender representations of Two-Spirit people (often discussed using the colonialist slur *berdache* as though it were a neutral term) also depict them as being in the past, having died out under colonialism by the early twentieth century. Morgensen argues that this depiction leaves the Two-Spirit role apparently free for the taking; if "real" Native Two-Spirit people ceased to exist more than a hundred years ago, some non-Native people argue, then anyone ought to be able to revive that role. This argument, as Morgensen makes clear, perpetuates and supports settler colonialism and cultural genocide in part by making those forces invisible to those enacting them; it absolves practitioners like the Radical Faeries of complicity in colonialism by erasing contemporary colonized people and making their realities into a romanticized history that anyone can reclaim, along with Native land.

Morgensen also asks whether it's possible to do things differently. Can non-Native queer and transgender folks ally with Native queer and Two-Spirit people in their efforts to decolonize, instead of perpetuating colonization by claiming Two-Spirit identities as their own? He argues that they can, and in his chapter on the Radical Faeries he suggests that by the late 1990s some Faeries had begun to approach their relationship to Native people and Native traditions differently. He describes two cases in which Native queer and Two-Spirit men approached Radical Faerie communities to offer religious leadership—not to hand over their religious authority, their identity, or their religious practices to the Faeries, but to allow them to participate on a onetime basis in a Native traditional practice. While there was still some reaction from the Faeries that hinted at a longing to appropriate these traditions and identities, Morgensen also notes in one case that the Native leaders had clearly stressed that the practice was not being given to the Faeries and was not "for discussion or representation outside of that space. As a result," Morgensen adds, "for the first time, I heard among Radical Faeries an articulate silence about a quality of Native culture that they desired. I also noticed increased discussion among Radical Faeries about their being non-Natives who bore a responsibility to Native people not to usurp Native culture."[27] Just as settler colonialism is learned, then, being an ally in decolonization can be learned as well—and in many ways this starts with learning to identify as non-Native, marking an unmarked category of identity in order to examine its power.

QUEERING RELIGION/RELIGIONING QUEER

While all three of the fields that flow into transgender and queer studies in religion engage in complex and thoughtful ways with identity, it may be the idea of social construction that proves most helpful at their confluence. Recall that social construction means that a concept is created by society, not individuals. There's a cultural choice, for instance, to understand human beings as having only two sexes despite the presence of a wide range of sexed embodiments in human life. There's also a cultural choice to determine sex on the basis of external genitalia and to make it a defining factor in how a culture treats any given person. Likewise, there's a cultural decision to identify certain aspects of a person's appearance—skin tone, hair color and texture, eye shape—as indicating "race," and to make those aspects of a person's embodiment central in determining how that person will be treated in the culture. Not all cultures in the world have made genitalia the determining factor in whether someone is a man or a woman; not all have restricted humans to only two sexes or genders; not all have divided people based on race or have even had the concept of race. Sex, gender, race, sexuality—yes, even religion—these concepts are social and cultural fictions even as their consequences for human lives are established facts.

By definition, the social construction of identity can't take place without some sort of social influence. There were multiple social influences and social constructs at work in the neo-pagan community that anthropologist Susan Harper participated in during the decade of the 2000s, for instance. Mostly white and young—between ages eighteen and thirty-five—these Texans espoused fairly liberal social values and placed a high priority on accepting many different sexual identities and practices. Both their neo-pagan perspectives and their participation in broader US mainstream culture shaped their understanding of sexual identity, which included a number of possibilities but mostly focused on the categories of heterosexual, gay or lesbian, and bisexual. When Harper began exploring sexual identities among this Neo-pagan community, though, she was intrigued to discover that more than 60 percent of the people who identified as women considered themselves bisexual, whereas almost none of those identifying as men did. "Men seemed far more likely to self-identify as gay or straight," she explains, while "women were more reluctant to identify as lesbian, choosing instead the label *bisexual* or *heterosexual*."[28] Why might this be? Harper explains that this community represented women's bisexuality as feminist, as a rejection of binary understandings of gender and sexuality, as quintessentially neo-pagan, and as "a 'more natural' form of sexuality."[29] But why would this be a value for women and not for men? Harper thinks it's because of some very old social constructs.

"There is a coexistence," Harper argues, "of . . . the 'fetishization of the hot bi Pagan babe,' a male-dominated encouragement of same-sex performances between women in public spaces such as festival fires [following on the popularity of the 'lesbian' genre in pornography made for straight men], and a construction of monosexuality [in women] as deviant and bisexuality as normative."[30] The valuing of bisexuality in women, the belief that, as Harper puts it in her title, "all cool women should be bisexual," puts so much sexual pressure on women who are attracted to men that even those who have no particular attraction to women still feel expected to identify as bisexual "or be made to feel guilty, less spiritual, or less feminine because they identify as heterosexual."[31]

So what can we learn from this study about gender, sexual, and religious identity? We might begin with the social constructs of gender, sexuality, and religion. In the community Harper participated in, these encompass the possible categories of "woman" and "man" (Harper doesn't discuss gender variance, and transgender people may not have been welcome or present in the community); "gay," "lesbian," "bisexual," and "heterosexual"; and "neo-pagan" (religious identity varied from person to person, but everyone in the community identified as neo-pagan in one way or another). Identifying as neo-pagan and as a woman, though, led to certain expectations about femininity, including not only aspects of gender presentation but also sexual identity. An intersectional analysis shows us that in this community, despite its feminist commitments, women were expected to be sexually available to everyone and to perform sexually in public. Not accepting the expected sexual identity and the sexual practices that were expected to go along with that identity challenged both of their other key identities within this community: their gender and their religion.

The interplay between gender, sexual, and religious identities in this community can't be fully understood without considering all three of these factors. For queer and trans studies to approach this neo-pagan community without the perspectives of religious studies would be to miss the important role that being neo-pagan plays in the creation and maintenance of these expectations and in women's obedience to them. For religious studies to approach this neo-pagan community without the perspectives of queer and transgender studies would be to miss the complexities of gender and sexual identities. Social constructs these all may be, but determining our identities and having them respected and validated matters deeply to many of us as human beings. Sometimes we're willing to pay a steep price for that validation from communities that we care about. Harper's study brings us back again not only to the importance of social construction and intersectionality but also to the interconnections between the themes in this book. Women felt pressure to be bisexual because of some of the sacred stories in their religious tradition; they observed and took part in conversations about bisexuality, often learning from these conversations that the community valued bisexual women over heterosexual women; they took part in practices that demonstrated and reaffirmed their identities, sometimes not in very positive ways; and none of this could have happened at all in the absence of communities—to which we now turn.

STUDY QUESTIONS

1. The opening part of this chapter argues that "essentialist and constructivist approaches to sexuality, gender, and religion aren't inherently liberatory or oppressive." Why? Can you think of examples of each case—where a constructivist approach is liberatory and where it's oppressive, for instance?

2. How does Justin Tanis's argument that gender is a calling change the terms of the debate over constructivist and essentialist approaches to identity?

3. What is transcorporeality, and how might it offer additional ways of understanding gender and selfhood?
4. What is liberal multiculturalism, and what do some people think is wrong with it? What does Ibrahim Abraham propose instead?
5. How do *hijras* in Hyderabad understand their Muslim identities? How do they navigate being Muslim when *hijras* are historically Hindu and they're dedicated to a goddess?
6. How did the Iranian government come to officially support transgender people but harshly condemn nontransgender, same-sex-attracted people?
7. What is cultural genocide? Why do some people think that non-Native people practicing Native religions are engaging in cultural genocide?
8. According to Susan Harper, why were women and not men in the neo-pagan community she worked with subjected to pressures to be bisexual?

FOR FURTHER THOUGHT

1. In the beginning of the chapter, we considered the idea of identifying *culturally* as part of a religion—culturally Jewish, for instance, or culturally Mormon. But you hardly ever hear about people identifying as culturally Protestant. Why do you think this is?
2. Regardless of your own perspectives on the divine (or lack thereof), what do you think about Tanis's idea of gender as a calling? Why?
3. How might a focus on Black Atlantic ideas of selfhood change queer and transgender studies? How might it change religious studies? Can you think of one example of something (other than Black Atlantic religious traditions themselves) that we might understand differently if we analyzed it from the perspective of transcorporeality or transgeneric selfhood?
4. Abraham offers his critique of the idea of liberal multiculturalism in the interest of thinking about how to create a more widely inclusive and egalitarian society. How does he think people should work toward this goal? What do you think of his critiques and his suggestions? How do you think people should work toward this goal? Why?
5. We've covered a lot of very complex identities in this chapter, identities that from the outside sometimes seem to be a result of oppression, false consciousness, confusion, or lack of education. What makes people on the outside make such assumptions? How might we think differently about other people in order to accept rather than dismiss their own understandings of themselves?

6. Some people think that the Iranian government is trying to eradicate gay men and lesbians through its support of medical transition for transgender people. Why do Elizabeth Bucar and Faegheh Shirazi think that's the wrong interpretation? What can we learn from this case about how identities are socially formed? If you were a same-sex-attracted, gender-variant person in Iran, how would you decide whether or not you were transgender?

7. What do you think of the argument that non-Natives practicing Native religious traditions is often not only appropriation but even cultural genocide? If you agree, at least in part, where do you think the line is? Is it ever acceptable for non-Native people to practice Native traditions? And if you disagree, what are your reasons?

8. What identity pressures exist in the religious community you're most familiar with? Who has access to religious identity at all, and how do they gain that access? Who doesn't have access to that identity? What kinds of expectations does the community have for its members' sexuality and gender?

RECOMMENDATIONS FOR FURTHER READING

Abraham, Ibrahim. "'Out to Get Us': Queer Muslims and the Clash of Sexual Civilizations in Australia." *Contemporary Islam* 3, no. 1 (2009): 79–97.

Bucar, Elizabeth M., and Faegheh Shirazi. "The 'Invention' of Lesbian Acts in Iran: Interpretive Moves, Hidden Assumptions, and Emerging Categories of Sexuality." *Journal of Lesbian Studies* 16, no. 4 (2011): 416–34.

Gilley, Brian Joseph. *Becoming Two-Spirit: Gay Identity and Social Acceptance in Indian Country*. Lincoln: University of Nebraska Press, 2006.

Harper, Susan. "All Cool Women Should Be Bisexual: Female Bisexual Identity in an American Neopagan Community." *Journal of Bisexuality* 10, nos. 1–2 (2010): 79–107.

Morgensen, Scott Lauria. *Spaces between Us: Queer Settler Colonialism and Indigenous Decolonization*. Minneapolis: University of Minnesota Press, 2011.

Najmabadi, Afsaneh. *Professing Selves: Transsexuality and Same-Sex Desire in Contemporary Iran*. Durham, NC: Duke University Press, 2014.

Reddy, Gayatri. *With Respect to Sex: Negotiating Hijra Identity in South India*. Chicago: University of Chicago Press, 2005.

Strongman, Roberto. *Queering Black Atlantic Religious Traditions: Transcorporeality in Candomblé, Santería, and Vodou*. Durham, NC: Duke University Press, 2019.

Tanis, Justin. *Transgendered: Theology, Ministry, and Communities of Faith*. Cleveland, OH: Pilgrim Press, 2003.

Tinsley, Omise'eke Natasha. *Ezili's Mirrors: Imagining Black Queer Genders*. Durham, NC: Duke University Press, 2018.

NOTES

1. Justin Tanis, *Transgendered: Theology, Ministry, and Communities of Faith* (Cleveland, OH: Pilgrim Press, 2003), 147.

2. Ibid., 156.

3. See Aisha M. Beliso-De Jesús, *Electric Santería: Racial and Sexual Assemblages of Transnational Religion* (New York: Columbia University Press, 2015); Elizabeth Pérez, "From the Throne to the Kitchen Stove: LGBT Lives in Black Atlantic Traditions," unpublished manuscript; Roberto Strongman, *Queering Black Atlantic Religious Traditions: Transcorporeality in Candomblé, Santería, and Vodou* (Durham, NC: Duke University Press, 2019); and Omise'eke Natasha Tinsley, *Ezili's Mirrors: Imagining Black Queer Genders* (Durham, NC: Duke University Press, 2018).

4. Strongman, *Queering Black Atlantic Religious Traditions*, 2.

5. Ibid., 3.

6. Pérez, "From the Throne to the Kitchen Stove: LGBT Lives in Black Atlantic Traditions," 14.

7. Tinsley, *Ezili's Mirrors*, 5.

8. Ibid., 43.

9. Ibrahim Abraham, "'Out to Get Us': Queer Muslims and the Clash of Sexual Civilizations in Australia," *Contemporary Islam* 3, no. 1 (2009): 79–97.

10. Ibid., 87.

11. Nikos Papastergiadis, "Hybridity and Ambivalence: Places and Flows in Contemporary Art and Culture," *Theory, Culture, and Society* 22, no. 4 (2005): 58.

12. Gayatri Reddy, *With Respect to Sex: Negotiating Hijra Identity in South India* (Chicago: University of Chicago Press, 2005), 99.

13. Ibid., 101.

14. Ibid., 103.

15. Such as Dhananjay Mahapatra, "Supreme Court Recognizes Transgenders as 'Third Gender,'" *Times of India*, April 15, 2014, https://timesofindia.indiatimes.com/india/Supreme-Court-recognizes-transgenders-as-third-gender/articleshow/33767900.cms.

16. See, for instance, Eesha Patkar, "India's Transgender Mayor: Is the Country Finally Overcoming Prejudice?" *Guardian*, March 3, 2015, https://www.theguardian.com/cities/2015/mar/03/india-first-transgender-mayor-overcoming-prejudice-hijra.

17. Afsaneh Najmabadi, *Professing Selves: Transsexuality and Same-Sex Desire in Contemporary Iran* (Durham, NC: Duke University Press, 2014)

18. Ibid.; see especially 160–62.

19. Ibid., 165.

20. Elizabeth M. Bucar and Faegheh Shirazi, "The 'Invention' of Lesbian Acts in Iran: Interpretive Moves, Hidden Assumptions, and Emerging Categories of Sexuality," *Journal of Lesbian Studies* 16, no. 4 (2011): 430.

21. Ibid., 429.

22. *Official Report of the Nineteenth Annual Conference of Charities and Correction* (1892), 46–59, reprinted in Richard H. Pratt, "The Advantages of Mingling Indians with Whites," *Americanizing the American Indians: Writings by the "Friends of the Indian" 1880–1900* (Cambridge, MA: Harvard University Press, 1973), 260–71.

23. Brian Joseph Gilley, *Becoming Two-Spirit: Gay Identity and Social Acceptance in Indian Country* (Lincoln: University of Nebraska Press, 2006); see especially 121–32.

24. *Lesbigay* is a term from the 1990s referring to lesbians, gay men, and bisexuals.

25. Scott Lauria Morgensen, *Spaces between Us: Queer Settler Colonialism and Indigenous Decolonization* (Minneapolis: University of Minnesota Press, 2011), especially chap. 4.

26. Ibid., 128.

27. Ibid., 158.

28. Susan Harper, "All Cool Women Should Be Bisexual: Female Bisexual Identity in an American Neopagan Community," *Journal of Bisexuality* 10, nos. 1–2 (2010): 84 (italics in original).

29. Ibid., 85.

30. Ibid., 94.

31. Ibid., 80.

Chapter Five

Communities

Human beings have a persistent tendency to exist in community. That doesn't mean that we always live together, or that people who live together are necessarily a community. It means that our thoughts and actions commonly take place in the context of a community. Communities aren't positive or negative, necessarily: They can welcome and they can shun, they can nurture and they can destroy. But because our communities are so often our reference points, they're powerful. Even people who live in solitude, like the religious **hermits** of Christian and Hindu histories, have a community, because they retreat to that solitude and avoid the company of other humans in order to focus more completely on sacred beings. Communities, then, don't have to be made up of humans. Communities are central influences in the lives of queer and transgender people; because religion is too, whether as a positive or a negative force, religious communities are sometimes doubly important. As Thelathia Nikki Young and Ashon Crawley tell us, the religious communities of black queer people can have a profound influence on them—and sometimes in unexpected ways.

In the United States, black religious institutions—historically churches, but especially since the twentieth century also mosques, temples, houses of African diasporic traditions, and even occasionally communes—have been central to black communities. Denied access by racial segregation to a variety of community resources, from burial societies and labor unions to simple human dignity and respect, black communities built their own networks of resources, and many of those grew from religious groups. Black religious communities have been among the few safe havens from racism for black people in the United States; at their best, they've been places where people look out for each other, offer critical resources for survival in a white supremacist society, and affirm that they are children of a loving God. For queer and transgender people, though, this affirmation has often been more complicated. One of racism's major forms, in the United States and elsewhere, is sexual oppression, expressed both through practices and through stereotyping. Under the United States's form of chattel slavery, the sexuality of enslaved people was nearly entirely co-opted by slave owners, who had complete sexual access as part of their property rights to enslaved black bodies. Many white people in the United States extended their idea of those sexual rights to all black and brown bodies, enslaved or not. Some still do. Enslaved people were denied the right to marry, and when they married anyway their marriages were considered negligible; enslaved families were often broken up on the owner's whim or even intentionally to try to keep the enslaved population more under control. These violent practices fed into, and were fed by, stereotypes of black people as sexually voracious. In women, that stereotype suggested that they were always sexually available; in men, it suggested that they were all sexual predators. False accusations of black men's sexual assaults against white women drove the lynch mobs of the nineteenth and twentieth centuries, while the combination of sexual stereotyping and racist restrictions on available work made many black women extremely vulnerable to sexual assault from the white men they worked for, particularly as domestic servants. Both of these stereotypes linger today, showing up in everything from celebrity scandals to ongoing violence against black bodies. The staggeringly high rates of assault and murder against black trans women show us what happens when **transmisogyny** (a combination of transphobia and sexism targeted at transgender women) is added to this volatile mix.

Black religious organizations have responded to these stereotypes by offering their congregations spaces where their own ideas of womanhood and manhood can be lived out; they have strived to create spaces free of the stereotypes and the violence that have characterized, and continue to characterize, the profoundly white supremacist culture around them. These have been powerful and important moves, but they've often carried with them the consequence that black sexuality has been silenced and any hint of nonnormative sexuality has been quashed. "The black church," writes womanist theologian Kelly Brown Douglas in a landmark article from 1994, "inherited a body-negating sexual ethic [from the form of Protestantism that most black churches are based in] and has employed it as the religious counterpart to the black community's social-cultural sexual narrative. It provides a sacred cover for the black community's standard of hyperproper sexuality, making violation of this hyperproper sexual standard not simply a social breach, but also a sin against God. Ironically, the black narratives of hyperproper sexual standards validate the same white cultural narrative they attempt to contest."[1] Because of this sexual standard, and because gender variance and same-sex desire have been associated for so long in the United States, both queer and trans people have traditionally been unwelcome in black religious organizations. As we'll see later in this chapter, black queer and trans people have pushed back powerfully against that exclusion, as have some of their straight and cisgender allies, resulting in growing inclusion in black religious spaces, but the question remains of how black trans and queer people can and should navigate the double exclusion of facing homophobia and transphobia in black, usually largely heterosexual and cisgender, religious communities and racism in queer, often largely white, religious communities.

Thelathia Nikki Young's 2016 book *Black Queer Ethics, Family, and Philosophical Imagination*, focuses on one queer approach to the creation of community: chosen families. This term, Young explains, "usually denote[s] a set of relationships that are purposefully, thoughtfully, and carefully selected. These families sometimes include but are not limited to biological relatives and friends. . . . Chosen families are often sites that allow for individuals to exercise freedom in developing behaviors, practices, and expectations that represent the dynamic nature of family that they experience."[2] In creating chosen families, Young argues, the black queer people she interviewed practice "creative resistance, . . . a mechanism by which marginalized people resist and eschew the internal and external disciplines and disciplinary powers that support and foster institutional assimilation." This allows "black queers to disrupt normative ideas of family and also resist the constraints of familial norms that limit their individual and collective moral agency as black queer people."[3] In these chosen communities, black queer people have the space and the opportunity to create new family values, a new, more inclusive, and more egalitarian vision of "the good life."[4] While the people Young interviewed created chosen families in which they could live out and collectively develop their own ethics, their own version of "the good life," many of them remained in contact with their families of origin as well, if nothing else through memories of the impact those families had on their lives, but typically through communication and visiting too. Those families, often supportive of them in some ways but less so in others, particularly around sexuality and gender, created a more traditional community for these black queer people—one that often included traditional religious communities.

Ashon Crawley's *Blackpentecostal Breath* approaches these communities from the other side, exploring the ways that the deeply socially conservative Black Pentecostal church tradition can be seen as queer and can provide more radical social possibilities than it seems on the surface to do. Crawley reminds us not to define religion solely on the basis of belief, even within the strongly creed-oriented Protestant Christian traditions. And after all, Pentecostal Christianity is defined very much on the basis of practice: the practice of connection with the Holy Spirit that first took place among the followers of Jesus two thousand years ago. Crawley turns especially to the aesthetics of this practice, the sensory aspect. Rather than what Black Pentecostal churches *say*, Crawley is interested in how they *feel*—and how they feel (and look, and sound, and smell, and taste), for him, is pretty queer. He challenges the idea that specific members or leaders of Black Pentecostal churches in some way "own" Black Pentecostalism, insisting that "Blackpentecostalism belongs to all who would so live into the fact of the flesh, live into this fact as a critique of the violence of modernity, the violence of the Middle Passage and enslavement, the violence of enslavement and its ongoing afterlife, live into the flesh as a critique of the ongoing attempt to interdict the capacity to breathe. The aesthetic practices [of Blackpentecostalism] cannot be owned but only collectively produced, cannot be property but must be given away in order to constitute community."[5] Black Pentecostal church members and organizations may violently reject queer and trans people, pushing the people out of the churches or the queerness and transness out of the people, Crawley says, but they can't stop trans and queer people from practicing. Through analytical reflection and experiential narrative, Crawley weaves together a profoundly queer Black Pentecostalism, not as a new development or a new community but as an aesthetic that was already there and perhaps has been there all along.

Chosen communities and traditional communities are two of the contexts in which transgender and queer people grow, develop, and live out their religious lives. Two others that we'll focus on in this chapter are queer- and transgender-specific religious communities and virtual communities. This chapter centers on people who define themselves at least partially within modern Western terms like *queer, transgender, gay, lesbian, bisexual,* and *same-gender-loving* or SGL, not because people who structure their gender and sexuality differently don't have communities but because there's such extensive scholarship on this topic among LGBTQ-identified people that even a brief overview of it will take up the full chapter. You can build your understanding of community among people who structure their sexuality and gender more through indigenous and Global South/Global East categories by returning to the examples in the previous chapters, many of which discuss community even though they don't focus on it.

CHOSEN COMMUNITIES

Religious practitioners have been creating chosen communities for millennia. Many of these are for full-time practitioners; some examples are convents, monasteries, and *beguinages* (communal houses in European Christian traditions for women who did not intend to take full religious vows and become nuns but who nevertheless wished to live together in chastity as laywomen and members of so-called tertiary orders). Some of these communities take larger forms, like Salt Lake City did when it was first built by members of the Church of Jesus Christ of Latter-day Saints, or Mormons, after they fled violent persecution farther east. Some are neither celibate nor gender segregated—like Salt Lake City, of course, but also like many other residential new religious movements and hippie communes. These also aren't exactly new, even though many people think of the 1960s and 1970s as the era of communes and religious experimentation. For example, the Oneida community, named for a region in New York state that, in turn, was named after the indigenous people whose ancestral lands it occupies, and now the namesake of a silverware company, was a Christian commune in the mid-nineteenth century that allowed its adult members to be sexually active with multiple (though always different-sex) partners provided they had the approval of the community leaders.[6] These religious communities, and other shared residential communities that aren't religious (other communes, for instance), are called **intentional communities**. From the perspective of queer and transgender studies, intentional communities look a lot like chosen families, so here we'll call all of them "chosen communities."

What does it do to think of queer and trans chosen families, and intentional religious communities like convents, as similar? Some readers will think immediately of the implied ties between **homosociality**, or socializing predominantly with people of the same sex, and homosexuality—implications so forceful that groups uncomfortable with same-sex eroticism often become surprisingly defensive about it. ("No homo, man," says the straight guy in an all-male space.) But same-gender loving takes many forms, and as Sister Bernice pointed out in chapter 3, some of them include celibacy in a convent. There's more to the story, that is to say, than sex. When we look at queer chosen families and religious chosen communities together, we can see that even chosen communities take shape within the bounds of social influence. We choose communities, often, on the basis of something shared like heritage, background, perspective on the world, practice, identity. Often, the people in our chosen communities understand what we've been through and how we approach life. Often we gain more than understanding from our chosen communities. They may offer us support, empathy, learning, comfort, peace, or growth, and we have things to offer in return. We also choose our communities for what they aren't and what they can protect us from. Historically, women have often chosen convents in a number of religions, such as Buddhism and Christianity, not only because they wanted to devote themselves full-time to their religion (though certainly this was true) but also because the convent wasn't marriage, and it could protect women from being forced into marriage—a social role that historically hasn't been particularly good for women's health or their intellectual and spiritual development. The black queer people Young interviewed chose their communities, their chosen families, not only for the positive and nurturing qualities of the people they

surrounded themselves with, but because they weren't a homophobic religious family or a racist queer community.

By considering queer chosen families and religious intentional communities together we also see that community comes in many forms, and not just
because queer chosen families take one form and religious intentional communities take another. Chosen communities may or may not be residential,
for instance, even if people spend a lot of time together. The Sisters of
Perpetual Indulgence call their chapters *houses* because they model themselves on Roman Catholic nuns, and a Sister house is definitely a chosen
community, but there's no physical space in which the members of a house
all live together. Some members may live together as partners or roommates,
and sometimes a house will designate a particular space where they often
meet or put on their habits as "the priory" or "the convent," but the order
itself isn't residential. The Radical Faeries, on the other hand, which have
historical connections to the Sisters and continue to maintain strong ties with
the order in many areas, are sometimes residential and sometimes not. While
many Faeries live on their own, or perhaps with other Faeries as partners or
roommates, there are also rural Faerie Gathering spaces called *sanctuaries*
where some Faeries live for extended periods of time. Radical Faerie houses
in urban areas are somewhere in between these two categories, since they're
intentionally formed as Faerie spaces, not just through a few Faeries who
know each other deciding to live together, but they're also not the intensive
retreat spaces that the rural sanctuaries are. And chosen community, even the
residential kind, can also be temporal, or time based. Again the Radical
Faeries provide a good example in terms of queer and trans chosen community: Faerie Gatherings are spaces and periods of time in which people come
from far and wide to live together in a chosen community for several days.
There are lots of other examples of short-term chosen communities, whether
religious or not; the Burning Man festivals are a good example, as are multi-
day music festivals, film festivals, destination sporting events like the FIFA
World Cup or the Olympics, and the like.

Chosen families are a form of chosen community that tends to be longer-
term. Transgender and queer folks refer to their chosen families as *families*,
and not more generically as *communities*, because in many cases they fill the
roles that families of origin are expected to fill in most people's lives: They
teach, support, nurture, and love. They're there no matter what, through the
ups and the downs of one's life, and they're there to stay. Though in some
parts of the world and in some subcultures families of origin are becoming
more accepting of their transgender and queer members, it was not all that
long ago that one could generally expect reactions ranging from stony silence
to physical violence when one revealed one's sexuality or gender to one's
family of origin. Still today, youth are kicked out of their caregivers' homes
when they come out and family members force their supposedly loved ones

into religious forms of "treatment" in an attempt to undo their gender or their sexuality. With this range of possible reactions, trans and queer folks are often denied some of the basic, positive functions of families: education about relationships, for instance, or material support as a young adult setting out into the workplace or heading off to university. Understandably, then, they find others who can fill these roles, emotionally if not financially. People often refer to their chosen family members with familial titles (like "my lesbian moms," who might be the lesbians a few decades older who helped a newly out woman learn about queer cultures), and *family* is still one of the code words for *queer* in some communities (as in, "Do you think he's family?"). Familial roles are especially important in the drag ball houses within queer and trans communities of color in the US, where mothers and fathers teach, nurture, and protect their daughters and sons. But here we come right back around to the connections between queer chosen families and intentional religious communities, because familial terms are also often used in full-time residential religious communities. Many Christian **renunciants** (monks and nuns), for example, use the titles "Sister" and "Brother." The Shakers, a communal Christian movement of the eighteenth through the twentieth centuries, called their founder "Mother" and each other "Sisters" and "Brothers." Even some nonresidential religious groups—a kind of chosen community, for many people—use these familial terms.

An especially interesting connection between queer chosen families and intentional religious communities is evident in ex-gay communities, especially residential ones. Ex-gays are usually Christian and more specifically conservative Protestant; they experience same-sex attraction but believe that God forbids them from acting on it. As we saw in chapter 3, unlike Roman Catholics with these beliefs, for whom celibacy is a viable and long-valued role in their church communities, for Protestants the only valued relational role an adult can have is that of heterosexual marriage—what Lynne Gerber calls "queerish celibacy." In order to reach that goal, same-sex-attracted people first have to prepare themselves as best as possible. For those who have only recently found the support of the ex-gay movement, preparation begins with an attempt, typically communal although it may or may not be residential, to reduce or eliminate one's same-sex desire.

As Gerber tells us, the various organizations and leaders in the ex-gay movement are divided on the question of whether same-sex-attracted people can be "reoriented"—that is, made into people who experience different-sex attraction. Attempts at such reorientation, called "conversion therapy" in popular discourse, have been determined by the American Psychiatric Association and the American Psychological Association to be not only ineffective but psychologically harmful. Some conservative Christians, however, are suspicious of this secular research and argue that God will create the changes that God wants to see in people, as long as they're dedicated and patient. Others are concerned by the scientific findings; they're more con-vinced that sexual desire can't be changed. But as we've discussed, essential-ist approaches to identity don't automatically equate to accepting ap-proaches. Conservative Christians who find it plausible that sexual desire can't be changed continue to assert nonetheless that same-sex sexual activity is not permissible in their understanding of Christianity. Following a track that's been taken for several decades, they liken same-sex desire to addiction.

As with addiction, this argument goes, one may inherit genetic tendencies toward same-sex desire. As with addiction, those genetic tendencies are not sufficient reason for people to indulge their desires, because to do so would be harmful. In fact, whether you believe that addiction is an inherited tenden-cy or a learned behavior, if you're concerned about addiction you may have several ideas about how to avoid, manage, or cure it. Today, no matter where you are in the world, some of these ideas come from the twelve-step move-ment that began with Alcoholics Anonymous. This movement, which now includes programs for a variety of addictions (but not for same-sex desire; in fact, there are twelve-step groups specifically for queer and transgender peo-ple dealing with addiction) as well as programs for people who are impacted by the addictions of those close to them, has its roots in the same thread of Protestantism as the ex-gay movement. Although the twelve-step movement as a whole works hard to present itself as open to all religions and to none at all—one only needs to be able to work with the idea of some sort of higher power—its underlying concepts of humanity, illness, and ultimate reality are rooted in an evangelical Protestant worldview. Given these roots and the cultural prevalence of the twelve-step movement, it's no wonder that the ex-gay movement so closely resembles it in some ways.

When attempting to recover from an addiction, the twelve-step movement recommends, one needs a mentor who's been through the process and who can also help to keep one accountable. In the movement, these are called sponsors. One should try to avoid social contact with people who engage in the behavior one is addicted to, for instance by avoiding bars or not going to all-you-can-eat buffets. And one should have a community of others who are struggling with similar challenges, all trying to live in what they consider to be healthier ways. This is precisely what ex-gay communities offer to their members. As Tanya Erzen writes about one residential ex-gay community, "The program members believe that [their] friendships [with each other] and the process of living together communally will fulfill the unmet needs of early childhood [which the ex-gay movement generally believes cause same-sex desire] and heal their homosexuality. . . . Elements of the program such as Straight Man Nights, the phase structure, the rigorous schedule, and the classes are designed to reinforce an insular ex-gay world, while group activ-ities like sports and camping become collective rituals designed to teach men and women how to be properly masculine and feminine."[7] Insular ex-gay communities such as this one, whether residential or not, are chosen communities, a combination of queer chosen families and intentional religious communities. Given Gerber's argument that even once married to someone of a different sex, ex-gays still practice a queerish celibacy, we might consider the possibility that residential ex-gay programs are themselves a queerish sort of monastery or convent. Here again, as both Erzen and Gerber show us, bringing the insights of queer theory together with those of religious studies produces a strikingly queer perception of religion and a strikingly religious understanding of queerness.

It's impossible in many transgender and queer spaces, though, to talk about chosen communities and even about religion without talking about bar culture. For decades—and in a few cases, centuries—bars, taverns, bathhouses or saunas, and parks were among the only places where gender-variant and same-sex-attracted people could gather together in larger numbers. Wealthier people could, at times, hold and attend private parties that served this purpose too, but for many people such luxuries were out of reach. And since secrecy and silence were especially important in parks, where one might be arrested or beaten (or both) at any moment for seeking out lovers and having sex in public, it was the bars and bathhouses that provided spaces for a more vocal, audible communal gathering. As some of the only places where people could be themselves, be with others like them, and celebrate together, these spaces often took on a joyfully sacred atmosphere.

In fact, they still do. In chapter 3 we considered Paul Gorrell's argument that circuit parties are a form of religion; many other writers have considered the sacredness of cruising grounds, bathhouses, and bars.[8] Such commentaries became particularly important, vocal, and poignant in the aftermath of the mass shooting at the Pulse nightclub in Orlando, Florida, on June 12, 2016. It was Latin Night at this gay bar, "a refuge within a refuge," as religious studies scholar Elizabeth Pérez puts it, for black and Latinx queer and trans folks seeking a place to gather where they might be relatively free from homophobia, transphobia, *and* racism.[9] Latin Night at the Pulse was sacred space, like circuit parties and cruising grounds and so many, many queer and trans dance clubs. Theologian Vincent Cervantes wrote the day after the shooting that

> Latin@ queer spaces were always spaces of healing—migratory spaces we journeyed to, to be in solidarity with one another in our shared pain and suffering, but also in our shared joy and triumph. We anointed one another with affirmation and laughter. We created fellowship and communion—because too many of us had traversed dangerous landscapes just to get there in the first place. The Spirit lived and carried through each and every one of us. We emerged from the shadows we worshipped in to survive and to be storytellers about our journeys. These are our sacred spaces.[10]

As Pérez and Cervantes point out, media coverage of the Pulse shooting discussed religion only in the context of the person wielding the gun—a man who claimed allegiance to the terrorist group ISIS and was therefore automatically deemed a "Muslim terrorist" despite the fact that he wasn't particularly familiar with Islam. In neglecting the religious aspects of the Pulse itself, and especially of Latin Night at the Pulse, the news coverage told a one-sided story about religion as violent and intolerant, and erased a deeply meaningful, diverse, inclusive religious community. It erased the religiousness—in whatever forms it took—of the people who died and of those who went on to live with the grief, trauma, and guilt that come all too often with survival. The Pulse story returns us again to questions we've been considering throughout this book: Who and what are religious? Who gets to say? What are the consequences of someone else defining you into or out of religion, spirituality, traditions, and lifeways? In the next section we turn to traditional religions to continue asking questions in the context of established, straight- and cisgender-dominant religious communities.

TRADITIONAL COMMUNITIES

Sometime around 2005, a prominent gay journalist came to speak at the school where I was teaching at the time. A colleague of mine in the gender studies program was showing him around campus when our paths crossed. The journalist was cheerful, happy to meet another queer studies scholar at the school, until my colleague explained that I studied religion in queer communities and that I had recently published a book on queer Christians. The journalist's affable smile faded to a scowl. "What?" he cried disbelievingly. "You mean to tell me there are *gay Southern Baptists*?!" "Yes, of course there are," I responded, a little startled by the sudden change. "What are they doing?" he scoffed. "Getting their *heads cut off*?"

There's a lot to unpack in this story. For one thing, the journalist seems to have immediately focused on gay men, despite the fact that my work had been represented to him as being about queer people more broadly; at the time, *gay* hadn't yet returned to its older use as a (or at least an ostensibly) gender-neutral term, so his use of it probably meant men specifically, and probably cisgender men at that. He also jumped from *Christian* directly to Southern Baptist, despite the vast diversity of Christian and even specifically Protestant groups (the subset of Christianity that Southern Baptists are part of) and the wide range of their opinions on queer people. And he assumed that all Southern Baptists are hostile to gay men—which also means assuming that none of them are gay themselves. None of these assumptions is accurate.

There are, in fact, gay Southern Baptists—and queer Southern Baptists, and transgender Southern Baptists, and lesbian Southern Baptists, and bisexual Southern Baptists, and nonbinary Southern Baptists, and so on. And while it's true that many Southern Baptist churches are unwelcoming to queer and transgender people, decapitation isn't usually in the contemporary Southern Baptist repertoire of responses to people they're unfriendly to. Moreover, Southern Baptist polity is *congregational*, meaning that technically each congregation decides for itself the correct way to do things. In practice, as you might imagine, there are limits to that polity; churches have been expelled from the Southern Baptist Convention, the official organization for Southern Baptist congregations, for such actions as ordaining an openly gay minister and marrying a same-sex couple.[11] So yes, there are gay Southern Baptists. Was the minister still a Southern Baptist after his congregation was kicked out of the Southern Baptist Convention? What about the married couple? Here's that question again: Who gets to say? If you were raised Southern Baptist, you have the same practices and beliefs as other Southern Baptists, and you consider yourself a Southern Baptist, does condemnation from the official organization make you not a Southern Baptist? These are the profound questions raised by our considerations of identity in chapter 4, but they return to us in full force when we consider communities.

Contrary to the assumptions of the gay journalist that day, gender-variant and same-sex-attracted people are present in nearly every religious community. Sometimes they're trying to suppress their sexual desires or their gender identity because they believe these violate the precepts of their religion, as we saw above with the ex-gay movement. Sometimes they're not suppressing anything but they're not open with their religious community about their sexual or gender identities, as we've seen is the case for some Two-Spirit people whose tribal communities are homophobic and transphobic. Sometimes their religious space is what people call a "glass closet," where everyone knows they're queer or trans but no one talks about it and other people still feel free to express homophobia and transphobia. Others openly live out traditional, indigenous sexual and/or gender identities in combination with their religious practices, like some Two-Spirit people, *bissu*, *hijras*, *māhū*, and *'yan daudu*. And in time periods and regions where same-sex-attracted people identify with terms like *queer*, *lesbian*, *bisexual*, and *gay*, and gender-variant people identify with terms like *nonbinary*, *transgender*, and *genderqueer*, people who use those terms for themselves live openly in and draw sustenance from many different kinds of religious communities. Some of those communities are designed by and for queer and transgender people, like Mayyim Hayyim, the egalitarian *mikveh* we discussed in chapter 3. We'll talk about those more in the next section. But many trans and queer people also take part in traditional religious communities that are inclusive of people of many different gender and sexual identities.

Ashon Crawley writes lyrically of the queer power of Black Pentecostal practices—sometimes so queer as to cause two men who were attracted to each other to let down their guard. "Would you be surprised to know," he writes in a diary-style interlude in *Blackpentecostal Breath,* "that my first time really, really touching Derrick was in a high-ceiling church?" He continues, "It was in August after we sang [in the choir] that I first noticed the grace of his body when he was shouting." Shouting is an ecstatic religious practice with deep roots not only in African American Christian traditions but, Crawley argues, in some Islamic mystical practices as well that may trace through the Muslims who were among those captured and enslaved during the transatlantic slave trade. Moved by the sight of Derrick and by the power of the music, Crawley writes, "I ran up next to Derrick and it was the spirit moving me, I promise, I had no idea what was occurring—and grabbed his left hand and we shouted together. . . . he knew it was me, though his eyes were shut tightly." As the service began to wind down, the two found themselves alone in a bathroom, kissing and holding their partially naked bodies together.[12] This was a socially conservative church, of course; if they'd been found there would literally have been hell to pay. And as Crawley tells it, Derrick never made contact after that day. But the aesthetic and religious power of the community that day made it a queer space, a space that opened up the possibility of black queer lives, even if just for a moment.

Unlike the church in Crawley's story, many traditional religious communities have come over time to welcome queer and, later, transgender people. The Unitarian Universalist Association, for example, a religious organization that welcomes people of many religious backgrounds and perspectives, passed a resolution in 1970 to end discrimination against homosexuals and bisexuals, in which it also encouraged its own congregations to work toward greater inclusion; the first openly gay Unitarian Universalist minister was ordained in 1979.[13] The United Church of Christ was the first Christian denomination to become inclusive, passing a resolution in favor of gay rights in 1969 and ordaining the first openly gay minister in 1972.[14] Also in 1972 the Union of American Hebrew Congregations (now the Union for Reform Judaism) became the first mainstream Jewish organization to recognize a gay and lesbian synagogue; in 1977 the Central Conference of American Rabbis, also a Reform organization, passed a resolution supporting gay rights. It would be Reconstructionist Judaism, though, that would move first to ordain gays and lesbians, in 1984, while Reform Judaism opened its ranks to gay and lesbian rabbis in 1990 and Conservative Judaism not until 2006.

The Episcopal Church, well ahead of the broader Anglican Communion, declared the full equality of "homosexual persons" in 1976; however, while the church consecrated its first openly gay bishop in 2003, it was 2012 before discrimination against transgender candidates for ordination was officially banned.[15] This is part of a long-standing pattern: Gay men often gain access to religious spaces first, followed by lesbians if and when women in general have such access; inclusion of bisexuals is often slower because of biased assumptions about bisexuality and promiscuity in religious groups that value monogamy; and transgender rights have been far slower in coming, though they're now becoming established in the more socially liberal religious groups. In 2006, for example, Elliot Kukla became the first transgender rabbi to be ordained in the Reform Jewish tradition.

QUEER AND TRANSGENDER COMMUNITIES

Same-sex-attracted and gender-variant people have had their own religious communities for millennia. In the Mediterranean and South Asia, for example, some goddesses have long been served by male-born people who live as women. *Bissu* and *hijras* are other examples, although given the prevalence of people assigned male at birth among *bissu* and the fact that *hijra* communities are solely for male-born people, it's worth noticing and wondering about the fact that many of these dedicated gender-variant communities are composed largely or entirely of people assigned male at birth. Why are there so few comparable communities of female-born gender-variant people?

If we turn to communities of self-identified transgender and queer people—including among those people who used older terms like *homosexual, bulldagger, fairy, transsexual,* and *invert* as well as the more familiar *lesbian, bisexual, gay, transgender,* and so on—when would you guess the first religious groups specifically for people with these identities were founded? You might be surprised by the answer.

The first known religious service specifically for self-identified homosexuals was held on July 1, 1946, in Atlanta, Georgia.[16] The group that formally began that day was founded by a former Roman Catholic seminary student and a Greek Orthodox priest who'd been kicked out of his church on charges of homosexuality. They named it the Eucharist Catholic Church, after the event that led to its founding: A Roman Catholic priest had refused to serve communion, also called the Eucharist, to a group of gay and lesbian Catholics. The timing of this church's founding is intriguing, since it came in the same year as the first appearance of the word *homosexual* in an English translation of the Bible. While it's probably not the case that the Catholic priest read the new translation and thought, "Oh! I need to deny communion to all those homosexuals now," at the same time both developments are part of the larger cultural shift that historian Heather White discusses, in which what had been simply one of a variety of sinful activities in earlier Christian communities and had become in nineteenth-century Western cultures a type of person and, by the end of that century, a possibly incurable illness, began to leach back into Christian culture as a particularly, perhaps even irredeemably, sinful type of person.

Over the course of about a hundred years, the definitions of same-sex desire and gender variance shifted from actions to types of people to illnesses to sinful proclivities. The shift from sickness to sin—all within the inversion model that defined same-sex desire and gender variance as symptoms of a much larger, fundamental form of human difference—would continue to pick up steam from the 1940s onward, culminating in the ex-gay movement's intertwining of the two approaches in its conceptualization of same-sex desire as a proclivity toward sin caused by an illness of gender identity resulting from childhood trauma. In the midst of these shifts, a Roman Catholic priest in Atlanta decided that homosexuals could not receive communion decades before the church leadership in Rome decided to weigh in on the issue. In response, a group of Christians who'd been rejected by Christian churches, a group whose members were "homosexual, heterosexual, black, white, Catholic, and Protestant," as White explains, decided to form a church that was more inclusive of all Christians.[17] In fact, its inclusion of openly lesbian and gay people may have been the least shocking aspect of the Eucharist Catholic Church, since at the time anti-Catholicism was still a significant force among Protestants in the United States, and Atlanta, like most US cities, was still deeply racially segregated.

Although the Eucharist Catholic Church lasted for only a few years, there were a handful of other support groups and ministries for gays and lesbians in the mid-twentieth-century United States, often run or at least advertised by the gay rights organizations of the time, which were known collectively as the **homophile movement** in an attempt to shift the focus of heterosexuals away from same-sex sexual activity toward same-sex love (*philos* means "love" in Greek). But the spark that really lit the fire of queer and transgender religious organizing was the creation of the Metropolitan Community Church in Los Angeles in 1968. The Reverend Troy Perry, its founder, had been ordained in the Pentecostal denomination known as the Church of God in Prophecy. When he realized that he was gay and informed his superiors, he was removed from the pulpit and his ordination was revoked. Several years later, he came to the realization that God wanted him to found a church for gay people. The first church service took place in Perry's living room with a congregation of twelve, but soon the church outgrew the living room and then several more spaces before the members bought their own building. People who visited Los Angeles and attended MCC, and members of the congregation who moved elsewhere, wanted to have the same opportunities in other cities, and MCC consequently began to grow. Today it's an international denomination, with a somewhat eclectic and unique approach to church services based on the many different branches of Christianity represented in the church since its founding, and still with a commitment to serve queer and transgender Christians.

Other movements followed hard on MCC's heels. In 1969 Father Patrick X. Nidorf, a Roman Catholic priest and psychologist working in San Diego, California, started a support group for lesbian and gay Catholics that he named after the quality he felt was missing from the lives of many of those he counseled: Dignity. Soon people were driving the two or more hours from Los Angeles to attend the group, and Father Nidorf—or Father Pat, as he was known—opened up an LA chapter. In the excitement following the modernization of the Roman Catholic Church at the recent Second Vatican Council, also known as Vatican II, some members of Dignity hoped that official acceptance of gay and lesbian Catholics was just around the corner. And since the year of Dignity's founding had also seen a sea change in gay and lesbian activist strategies with the founding of the radical Gay Liberation Front (GLF) in the midst of the Stonewall riots, some thought they should demand that acceptance openly. Their attempt failed, and the Los Angeles archbishop barred Father Pat from further work with the group. Later Vatican policies targeted Dignity directly. But fierce official opposition may have also benefited the group, as it became more openly supportive of progressive causes in the church, working not only for the full inclusion of lesbian, gay, bisexual, transgender, queer, and intersex Catholics but also for women's ordination. [18]

In 1972 the first group for gay and lesbian Jews was formed, also in Los Angeles. Meeting at MCC, the members modeled their new group on the church and initially called themselves Metropolitan Community Temple. Within several months, early in 1973, they adopted a Hebrew name for the congregation: Beth Chayim Chadashim (BCC), or the House of New Life. With support from MCC and Troy Perry, from their own members, and also from key leaders in the Reform movement of Judaism, BCC grew and thrived. Within five years the congregation had already raised enough money to buy a building of their own, and within another five years, in 1983, they hired their first rabbi. [19]

Have you noticed a pattern in these stories? All three of these early gay and lesbian (those were the words used at the time) religious groups were started in Southern California, and all three found their greatest foothold in Los Angeles. They weren't the only such groups to begin there, either—the Mormon group Affirmation took root in LA in 1978, although its initial founding was in Salt Lake City several months earlier, and both the Radical Faeries and a separatist feminist, largely lesbian, neo-pagan movement known as Dianic Wicca also had their roots there. The founder of Dianic Wicca, Zsuzsanna Budapest, lived in the greater Los Angeles area and her first coven, the Susan B. Anthony Coven #1, took shape there in 1971, while the Radical Faeries were founded in 1979 by LA residents even though their initial Gatherings were in Arizona.

But religious organizing was also happening far beyond Los Angeles. A group of gay and lesbian Jews began meeting in London in 1972, for instance, and on February 9, 1973, the group that became Congregation Beth Simchat Torah held its first Shabbat service in the gay-friendly Church of the Holy Apostles in New York City. MCC opened its doors in San Francisco in 1970, then in Chicago, San Diego, and Honolulu that same year; by 1973 it was moving outside the United States with the founding of MCC Toronto. The first meeting of the Gay Christian Movement, which eventually became OneBodyOneFaith, took place in London in 1976. Congregation Sha'ar Zahav in San Francisco began in 1977, and after international conferences for gay and lesbian Jews began in 1976, the World Congress of Gay and Lesbian Jewish Organizations (now Keshet Ga'avah) was formed in 1980.

Although queer- and transgender-specific religious organizing has been most common in Christianity, Judaism, to a certain extent neo-paganism, and more recently Islam, there are also networks of queer and transgender Buddhists, especially but not solely in the Global North/Global West. One of the oldest such groups is San Francisco's Gay Buddhist Fellowship, founded under the name of Maitri in 1980 by lay practitioners and supported until his death by beloved gay monk and former drag performer Issan Dorsey. Maitri also organized a hospice, initially designed specifically to serve people dying of AIDS, who were being turned away from both hospices and hospitals as well as by their families of origin during the worst years of the epidemic. Although queer and transgender Hindus, Sikhs, and Jains typically organize more around ethnic and racial identity than around religious identity, within some Hindu-based new religious movements there is occasionally gay and lesbian organizing. One example of such organizing is GALVA-108, the Gay and Lesbian Vaishnava Association, whose members hail mainly from the socially conservative, Hindu-based new religious movement known as the International Society for Krishna Consciousness (ISKCON), and popularly known as the Hare Krishnas.[20]

By the early 1970s, lesbian and gay groups had also begun to take shape within traditional religious organizations. The first three, all formed in 1974, included Integrity, a group for gay and lesbian Episcopalians; Lutherans Concerned; and More Light Presbyterians. Evangelicals Concerned, a support group for gay and lesbian evangelical Christians, formed in 1975, followed by Kinship International for Seventh-day Adventists, the United Methodist group called Affirmation, and the Brethren-Mennonite Council for Lesbian and Gay Concerns. Although some of these groups, like Integrity, More Light Presbyterians, Lutherans Concerned, and the Unitarian Universalist group Interweave, are now officially recognized and often even supported by their denominations, the organizations that support queer and transgender people from more conservative religious backgrounds usually are not. In fact, some conservative Christian denominations have started their own support groups that are ex-gay movements but have similarly welcoming names; for instance, while Affirmation welcomes and supports openly queer and transgender Mormons and is not recognized by the LDS Church, Evergreen supports those Mormons seeking to change their sexual desires and their gender expression toward cisgender heterosexuality and is very much supported by the church. In Roman Catholicism, while Dignity remains not only unrecognized but actively combatted by the church, Courage offers ex-gay-style support from within the church's embrace. New Ways Ministry, founded by Sister Jeannine Gramick and Father Robert Nugent, walks a line between the two; it's recognized by the church but regarded with suspicion for its stress on the role of individual discernment over church doctrine in determining properly moral action.[21]

As religious congregations and support groups were springing up for queer and transgender people who were being excluded from their traditional congregations, the new groups also faced challenges of inclusion. Many, for instance, were called to task early on by women who expected inclusion not only around sexuality but also around gender. They demanded what was understood as gender-inclusive language at the time—using "she and he" instead of "he," for instance, and "women and men" instead of "men"—in everything from bylaws to sacred texts, and they also challenged these groups to include women equally in leadership. As the transgender rights movement gained momentum in the 1990s, and as bisexuals also began to demand a seat at the table, these groups too pushed what had begun as gay religious groups to live up to their early principles of inclusion.

Also at issue was race. Queer and transgender congregations often formed in the best-known "gayborhood" of a city, but although these neighborhoods were run-down and marginal while gender variance and same-sex eroticism were still illegal, as police persecution began to ease for some members of these communities the gay neighborhoods quickly gentrified. They became economically inaccessible as residential neighborhoods to those without significant resources, but they also became increasingly white and male—not that they'd ever been enormously diverse in terms of either race or sex. The religious congregations formed in these neighborhoods were easiest for white, often cisgender, gay men to access, so they were both attended and led often by those same white, cisgender, gay men. In turn, their cultures formed around this group in particular, and quickly came to feel exclusionary and off-putting to women, transgender people, and people of color.

People who felt marginalized or excluded by these religious communities tended to respond in one of three ways. As we've seen, some stayed in the congregations and worked for greater inclusion by speaking up, demanding better representation, and when possible even becoming ordained themselves so that they could lead more inclusive congregations and religious services. Some simply left the religion entirely, pursuing other forms of spiritual and religious practice where they found greater equality. Some queer and trans Christians of color preferred homophobia or the "glass closet" in their religions of origin to the subtle and blatant forms of racism and exclusion they encountered in white-dominant queer churches. And some started their own welcoming congregations. Among the first to do so was Reverend Dr. James Tinney, a Howard University journalism professor who founded Faith Temple in Washington, DC, in 1982. A member of the prominent Black Pentecostal denomination the Church of God in Christ, Tinney had been publicly outed by his minister in the 1970s when the minister tried to pray what he thought were the demons of homosexuality out of Tinney. Tinney's sexual desires didn't change, and he quickly concluded that there were no demons. He was simply gay, and God had made him that way and loved him just as he was. Having been ordained at the age of eighteen and wanting other gay men and lesbians to have a place to hear the same message, Tinney founded a congregation where that could happen. [22]

In the same year on the opposite coast, famed gospel singer Carl Bean—known especially for his 1977 recording of "I Was Born This Way"—made the same move as Tinney. From his garage in the historically black Crenshaw District of Los Angeles, Bean began holding the services that would grow into the Unity Fellowship Church and, as new congregations of the church started around the United States, the Unity Fellowship Church Movement. [23] Open to people of all sexualities, genders, and races, the Unity Fellowship Church Movement has a predominantly black following and holds services that are in many ways indistinguishable from other traditional black church services, save for the clear and insistent message that "God is love and love is for everyone"—including queer and transgender people. In 1985, responding to the fact that HIV/AIDS services were also concentrated in largely white gay neighborhoods that were especially inaccessible in LA's car culture, with its extremely limited public transit, to those with the visual impairment and mobility restrictions that are part of the complications of AIDS, Bean founded the Minority AIDS Project (MAP), as a paired project with the church to provide supportive and welcoming HIV and AIDS services to those living in and around the Crenshaw District.

In addition to Unity, another, now more widespread movement of inclusive black churches also began in California—but at the other end of the state. In 1991 Reverend (now Bishop) Yvette Flunder started City of Refuge Church in San Francisco, feeling that the inclusive black church she attended wasn't as fully inclusive of queer and transgender people as she wanted it to be. City of Refuge eventually moved to the historically black community of Oakland, across the bay from San Francisco, and in time it affiliated with the United Church of Christ, but as it began to grow and to gather interest from individuals and congregations in other regions Bishop Flunder developed the Fellowship—a loosely structured network of welcoming black churches. In 2011, in an effort to broaden the "radical inclusivity" that Bishop Flunder believes is at the heart of Christian teachings, the Fellowship became the Fellowship of Affirming Ministries (TFAM), building bridges with a variety of congregations, denominations, and other groups that share Bishop Flunder's vision.[24]

A more recent development in the founding of queer and transgender religious organizations is the creation of inclusive mosques, including the People's Mosque in Cape Town, South Africa, which was founded by Imam Muhsin Hendricks; the Toronto Unity Mosque organized in 2009 by Imam El-Farouk Khaki, Laury Silvers, and Troy Jackson;[25] Masjid Nur Al-Isslaah, organized in Washington, DC, by Imam Daayiee Abdullah in 2011; the Paris mosque organized in 2012 by Ludovic-Mohamed Zahed; and Masjid Ibn Rushd-Goethe in Berlin, which formed a few years later.[26] The Toronto Unity Mosque has organized a network of inclusive mosques called the El-Tawhid Juma Circle, which as of a 2015 blog post had six member congregations in Toronto, Montreal, Halifax, Calgary, Vancouver, and Boston.[27] Likewise, Masjid Ibn Rushd-Goethe was supported in its organization by Ludovic-Mohamed Zahed, who together with the Berlin mosque's founder, Seyran Ates, is working to create a network of inclusive mosques in Europe. Like many other queer and transgender religious organizations, these inclusive mosques not only welcome queer and transgender people, they also practice inclusive forms of worship by integrating genders during services and having women as well as men lead prayers.

The overall picture of queer and transgender religious communities continues to shift. When Troy Perry first founded MCC his goal was to work himself out of business, for the church to be so successful in its struggle for gay inclusion in Christianity that it was no longer needed. Clearly that goal hasn't yet been reached in many religions, and certainly not in Christianity. Some people continue to seek out transgender and queer religious communities because their home communities are unwelcoming or insufficiently inclusive. Some are involved with both. Some whose home communities have moved even partially toward inclusion remain in or return to those communities because the other options just don't "feel right." Often this is less about who's attending and more about the blending of traditions that queer and transgender religious communities have to practice in order to serve everyone. At Beth Chayim Chadashim, for example, the services follow a Reform Jewish model, but people who attend the synagogue come from a much wider range of backgrounds. People who were raised in Orthodox Judaism are often taken aback by the informal style at BCC, and some miss the ritual forms of prayer in Orthodox synagogues.

Sometimes even a single word can matter; Christians typically say a very important prayer, the Lord's Prayer, during their services, but in English there are two slightly different versions of the prayer. Sometimes changing the word *debts* to *trespasses* in this prayer, or vice versa, is enough to make things feel a little bit off. All of these discrepancies, from slight to glaring, can impact people's choices about where to attend, as can location; the availability of transportation; inclusion along the lines of gender, gender identity, race, class, non-homonormative sexualities; and so on. Despite the growth in inclusion, then, especially in Christianity and Judaism, queer and transgender congregations aren't going anywhere. They continue to change, as Bishop Flunder's Fellowship broadened out to include a network of groups with "radically inclusive" vision, but they aren't likely to fade from the scene any time soon.

VIRTUAL COMMUNITIES

What do people do who want a queer and/or transgender religious community but can't access one? Despite the existence of traditional gender-variant and same-sex-attracted religious communities, the importance of families of choice, and the growth of both welcoming congregations and queer and transgender religious communities, even in fairly small towns and rural areas, for many people the right community still isn't available. What then? Increasingly, people are turning to virtual communities.

Religious communities have always been virtual in some ways. Buddhist nuns and monks who could trace their lineage back to the earliest followers of the Buddha could see themselves as part of a larger **sangha**, or community of Buddhists; through studying shared sacred texts and writing letters they could even take part in that sangha across vast distances. Muslims hearing the call to prayer have for centuries taken part in a virtual community, knowing that thousands if not hundreds of thousands of people in their city alone, and many more farther afield, were all laying out their prayer rugs and facing Mecca together to pray. The ability to take part in a virtual religious community expanded with the invention of radio technology, and religious groups took advantage of that technology quickly, with Christian leaders broadcasting religious services quite early in the twentieth century. In fact, radio played an important role in the rise of twentieth-century revivalist preachers like Billy Graham, but television did even more. Even Zsuzsanna Budapest, the founder of Dianic Wicca, had her own TV channel for a period of time.

Radio and television, though, are pretty much one-way communities. You can write in to a religious leader who has a TV show and communicate with that one person in that way, but you have to hope that your letter is one of the ones selected or trust that it's in the stack of letters that's being prayed over on TV. You might sing or pray along with the religious leader on the radio or the TV, but that leader can't see or hear you. Radio and TV audiences participate in real time, but unless it's a call-in show the people in the sound booth and on the TV set aren't really part of a real-time community in the same way. The internet, though, changed all that. Even in the early days of the internet, in the late 1980s and the early 1990s, an early form of chat rooms called bulletin boards allowed people to converse—though slowly—in a public forum. As internet speeds and data capacities increased, and as online gaming started to come into being, other forms of online interaction took shape. Neo-pagans' world concept is well suited to virtual religious community, and neo-pagans also are often more isolated from their coreligionists than people who practice larger or more socially dominant religions, so they in particular began to experiment fairly early on with virtual religious practice. In a virtual circle, a group of people in different places set up their own altars, then work together to create sacred space and perform the ritual. Over time, not only did many different religious traditions develop online forums for real-time religious practice and other forms of religious community, but the internet also became a major resource for queer and transgender religious people. For some, virtual community simply means having other people like you to talk with, even if they live thousands of miles away. It means finding resources to help you understand your gender and sexuality from your own religious perspective, when your queer and transgender friends may not share your religion and your religious friends may not know you're queer or trans. But as the technology developed, it also meant being able to take on an online persona and walk (virtually) into a religious community to join in a worship service.

One space where this sort of virtual religious practice has taken place, especially in the mid-2000s, is Second Life. This space is in many ways exactly what its name says: a place where you can live a second, but not necessarily double, life. Second Life is an online world; though it's technically a massively multiplayer online role-playing game (MMORPG), it's not quite the same as many other such games because it's often more mundane. There's no goal in Second Life, no points (though you can earn money, and spend it again). Basically, it's life, just lived online. In Second Life you choose your avatar's name, what they look like (including what species they are), where they live, how they dress, and what they do. There are social expectations from other players, just as there are in real life, and of course they may not always be pleasant, but in Second Life more than in real life you can choose where you go and whom you hang out with. Second Life provides a haven for some transgender and queer people to whom real life doesn't have much to offer—and also for those to whom it does.

In 2008 Kate O'Riordan and Heather White set out to study the spiritual practices and experiences of queer and transgender Second Life participants.

They found that the people they interviewed generally felt less judgment from those they interacted with in Second Life than they felt in real life (or, as some participants called it, Real Life or RL). Rivka, for example, is a Jewish intersex person who uses the gender-neutral pronouns *ze* and *hir* (pronounced "zee" and "hear") and who is interested in Taoism. Rivka told White that ze likes the Torah study ze attends in Second Life because it brings together into one space experts from different branches of Judaism who might not spend time in the same RL space, and people were excited to be there because they really had to put in effort to go, so they were there because they wanted to learn Torah. "Nobody's there," Rivka explained to White in an interview, "just to look good in the eyes of their neighbors or parents . . . and the hierarchies that are common in RL are missing. The deference to the older or more male or more rich or better family or whatever."[28] Because people aren't as inclined in Second Life to do things just to please others, Rivka felt, and because Second Life could bring people together from different regions for free, a Second Life Torah study was richer and better focused than one in RL.

Another participant, Jubilant, was able to exist in Second Life in female form even though she hadn't yet transitioned in RL. Being able to live as the gender she identified with also freed Jubilant to develop her spirituality, she told White. The freedom that living virtually as Jubilant offered her allowed her to begin connecting with other virtual transgender communities, and in exploring spiritual groups in those communities she found debates over spirituality that got her thinking. As a result, when she began a blog about her transition, Jubilant's first entry was what she called "a 'spiritual manifesto.'"[29] Second Life and other online spaces, then, can provide critically important resources for transgender, intersex, and queer people who are seeking religious community but can't easily find it in the RL world around them.

QUEERING RELIGION/RELIGIONING QUEER

In this chapter we've connected queer studies, transgender studies, and religious studies from the beginning. All of these fields have a great deal to say about community, whether it's the unique ways in which queer and transgender people create communities or the particular forms that religious communities take. Another area in which these fields can helpfully inform each other has to do with the apparent divide between public and private, which is closely related to the apparent divide between the sacred and the secular; both of these divides have a lot to do with communities.

To many people, the divide between public and private realms is clear. Families, households, relationships, sexuality—these are private affairs. The home is a space of privacy. Governments, cities, stores, parks, rallies, concerts, and the like are all public spaces. Many countries have laws pertaining to the right to privacy; European legal developments regarding the "right to be forgotten" on the internet—to have old posts removed from search results, for example—are indications of the navigation of privacy rights within new, virtual public spaces. But what are religious spaces—public or private? Some are fairly clearly private, like a meditation room or altar space in someone's house. Some are obviously public, like the annual Easter Mass at the Vatican. But what about your local synagogue? What about sacred spaces, like a Mormon temple or Mecca, that are accessible only to followers of the religion to which they're sacred? Millions of people visit Mecca each year, making it a very public space, but if we understand *public* to mean "accessible to all" then Mecca isn't public. We could ask similar questions of all kinds of religious institutions, even if they don't restrict entry. Is a small storefront church a public space or a private one? What about the Mormon Tabernacle in Salt Lake City? Can the same place be both public and private? What kinds of expectations do we place on public spaces and on private spaces? How do those expectations shape our understanding of religion? How does our understanding of religion shape our expectations about public spaces and privacy?

Queer studies has had quite a lot to say about public and private spaces— and **publics**, imagined communities in historian Benedict Anderson's terms, whose members don't necessarily know each other but share (or believe they share) values, identities, practices, and the like. In a well-known article from the 1990s called "Sex in Public," Lauren Berlant and Michael Warner argue that Western cultures promote sex, "intimacy," as a private and apolitical act, yet in fact heterosexuality is highly public, splashed across movie screens and sober newsmagazines alike.[30] Queer sex, on the other hand, is expected to be private: "Keep it in the bedroom," some people still admonish. Yet this enforced or expected privacy is also, Berlant and Warner argue, a form of isolation. Queer sex in public—in parks, public restrooms, and sex clubs, among other spaces—has a history of creating communities and **counterpublics**—publics that resist the dominant norms and values. After all, throughout the 1960s (and not just at the Stonewall Inn in New York City in 1969), bars and other public gathering spaces such as cafeterias were the flashpoints of transgender and queer activism. Berlant and Warner argue that forcing queer and transgender people's sex, and other forms of nonheteronormative sex, into the private realm while allowing heteronormative sex free rein in public shatters queer and transgender communities and forces queer and transgender people to adopt heteronormative values and "keep it in the bedroom."

Writing several years later, queer theorist Lisa Duggan would call this queer and transgender adoption of heternormativity by the name of *homonormativity*. Duggan expanded on Berlant and Warner's argument, and the work of others in this area, by elaborating on the point that there are ties between the heteronormative value of privacy and the value placed on privatization—that is, transferring resources and services like national parks and healthcare from the control of the government to the control of private corporations—in the contemporary global economic system known as neoliberal capitalism.[31] Queer theorist Jasbir Puar, in turn, built on Duggan's work by demonstrating the connections between homonormativity and nationalism, arguing that certain queer people gain acceptance into the "public" of countries like the United States by combining homonormativity with patriotism.[32] Crucially, Puar also makes clear that not all queer people, and certainly not all transgender people, even have access to the kind of inclusion and privacy alluringly offered by what she terms ***homonationalism***. Poor people, for instance, have very little access to privacy regardless of their sexual or gender identity; the same is true for many people of color, especially those who are racially profiled in the twenty-first century as "terrorists." For Puar, this includes people from specific religions, especially Muslims and Sikhs. In bringing religion into the picture, Puar is one of only a few queer theorists outside of religious studies to acknowledge the ways that religion is intertwined with many of the issues of power that queer theory and transgender studies are concerned with—for this reason, we'll discuss her work at more length in the next chapter. But in raising the question of which religions are *allowed* privacy, and which religions are as public as heteronormativity, Puar also brings her work into conversation with religious studies scholars who were already pursuing such questions in tandem with an analysis of religion in public: Janet Jakobsen and Ann Pellegrini.

We've already considered Jakobsen and Pellegrini's ideas in chapter 2, but it's worth returning to their book *Love the Sin* and also drawing on their important edited collection *Secularisms* as we consider how an analysis of communities at the intersection of queer studies, transgender studies, and religious studies might offer new insights into the roles of religion, secularism, public, and private in contemporary cultures. In *Love the Sin* Jakobsen and Pellegrini take a queer studies approach to a question that a few scholars of US American religions had already been asking: Just how secular is the United States, actually? The country is known worldwide for having a "separation of church and state" written into its founding documents; yet, as we've seen, Protestant Christianity is woven throughout US culture, law, history, and even government practices. Some people in the United States, who think of the country (probably correctly) as a "Christian nation" and would like to see it become even more explicitly Christian, bemoan what Lutheran pastor Richard John Neuhaus called in 1984 "the naked public square."[33] They claim that US mainstream culture and US government are devoid of religion; so do many people who think that's a great thing. Religion, people in many Global North/Global West countries today say, should remain in private, oddly like sexuality.

And that connection should make us think a bit more. If religion is under the same command to "stay in private" as sexuality is, but it turns out that only certain forms of sexuality are required to be private while others either are on constant public display or are denied any right to privacy whatsoever, is the same true for religion? Puar argues that Sikhs and Muslims have little to no access to religious privacy in the United States; the same could be said, especially for Muslims, in Europe. Jakobsen and Pellegrini argue that Christianity is on constant public display, either blatantly or subtly, in the United States; again, similar forces may be at play in other European and European-derived cultures. So it appears that certain religions are indeed both allowed and expected to remain in private, while others are denied privacy and still others—predictably, the dominant religion—are constantly on display, just like with sex. What appears to be "secular," as Jakobsen and Pellegrini note in *Secularisms*, is actually the invisibility of the unmarked, dominant category of Protestant Christianity.[34] What are the consequences of this differential treatment for these religions? What are the consequences for queer and transgender people? What are the religious consequences of the differential treatment of sex? What can we learn about religion, gender, sex, and power when we take both religion and sex seriously? This is the topic of the next, and final, thematic chapter.

STUDY QUESTIONS

1. What is a chosen family, and why might someone want to choose one? What are intentional communities? How are these two concepts related?

2. When did traditional religious communities first become open to gays and lesbians? When did mainstream religious communities start opening up to transgender people? Why do you think these dates aren't the same? Look up the official positions on queer and transgender people of the religious organization(s) you're most familiar with. How do they explain these positions? How do their explanations fit in with the stories and histories you're learning in this book?

3. Make a list of the queer and transgender religious organizations discussed in this chapter, and their various founding dates. Since most of these were in the United States, now look at two other important dates in US queer and transgender history: the Stonewall riots (1969) and the vote that removed homosexuality from the American Psychiatric Association's *Diagnostic and Statistical Manual* (1973). How do

these dates fit together? Do you think the various events impacted each other? How, or why not?

4. Why did black queer religious leaders like James Tinney, Carl Bean, and Yvette Flunder start their own churches?

5. How did the invention of the internet change virtual religious communities? What resources does the internet offer for queer and transgender people who are religious?

6. What is heteronormativity? Homonormativity? Homonationalism? How do they relate to each other?

FOR FURTHER THOUGHT

1. What chosen communities exist in your life? What roles do they play for you? Are they religious? Secular? Something else?

2. What do you think about the argument that, following Lynne Gerber, we could consider residential ex-gay communities to be queerish monasteries and convents? Develop an argument to support your evaluation.

3. If, as so many commentators have argued, gay bars offer a form of chosen religious community for transgender and queer people, then we could argue by analogy that violence at gay bars is a form of antireligious violence, similar to shootings and bombings at churches, synagogues, mosques, gurdwaras, and the like. Do you think it would change mainstream representations of violence at gay bars if it was represented in this way? If so, how? If not, why not?

4. Ashon Crawley argues that despite their homophobia, Black Pentecostal communities can be profoundly queer. In what ways? What do you think of his argument, and why?

5. In what ways have some queer and transgender people experienced exclusion from queer and transgender religious groups? How have they responded, and why? Do you think there are any limits to the inclusion that queer and transgender religious organizations should aim for? If so, what are they and why? If not, why not?

6. What do you think the future of queer and transgender religious communities is? Are they going to fade out as more mainstream organizations become increasingly inclusive? Will they adapt to those changes and take on new forms? Will they continue to exist in their current forms? Why?

7. In the final section of this chapter, we returned to some important themes in queer studies and in religious studies, and drew them together through a consideration of privacy. Recap this argument, if you can. Do you find it persuasive? In your own country, or the country where

you're living right now, is religion public, private, or both? Are different religions treated differently with regard to privacy? What about different sexualities? What relationships can you perceive, in the culture(s) you're most familiar with, between religion, sexuality, and privacy?

RECOMMENDATIONS FOR FURTHER READING

Berlant, Lauren, and Michael Warner. "Sex in Public." *Critical Inquiry* 24, no. 2 (1998): 547–66.

Cervantes, Vincent. "Sacred Geography: A Queer Latino Theological Response to Orlando." *Religion Dispatches*, June 13, 2016. http://religiondispatches.org/sacred-geography-a-queer-latino-theological-response-to-orlando.

Crawley, Ashon T. *Blackpentecostal Breath: The Aesthetics of Possibility*. New York: Fordham University Press, 2017.

Douglas, Kelly Brown. "Black and Blues: God-Talk/Body-Talk for the Black Church." In *Sexuality and the Sacred: Sources for Theological Reflection*, edited by Marvin M. Ellison and Kelly Brown Douglas, 48–66. Louisville, KY: Westminster John Knox, [2004] 2010.

Duggan, Lisa. "The New Homonormativity: The Sexual Politics of Neoliberalism." In *Materializing Democracy: Toward a Revitalized Cultural Politics*, edited by Russ Castronovo and Dana D. Nelson, 175–94. Durham, NC: Duke University Press, 2002.

Fogarty, Robert S. *Desire and Duty at Oneida: Tirzah Miller's Intimate Memoir*. Bloomington: Indiana University Press, 2000.

Griffin, Horace L. *Their Own Receive Them Not: African American Lesbians and Gays in Black Churches*. Cleveland, OH: Pilgrim Press, 2006.

Leong, Pamela. *Religion, Flesh, and Blood: The Convergence of HIV/AIDS, Black Sexual Expression, and Therapeutic Religion*. Lanham, MD: Lexington Books, 2015.

Lewin, Ellen. *Filled with the Spirit: Sexuality, Gender, and Radical Inclusivity in a Black Pentecostal Church Coalition*. Chicago: University of Chicago Press, 2018.

O'Riordan, Kate and Heather White. "Virtual Believers: Queer Spiritual Practice Online." In *Queer Spiritual Spaces: Sexuality and Sacred Places*, edited by Kath Browne, Sally R. Munt, and Andrew K. T. Yip, 199–230. Burlington, VT: Ashgate, 2010.

Pérez, Elizabeth. "For All that is Good and Holy: Reclaiming Religion for the Black and Latinx Victims of the #pulseorlando Massacre." *Marginalia*, June 12, 2016. https://marginalia.lareviewofbooks.org/good-holy-reclaiming-religion-black-latinx-victims-pulseorlando-massacre/.

Puar, Jasbir K. *Terrorist Assemblages: Homonationalism in Queer Times*. Durham, NC: Duke University Press, 2007.

Young, Thelathia Nikki. *Black Queer Ethics, Family, and Philosophical Imagination*. New York: Palgrave Macmillan, 2016.

NOTES

1. Kelly Brown Douglas, "Black and Blues: God-Talk/Body-Talk for the Black Church," in *Sexuality and the Sacred: Sources for Theological Reflection*, ed. Marvin M. Ellison and Kelly Brown Douglas (Louisville, KY: Westminster John Knox, [2004] 2010), 56. Thanks to Aaron Brown for bringing this article back into my awareness.

2. Thelathia Nikki Young, *Black Queer Ethics, Family, and Philosophical Imagination* (New York: Palgrave Macmillan, 2016), 15.

3. Ibid., 111.

4. Ibid., 138.

5. Ashon T. Crawley, *Blackpentecostal Breath: The Aesthetics of Possibility* (New York: Fordham University Press, 2017).

6. See, for instance, Robert S. Fogarty, *Desire and Duty at Oneida: Tirzah Miller's Intimate Memoir* (Bloomington: Indiana University Press, 2000).

7. Tanya Erzen, *Straight to Jesus: Sexual and Christian Conversions in the Ex-Gay Movement* (Berkeley: University of California Press, 2006), 88.

8. See, for instance, E. Patrick Johnson, "Feeling the Spirit in the Dark: Expanding Notions of the Sacred in the African-American Gay Community," *Callaloo* 21, no. 2 (1998): 399–416; Donald L. Boisvert, *Out on Holy Ground: Meditations on Gay Men's Spirituality* (Cleveland, OH: Pilgrim Press, 2000); Mickey Weems, *The Fierce Tribe: Masculine Identity and Performance in the Circuit* (Logan: Utah State University Press, 2008); Jafari Sinclaire Allen, "For 'the Children' Dancing the Beloved Community," *Souls* 11, no. 3 (2009): 311–26.

9. Elizabeth Pérez, "For All That Is Good and Holy: Reclaiming Religion for the Black and Latinx Victims of the #pulseorlando Massacre," *Marginalia*, June 24, 2016, https://marginalia. lareviewofbooks.org/good-holy-reclaiming-religion-black-latinx-victims-pulseorlando-massacre/.

10. Vincent Cervantes, "Sacred Geography: A Queer Latino Theological Response to Orlando," *Religion Dispatches*, June 13, 2016. http://religiondispatches.org/sacred-geography-a-queer-latino-theological-response-to-orlando.

11. Keith Hartman, *Congregations in Conflict: The Battle over Homosexuality* (New Brunswick, NJ: Rutgers University Press, 1996), 25–65.

12. Crawley, *Blackpentecostal Breath*, 129–34.

13. Unitarian Universalist Association, Unitarian Universalist LGBT History Timeline, https://www.uua.org/lgbtq/witness/policy/timeline.

14. United Church of Christ, LGBT History Timeline, http://www.ucc.org/lgbt_lgbt-history-timeline

15. The Episcopal Church, LGBTQ in the Church, https://www.episcopalchurch.org/page/lgbt-church.

16. Extensive resources on these histories, including digital archival exhibits and oral histories, can be found on the website of the LGBT Religious Archives Network, http://www.lgbtran.org.

17. Heather R. White, *Reforming Sodom: Protestants and the Rise of Gay Rights* (Chapel Hill: University of North Carolina Press, 2015), 67.

18. On Dignity, see Michelle Dillon, *Catholic Identity: Balancing Reason, Faith, and Power* (Cambridge: Cambridge University Press, 1999), 115–63; http://www.dignityusa.org.

19. For a history of BCC, see Beth Chayim Chadashim, History, http://www.bcc-la.org/about/history/.

20. GALVA-108, About GALVA-108, http://www.galva108.org/about-galva-108.

21. New Ways Ministry website, http://www.newwaysministry.org.

22. Horace L. Griffin, *Their Own Receive Them Not: African American Lesbians and Gays in Black Churches* (Cleveland, OH: Pilgrim Press, 2006), 185–206.

23. Pamela Leong, "Religion, Flesh, and Blood: Re-creating Religious Culture in the Context of HIV/AIDS," *Sociology of Religion* 67, no. 3 (2006): 295–311; Pamela Leong, *Religion, Flesh, and Blood: The Convergence of HIV/AIDS, Black Sexual Expression, and Therapeutic Religion* (Lanham, MD: Lexington Books, 2015).

24. Ellen Lewin, *Filled with the Spirit: Sexuality, Gender, and Radical Inclusivity in a Black Pentecostal Church Coalition* (Chicago: University of Chicago Press, 2018).

25. Davide Mastracci, "What It's Like to Pray at a Queer-Inclusive Mosque," *BuzzFeed*, April 4, 2017, https://www.buzzfeed.com/davidemastracci/toronto-lgbt-unity-mosque?utm_term=.kyNk0Py90A#.tijjyrE4y3.

26. Damien McGuinness, "The Berlin Mosque Breaking Islamic Taboos," BBC News, August 7, 2017, https://www.bbc.com/news/world-europe-40802538.

27. El-Tawhid Juma Circle website, http://www.jumacircle.com/; El-Tawhid Juma Circle blog, http://jumacircle.blogspot.com/.

28. Kate O'Riordan and Heather White, "Virtual Believers: Queer Spiritual Practice Online," in *Queer Spiritual Spaces: Sexuality and Sacred Places*, ed. Kath Browne, Sally R. Munt, and Andrew K.T. Yip (Burlington, VT: Ashgate, 2010), 221.

29. Ibid., 225.

30. Lauren Berlant and Michael Warner, "Sex in Public," *Critical Inquiry* 24, no. 2 (1998): 547–66.

31. Lisa Duggan, "The New Homonormativity: The Sexual Politics of Neoliberalism," in *Materializing Democracy: Toward a Revitalized Cultural Politics*, ed. Russ Castronovo and Dana D. Nelson (Durham, NC: Duke University Press, 2002), 175–94.

32. Jasbir K. Puar, *Terrorist Assemblages: Homonationalism in Queer Times* (Durham, NC: Duke University Press, 2007).

33. Richard John Neuhaus, *The Naked Public Square: Religion and Democracy in America* (Grand Rapids, MI: Eerdmans, 1984).

34. Janet R. Jakobsen and Ann Pellegrini, eds., *Secularisms* (Durham, NC: Duke University Press, 2008).

Chapter Six

Politics and Power

As you may already have noticed in the previous chapters, studying power is central to studying gender, sexuality, and religion. Scholars in transgender studies, queer studies, and religious studies use a variety of approaches to understand power in a broad sense; they combine these perspectives with the insights they gain from studying particular axes along which power travels, such as gender, sexuality, and religion themselves but also race, colonialism, ability, and the like. Three of the most common approaches to the study of power in these fields are critical theory, derived in particular from the thought of Karl Marx; psychoanalytic theory, derived initially from the work of Sigmund Freud; and poststructuralist theory, derived especially from the work of Michel Foucault. The latter two bodies of theory have been taken up especially broadly by scholars of queer and transgender studies in religion, whereas critical theory has been most important so far for queer Christian theology. In this chapter, we'll go over the central insights of each area of theory before discussing some of the ways that these theoretical perspectives have informed the work of scholars in queer and transgender studies in religion.

MARXIST THOUGHT AND CRITICAL THEORY

Perhaps one explanation for the limited engagement of queer and transgender studies in religion with critical theory is Karl Marx's dismissive approach to religion. Certainly this is one possible explanation for the near-total neglect of religion within queer and transgender studies more broadly. Marx is famous for calling religion "the opium of the people." But what did he mean by that? In Europe during Marx's life in the nineteenth century, opium had varied uses. Some people think immediately of the famed "opium dens" that

171

formed when opium became increasingly available as a recreational drug. Because opium poppies grow in the Middle East and Asia, and because many of the opium imports at the time were coming through China to Europe and North America, the image of the "opium den" is deeply Orientalist, based on stereotypes of Asians as lazy, criminal, devious, seductive, and dangerous. In fact, opium was both used and sold as a recreational drug by a variety of people during Marx's time. But that's not what Marx is trying to say. Religion, for him, isn't a recreational drug. It's a painkiller.

Opium was also prescribed by doctors in Marx's time to treat pain. It was so effective that pharmaceutical companies later worked to create and patent medications derived from opium that would have the same effects. Today, those medications are called opioids; they're still closely enough related to opium that they have similar addictive properties, and their overuse has led to widening addictions not only to opioid painkillers but also to their stronger street-drug cousin, heroin. Rather than saying that religion is the ecstasy or the meth of the people, then, Marx was saying something more like religion is the morphine of the people. Why would he say that?

Marx was concerned above all with a class-based perspective on power and injustice. He argued for what he and his frequent coauthor Friedrich Engels called a *materialist analysis*, one that considered the material conditions of people's lives. "It is not consciousness that determines life," Marx famously wrote in *The German Ideology*, "but life that determines consciousness." If you struggle to get enough to eat, for instance, or if you live crammed into a one-bedroom apartment with fifteen other people and have no access to healthcare, your perspective on the world and how you think about things will be very different than it would be if you never worried about where your next meal was coming from and had a comfortably large and uncrowded home. Other thinkers at the time were idealists, meaning not that they thought everything was perfect (that's our current use of the term) but that they thought ideas came before material realities. Marx reversed that equation in his materialist analysis.

Closely tied to this materialist perspective was Marx's passionate concern for the liberation of working-class people. The Industrial Revolution was in full swing in Western Europe during Marx's lifetime, and economic systems were shifting from a mercantile form of capitalism, in which goods were produced and sold by artisans, people we might call small business owners today, to an industrial form of capitalism in which most working-class people earned money by standing on a factory assembly line or sitting at a sewing machine, doing exactly the same task over and over all day and never seeing or being able to take pride in the finished product. Changes in the form of production had rapidly outpaced legal changes, so workers had few to no rights and people often were injured, contracted chronic or terminal illnesses, or even died on the job where they worked sometimes fourteen or sixteen hours a day, six or even seven days a week. The Industrial Revolution was built on the broken bodies of working-class people, and Marx, along with other intellectuals and activists like him, wanted to put a stop to it.

But how to stop the runaway growth of industrial capitalism? Rather than try to undo it, Marx wanted to push it along because he had what Christian theologians and Christianity scholars call a **teleological**, or end-time-focused, view of time. Considering the economic history of the world as it was understood in Europe at the time, Marx believed that economic systems evolved in a way that was fairly inevitable. One economic system would develop as far as it could, then it would cause changes that led to the development of the next economic system. Capitalism, he thought, was creating its own doom because its principles required the exploitation and oppression of workers. Over time, Marx argued, the oppression would become too burdensome and the workers would revolt, ushering in the next and perhaps the final economic system: communism, in which people pooled their resources and supported each person equally so that no one had to work harder or get paid less than anyone else.

Why hadn't the revolution already happened? Marx explained that there were certain social systems keeping capitalism in place; he called these the superstructure. Such systems taught people to be good capitalists, rewarded them for their contributions to capitalism, and convinced them that capitalist systems were the best but also the only real choice when it came to economic structures. The superstructure had to be dismantled or at least weakened, Marx believed, before the revolution could take place. Religious institutions were part of this superstructure, teaching people that their rewards would be in heaven rather than on earth and that they should therefore accept their misery on earth in order to reap the greatest reward for all of eternity. But religion received special criticism from Marx because it had a very specific role in the maintenance of capitalism and the prevention of the revolution: its pain-killing properties. If the revolution is expected to take place because the working classes can't take their oppression any longer, then a painkiller would be a pretty effective way to prevent the revolution, wouldn't it? As it turns out, opium was an even better metaphor for this theory than Marx knew, because neurochemists today tell us that opium and its derivatives work as painkillers not by addressing the cause of the pain—reducing inflammation, for instance—but by convincing the brain that it feels no pain. Opioids don't address the cause of suffering, they simply make us numb to it—just like Marx thought religion did.

Marx's work proved extremely influential; through the work of later generations of Marxist thinkers he inspired the formation of the communist and socialist economic systems around the world today. Although economic centralization—the pooling of resources—has often led to political centralization—the concentration of political power—in ways that encouraged dictatorial and repressive regimes, capitalist economic systems have also at times gone hand in hand with repressive forms of government like fascism. It's important, therefore, to consider ideas about economic structures separately from the political systems they may be associated with even as we also ask questions about how such associations form.

Many of the governmental systems that formed under Marxist inspiration took seriously Marx's concerns about religion and sought to eradicate it through violence, prohibitions, and countereducation. Whether intentionally or not, many of these governments replaced traditional religions like Christianity and Buddhism with devotion to the nation; after all, nationalism functions very similarly to a religion. But already by the second generation of Marxist thinkers some were approaching religion in a more nuanced way than Marx did, even if marginally and cautiously. The best-known of these thinkers was Antonio Gramsci. A Marxist intellectual and activist in Italy during the early twentieth century, Gramsci was one of the second-generation Marxist thinkers who puzzled over why, despite their best efforts, the revolution wasn't occurring in some places as Marx had predicted it inevitably would. The working classes were suffering, and communist activists were working hard to dismantle the superstructure and to educate the workers about the true cause of their suffering and the fact that it wasn't inevitable; so why were people still not rising up *en masse*? Gramsci suggested that what he called **hegemony** was to blame.

Hegemony is a form of power so complete that it appears natural and normal even to those who suffer under it. If people believe their oppression is natural and normal, then they aren't likely to try to change it. And such beliefs are rooted in world concepts, so they're quite difficult to change. Gramsci, though, thought that a counterhegemony could be created that not only challenged the naturalness and normalcy of oppression but also taught people to see freedom and equality as natural and normal. Both hegemony and counterhegemony, for Gramsci, could be carried and reinforced by the institutions that Marx had identified as the superstructure, including religion. Gramsci was very clear that the dominant religion couldn't serve as a source of counterhegemony, but he was interested in the power of influences that came from within the oppressed group, and he was willing to concede that the religions of the people, of the working classes, might hold within them some of the tools for counterhegemony and therefore for the revolution.

As Marxist thought continued to develop and spread, it connected with other ideas and created the school of thought known today as critical theory. Among some religious leaders, though, it took a different form. In the second half of the twentieth century, first Latin American thinkers and then people concerned with religion, power, and oppression around the world drew on Marx's ideas in ways that would probably have shocked him. Instead of discarding religion as the opium of the people, they claimed it as a tool for economic—then racial, anticolonial, gender, and sexual—justice. This movement began with the teachings of Peruvian Catholic theologian Gustavo Gutiérrez, who developed what he called "liberation theology" and claimed that God was particularly concerned with the plight of the poor—what he called God's "preferential option for the poor." The God of Christianity, Gutiérrez argued, was a "God of the oppressed," and those who served that God could do so only by working together with poor and indigenous communities for greater economic justice. [1] In the United States, theologian James Cone drew on Gutiérrez's ideas to create a black liberation theology; later, feminist, womanist, *mujerista*, queer, and transgender theologians—mostly but not entirely those working within Christianity—would also build on Gutiérrez's work and on each other's ideas to create new theologies. These new kinds of Marxist analysis even made their way into sociology, with Venezuelan-born scholar Otto Maduro's systematic analysis of the interactions of religion, power, and oppression in his 1982 book *Religion and Social Conflicts.*

Building from the increasingly well-developed literature in liberation theology, feminist and queer Argentinian theologian Marcella Althaus-Reid challenged the narrowing and romanticizing of the concept of the poor in much of that literature. In classic liberation theology the poor are quietly suffering people, virtuous and innocent from a Catholic perspective, generally men, living traditional lifestyles in rural areas. But how many poor people in Argentina—or anywhere—actually live that way? What does liberation theology have to say, Althaus-Reid asks, to women who are marginalized by the church? What does it have to say about people's lives beyond their poverty, about their embodiment, about poor people who live in the city, about poor people who are queer and transgender, about sex? As provocative as liberation theology has been to the Roman Catholic hierarchy—many people have observed, for instance, that it's no accident that Pope Francis rose as rapidly as he did through that hierarchy as a Latin American Catholic leader who actively dismissed and marginalized liberation theologians—it nonetheless has presented a cisnormative, heteronormative, male-dominant, and pacified vision of the poor for whom God has a preferential option. What about everybody who doesn't fit this mold?

In her book titled *Indecent Theology*, Althaus-Reid provocatively recommends "doing theology without underwear." Some people are uncomfortable with this challenge, finding it inappropriate and even disrespectful. Remember our discussion in chapter 3 about cultural assumptions that sex and religion don't go together except in exoticized Other religions? Some of Althaus-Reid's readers had exactly this reaction. But that's her point, in much the same way as showing Guadalupe's body in *Our Lady* was exactly Alma López's point. What does eradicating sex from theology do to sex workers? Does God not have a preferential option for them even though they're poor? Is God's preferential option only for poor women who are virgins? Where are the lines? In bringing feminist theology, queer theology, and liberation theology together in a profoundly Marxist analysis, Althaus-Reid proposes what she calls an "Indecent Theology[:] . . . a theology which problematizes and undresses the mythical layers of multiple oppression in Latin America, a theology which, finding its point of departure at the crossroads of Liberation Theology and Queer Thinking, will reflect on economic and theological oppression with passion and imprudence. An Indecent Theology will question the traditional Latin American field of decency and order as it permeates and supports the multiple (ecclesiological, theological, political, and amatory) structures of life in my country, Argentina, and in my continent."[2]

PSYCHOANALYTIC THEORY

Sigmund Freud, the founding thinker of psychoanalysis, didn't set out to create a body of theory that would be used in the humanities for all kinds of analytical purposes. Ironically, scholars in the humanities are probably the ones who rely on his ideas the most today; although psychoanalysis is still a respected approach to clinical psychology, Freud's many intellectual descendants moved the field in new directions and made him more important as a forebear than as a current influence. Nonetheless, contemporary theorists who make use of Freud's work also rely on those who came after him, particularly Jacques Lacan.

As with each of the schools of thought covered in this chapter, this brief discussion can't hope to do justice to the complexity and breadth of psychoanalytic theory. Thus, this section focuses primarily on psychoanalytic concepts that have so far proven most useful to scholars of queer and transgender studies in religion. Interestingly, these are generally not Freud's writings on religion, which are fairly dismissive. Whereas Marx thought religion was an opiate, Freud argued that it was a neurotic illusion, held in place by people's unwillingness to grow up and stop relying on father figures to keep them accountable for ethical behavior. As you might imagine, religious studies scholars find that perspective to be a bit limited and inaccurate. Instead, they follow the lead of feminist and queer theorists in drawing from psychoanalytic ideas about sexuality and desire.

Freud is well known for arguing that much of human psychology is driven by early childhood experiences, and that many of these experiences are related in some way to desire, genitalia, and the erotic. In his theory of the Oedipal complex, for instance, he drew on the classical Greek story of Oedipus, who unknowingly murdered his father and married his mother, to suggest that little boys face a profound dilemma as they become increasingly aware of the world around them. Having initially developed a deep emotional attachment to their mothers (whom Freud assumed were their primary caregivers, a reasonable assumption in well-to-do intellectual circles in turn-of-the-century Vienna), boys eventually became aware that their fathers were rivals for their mothers' affections. How and whether they resolved that crisis, Freud thought, could significantly impact their psychology well into adulthood. A healthy resolution, in his opinion, took place when the boy began to identify with his father and generalized his desire for his mother to a desire for women in general. If you're thinking there's a strikingly gendered aspect to this theory, you're right; some psychologists used this idea later in the twentieth century to argue that poor resolution of the Oedipal conflict led to inversion in boys and men, and they even ran experiments to try to intervene in the process and "cure" boys they considered to be "proto-homosexuals."[3] In fact, these are the very theories that ex-gay psychology still relies upon.

In the mid-twentieth century, psychoanalyst and philosopher Jacques Lacan began publishing new approaches to psychoanalytic theory that were so controversial he was banned in 1962 from the International Psychoanalytic Association. Nevertheless, his ideas proved profoundly influential to some psychoanalysts and especially to many scholars of culture, power, and politics—including some who study religion. Among Lacan's ideas that have influenced queer studies, transgender studies, and religious studies are his interpretation of the symbolic role of the phallus and his ideas about the Law. In Lacan's terminology, neither of these words holds the same meaning as it does in popular usage. On a basic level, we can understand the Law or, as it's often called, the Law of the father, as referring to the norms and expectations of society. Though children learn this Law through their parents, the parents are also subject to it, though sometimes in different ways. Like the Law, the phallus is a complicated concept in Lacan's thought, but the important thing to know about it for our purposes is that it's not the same as the penis. The phallus is more about imagination and symbol than it is about flesh, representing male or masculine power in male-dominant societies.

What may be the first book to bring the nascent field of queer theory together with the study of religion did so through an engagement with psychoanalytic theory, which some scholars in each field were taking up at the time. Jewish studies scholar Howard Eilberg-Schwartz had studied with the well-known historian of religions Wendy Doniger at the University of Chicago. Doniger has an abiding interest in sexuality and gender in religion, which she approaches comparatively using the tools of philology (the study of written language) and psychoanalytic theory. Eilberg-Schwartz brought these same tools of linguistic analysis and psychoanalysis to his own work on ancient Judaism. In a book entitled *God's Phallus and Other Problems for Men and Monotheism*, he asked a central question about Judaism: Why is the depiction of God forbidden?[4]

Some religions, such as Christianity and Hinduism, depict the divine on a regular basis. In Hinduism the deities inhabit statues, so the depiction of goddesses and gods is an important part of interaction with them. In Christianity, although God the Father is less often depicted than Jesus (who, to most Christians, is also God), nonetheless depiction of the divine is perfectly acceptable. In Judaism, though, as in Islam, it's not. Unwilling to simply accept this situation as fact, Eilberg-Schwartz wanted to know why it happened in the first place. Other cultures in the ancient Near East depicted their deities; why were the ancient Israelites different? In fact, it's not only depictions that are banned; Moses himself, who actually saw God on Mount Sinai according to the Torah, was allowed to see only certain parts of the deity. Not only were the ancient Israelites banned from depicting God, then; they couldn't see God in entirety either.

Eilberg-Schwartz argues that the explanation for this avoidance of seeing God lies with the repeated depictions in the Torah of the people of Israel as God's spouse. The ancient Israelites interacted most closely with God by making offerings through priests at God's temple; this was a religion in which worship looked different than Jewish services look today. Because the priests were all male, because in other ways, too, it was men who represented the Israelite people in their interactions with God, and most importantly because God was conceived of as male, Eilberg-Schwartz argues that the metaphor of marriage became problematic in a religion that seems to have forbidden at least certain forms of sex between men. If Israel was married to God, that is, and men represented Israel in its interactions with the deity, then the homoerotic undertones of the relationship between priests and God become fairly clear—yet there are indications that homoeroticism was frowned upon in this culture. Eilberg-Schwartz suggests that these tensions were managed by studiously avoiding thinking about the body of God, and especially what might lie between God's legs. Resisting the urge to look at God, and to create images of God to look at, avoids the problem that God's presumed-male body creates for his male functionaries.

Two years after the release of Eilberg-Schwartz's book, Talmud scholar Daniel Boyarin published a book that engaged with psychoanalytic theory, gender theory, and queer theory to evaluate the ancient rabbinic commentaries known collectively as the Talmud. Writing about a story in the Talmud that recounts the relationship between a rabbi and a student, for instance, Boyarin relies on psychoanalytic interpretation of phallic symbols (here, especially a lance) to explore the ways the story addresses distinctions between Roman and Jewish ideals of masculinity at a time when the rabbinic authors of these texts were living under Roman rule.

In other chapters of the same book Boyarin turns the analysis on the analyst, using a psychoanalytic approach to explore connections between Freud's theories and his gendered, sexual, and racialized experiences as a

Jew in turn-of-the-century Vienna: the city in which Hitler was growing up and from which Freud would be forced to flee in 1938 after it was annexed by Nazi Germany. Boyarin argues that Freud's perspectives were shaped in part by his experiences of tension between the eastern European Jewish gender norms that had deep roots in his family and the mainstream European Christian gender norms against which he and his family were judged by the society around them. Traditionally, gender norms for Ashkenazi (northern and eastern European) Jews had valued quiet, gentle studiousness in men and practical, organizational abilities in women; the ideal situation for a hetero-sexually married couple was for the man to spend his days studying the sacred texts and praying, and for the woman to manage the household's worldly affairs. But in turn-of-the-century Christian European society, the ideal for women was to remain in the home with the children while men engaged in public affairs such as business and politics. Religion was still important for some of these societies, to be sure, but it was women's sphere. Men who were too bookish or pious were feminine; women who were too worldly were masculine. Still today, stereotypes abound of Jewish men as feminine and Jewish women as masculine. But at a time when the concept of the invert had free rein, allegations of Jewish male femininity edged over quickly into allegations of Jewish male homosexuality. Freud, a successful man but also a bookish intellectual with controversial new ideas about sex, living in a city that harbored deep nationalism and anti-Semitism that would make the Nazi takeover relatively smooth, was in Boyarin's reading determined to assimilate, and to take the rest of Judaism with him.

Though Freud was a fan of the early Zionist movement, Boyarin explains, this too was part of his larger drive to assimilate into mainstream culture. Provocatively, Boyarin suggests that the desire of the Zionist movement for a Jewish homeland was rooted in a desire to be like other Europeans. Other Europeans in the early twentieth century had a nation that they were a part of: The Germans had Germany, the French had France, the English had England. Jews, though, were persistently told that they weren't German or French or English; these nationalisms also included a religious identification, or at least a cultural history, with the religion of Christianity. So Jews, too, wanted a nation, Boyarin argues; it's no accident that they renamed their portion of Palestine as Israel. Now the French had France, the Germans had Germany, the English had England, and the Jews had Israel.

But Boyarin goes further, arguing that supporters of the early Zionist movement were also drawn to the validation of Jewish strength (and mascu-linity) as a nation that was provided by having their own colony. Every European nation, and some European settler colonies, were busy becoming empires; Jews, a small nation, just wanted one colony (was that so much to ask?). Zionist publications and art of the time lauded the brawny colonial Jewish man, bronzed by the sun and endowed with rippling muscles that displayed his hearty, masculine, heterosexual, outdoor lifestyle. Ultimately, Boyarin argues, "for Freud, Zionism was motivated as much by the Oscar Wilde [obscenity] trials as by the Dreyfus trial [a recent and infamous case of anti-Semitism in France]. It was a return to Phallustine, not to Palestine. . . . It is impossible to separate the question of Jewishness from the question of homosexuality in Freud's symbolic, textual world." Connecting stereotypes of male femininity and suspicions of homosexuality even more clearly together, Boyarin later argues that **diaspora**—a situation in which people from a shared homeland are scattered to live in distant places—is a position of political weakness and was understood in Freud's time as emasculating men. Because of the connection between gender and sexuality in the theories of the era, Boyarin adds, "Diaspora is essentially queer, and an end to Diaspora would be the equivalent of becoming straight. The fact, then, that political Zionism was invented at the time of the invention of heterosexuality is entirely legible. . . . Freud's Zionism outs itself as homophobia."[5]

Although engagement with psychoanalytic theories in both queer studies and religious studies—and at their intersections—was especially marked in the 1990s, this way of approaching questions of power and oppression remains influential. Queer studies in religion scholar Kent Brintnall is among those making use of it today; his work also demonstrates the promise of more theoretically eclectic approaches to queer studies in religion, since his analysis draws on all three of the schools of thought discussed here through his engagement with psychoanalytic theory and his primary focus on the work of French philosopher Georges Bataille.

Brintnall's book *Ecce Homo* draws its title from the words spoken by the Roman prefect of Judea, Pontius Pilate, when he presented a tortured Jesus of Nazareth to the people of Judea prior to Jesus's execution by crucifixion. Across the centuries, many European visual artists have represented this scene in paintings that take these words as their title. Brintnall is interested less in the Christian force of this image, though theological reflection isn't entirely absent from his book, than in the symbolic impact of images of the male body in pain, and his analysis ranges over a variety of contemporary images that are at first glance not religious at all. This is because he's working with religious studies concepts and their broader application, rather than with specific, identifiable religious traditions, even while the image of Jesus's tortured body remains in the background and sometimes more explicitly in the foreground throughout the book. While Christians often represent Jesus's suffering as redemptive, a sacrifice made by God to redeem the sins of humanity, Brintnall considers how, in his words, "certain ways of representing the male-body-in-pain have the capacity—not without complexity, not without risk, but the capacity nonetheless—to disrupt cultural fantasies of masculine plenitude that ground the social orders of masculine power and privilege."[6]

Brintnall's analysis begins with male heroes' bodies in pain in action films (including, appropriately, Mel Gibson's intensely violent 2004 film *The Passion of the Christ*). From these representations, he argues, "we see how action films, Westerns, war films, disaster films, Christian theological discourses, and a number of other cultural forms work together to present an image of the masculine subject as capable of enduring astonishing injury and still surviving. Placing the action genre's suffering-triumph narrative alongside Christianity's crucifixion-resurrection narrative reorients us to how the Christian tradition supports and sustains masculine domination."[7] In seeking the chink in the armor of this masculinist narrative Brintnall turns next to psychoanalysis, arguing ultimately that this perspective helps us to see how vulnerable the claims to masculine domination and authority actually are; once identified, these vulnerabilities become the route to follow in exploring the potential of alternative images of the male body in pain for feminist and queer politics. In his final chapters, Brintnall explores some of these alternative images, including the photographs of Robert Mapplethorpe and the paintings of Francis Bacon and George Dyer.

POSTSTRUCTURALIST THEORY

Georges Bataille, Brintnall's central source of theoretical inspiration, was also one of the forerunners of the late-twentieth-century school of thought known as poststructuralism. Since this is a broad field, many thinkers are considered to contribute to poststructuralist theory. For queer studies, however, one of the most influential of these is French philosopher Michel Foucault. Foucault engaged in a method of study that, following the philosopher Friedrich Nietzsche, he called "genealogy." Unlike the family genealogy you might research online for a class project or compile by interviewing elders in your family about their own elders, Foucault's and Nietzsche's genealogy is a cultural one, exploring the ancestry of cultural ideas and institutions. Foucault studied medical clinics, psychiatric hospitals and the concept of "madness," prisons, and sexuality, among many other topics. Through it all, he was profoundly interested in power.

Foucault thought about power a little bit differently than many people do. In popular usage, power is thought of as finite and fairly concrete. Some people have power; other people don't. People can become empowered—they can gain power—or they can become disempowered—they can lose it. We also often think of power as a zero-sum game, in that if one person has it, then another doesn't. It's like there's a law of the conservation of power that says there's a finite and fixed total amount of power in the universe, so when power increases in one place it has to decrease elsewhere by some sort of law of physics.

But Foucault thought about power really differently from this. If the finite and concrete version of power imagines it as being like money or land—tangible and limited—we might describe Foucault's understanding of power as being more like air. Air is all around us, but we can't grab it. Although technically it's finite since there's only so much air in the earth's atmosphere, in human experience it isn't limited in the way your paycheck or the amount of cash in your pocket is limited. If I sit next to you and take a breath, I won't take away your air; you'll still be able to breathe even when I'm breathing next to you, unless I do something else to you. What's powerful about air, in human experience, isn't so much the ability to hold, keep, or store it; it's the ability to mobilize it. Air affects our lives through the routes by which it travels. A strong enough wind can blow someone off their feet, destroy a building, or level a forest. And while those are natural phenomena, perhaps impacted by human actions such as those causing climate change, humans also have technologies for mobilizing air, from blowing it out of our mouths to using giant wind tunnels and fans to using it to keep aircraft afloat. Power is like that, for Foucault: The key questions are not "Who owns it?" and "How much do they have?" but "What channels does it travel along?" and "How is it mobilized?"

Foucault was particularly interested in the ways that government institutions, also called the state, mobilize power. He argued that the central mode of state power in Europe shifted a couple of hundred years ago from what he called **necropower** or **necropolitics**, a mobilization of power through state control over death, to **biopower** or **biopolitics**, a mobilization of power through state control over life. In a nutshell, for Foucault, necropower is the state's control of those under its power through its ability to make someone *die* or allow them to *live*; biopower is the state's control of those under its power through its ability to make someone *live* or allow them to *die*. Furthermore, according to Foucault the advent of biopower brings in the idea of the "population" as a focus of control and a channel for power. Lives, bodies, and populations are "managed" by biopower—disciplined, regimented, and normed. The statistical norm, in this context, becomes the measure of human perfection and the goal for all bodies. Being "normal" becomes the path to the good life, and people are so caught up in pursuing the norm that they become docile, easily governable by the state, a phenomenon that Foucault called **governmentality**.

Later commentators have added further complexity to Foucault's systematization of power. Cameroonian philosopher Achille Mbembe, for instance, has pointed out that necropower didn't disappear with the coming of biopower; instead, states control different populations through different modes of power. Those who are valued by the state are subjected to biopower, whereas those considered to have no value—the colonized in a colonial state, for example—remain instead under a regime of necropower.[8] Feminist and queer theorist Jasbir Puar, whose work we've encountered already in this book, has suggested that in the context of settler colonial states—she uses mainly the example of Israel/Palestine—there may be a third mode of power: maiming. Biopolitics and necropolitics both turn on state control over life and death; yet, Puar points out, maimed bodies neither die nor do they live in the biopolitical sense of being disciplined into docile, productive, governable citizens. Neither necropolitics nor biopolitics seems to fit here. In fact, a settler colonial state may use maiming as a tool to create docility and the appearance of acceptance among the victims of their colonization. Considering tactics like cultural genocide, land theft, boarding school abuses, and other forms of state control of Native American and First Nations people in the United States and Canada, we can understand the broader applicability of Puar's argument.

Because Puar's writing about what she calls "the right to maim" focuses primarily on Israel/Palestine, there is an intrinsic tie to religious studies in this work, as there is in her earlier writing on homonationalism, not because all Israelis are Jewish or all Palestinians are Muslim—they aren't—but because the conflict is often represented as a religious one. We'll come back to discuss both of these aspects of her work in the context of poststructuralism, but first let's consider a religious studies scholar who's sought to draw out the rich undercurrent of religious themes in Foucault's own work. This marks a particularly important intervention, because despite the prominence of Foucault's ideas in queer studies and transgender studies and the marked presence of religion threading itself throughout Foucault's writing, queer and transgender studies scholars rarely even mention religion, much less analyze it. Yet the tools to do so exist at the heart of some of the field's most formative texts.

A good place to start exploring the place of religion in Foucault's work is the practice of confession. Foucault, who focused his historical explorations largely on Europe and often specifically on France, saw the Roman Catholic practice of confession as one site for the development of European approaches to power. In the confessional, a person tells truths about themselves—their actions, but also their thoughts and desires—to a figure of authority, who responds by prescribing penance and absolving the person of their sins. As science came increasingly to be more authoritative than religion in determining the truth about people, Foucault argues, the location of the rite of confession shifted from the confessional booth to the doctor's office, be it that of a psychologist or a physician.

In a way, Christianity's traditional understanding of humanity and of the world beyond the human encodes a kind of necropower: God, as sovereign ruler, has the ability to make people die (eternally, that is, through condemning them to hell) or to let them live (again eternally, by allowing them into heaven). The psychologist and the physician, however, are purveyors of biopower, managing people's minds and bodies for optimum results and at times possessing the power to make people live or allow them to die. Some governments, including the United States, mandate mental and medical health providers to intervene, using law enforcement if necessary, when someone tries to take their own life. There are also mandates in medical ethics to preserve life, which is why advance healthcare directives are so important for people who would prefer not to have their lives preserved at all costs. Still, the authority remains with the medical personnel, and ultimately with the state through the laws that govern them, to make people live or let them die. Foucault argues that one entry into all of these procedures—the necropolitical control of God and the biopolitical control of modern medicine and psychology—is through the rite of confession. Admission into the care of a doctor or psychologist, from a Foucauldian perspective, is profoundly biopolitical: Data are gathered from the patient and from the patient's body, a file is created for management purposes, and when the provider finally arrives after lower-ranking staff have completed many of these procedures, the expected interaction is one in which the patient relates their experiences, thoughts, and actions and the provider responds by explaining the truth of the patient's body or mind and prescribing appropriate responses on the part of the patient. Confession remains, Foucault claims; its location has simply shifted.

But while confession is an obvious religious theme in Foucault's work, set right out for any reader to see, Mark Jordan argues in *Convulsing Bodies* that the sensibilities of a religious studies scholar can show us many more instances where Foucault's work is threaded through with, underlain by, or even haunted by religion. Just as scholars whose work focuses on gender become so finely attuned to its presence that they notice it where others don't, just as queer studies scholars are so experienced in studying subtle presences of sexuality that they discover it woven through all kinds of seemingly nonsexual things, so too religionists often spot themes of religion, ritual, and the sacred where others see only the secular. This is precisely what Jordan shows us in his analysis of Foucault's work.

In his early writings, Jordan argues, Foucault is interested in other philosophers' pursuit of the sacred, particularly that found in the work of Georges Bataille, Pierre Klossowski, and Maurice Blanchot. Foucault writes about power in ways that echo Christian ideas about God—all-knowing, all-powerful, inscrutable—maybe because these models still resonate with his audiences, and perhaps also with him. He writes about Christian practices and about Christian bodies, relying for instance on a famous eighteenth-century French case of possessed nuns whose exorcism rituals became a public spectacle to explore the reactions of the body to the rising compulsion to speak. He writes in "lyrical" ways, Jordan argues, that remind one of liturgy. He returns repeatedly to Christian history, and sometimes gets it wrong. But,

Jordan writes, "Foucault mistaken often asks more interesting questions about Christian power than most specialists do."[9] Foucault begins writing about spirituality toward the end of his life, but not in ways that might make us read him as a religious or spiritual person. No, Foucault is pious, Jordan insists, about the speechless, convulsing bodies—often the bodies of the marginalized even as Foucault concentrates on the writings of elites—that thread their way throughout his work. Theological it's not, at least not in the strict sense, yet Jordan believes that we can learn something from the piety of Foucault.

In some ways, Jasbir Puar's writing couldn't be farther from Jordan's. She focuses on elites only when this focus helps her to disentangle the forces that marginalize, maim, and kill queer people, people of color, and colonized people. Rather than find religion everywhere, she finds the traces of power, routed through religion certainly but also through gender, sexuality, nationalism, disability, and, above all, embodiment. When she discusses voiceless, convulsing bodies it's not to consider a philosopher's fascination with them but to demand to know who silenced their voices, what caused the convulsions, and why. Both writers are focused on the creation of greater justice; both do their work to make change in the world, but they do it very differently. Nonetheless, both bring poststructuralist theory together with the study of religion. We've considered Puar's work in both *Terrorist Assemblages* and *The Right to Maim* in other parts of this book, but we haven't paid as much attention yet to how her engagement with poststructuralism allows her to trace the workings of power through and on religion. Let's turn to that topic now.

Even before publishing *Terrorist Assemblages*, Puar was writing about the symbolic figure of the "terrorist" and how it was represented in US mainstream discourse, especially after the terrorist attacks of September 11, 2001. She noticed that "terrorists" in this discourse were always male, Arab, Muslim, and—an aspect that really hadn't been thoroughly analyzed before—feminine and sexually perverse. In the days, months, and years following the attacks, for instance, numerous representations of al-Qaeda leader Osama bin Laden in US popular culture showed him bent over, suggesting in their drawings and their messages that he was inviting anal rape. Missiles used against al-Qaeda forces during the US invasions of Afghanistan and Iraq sometimes had messages written on them that likened the missile to a rapacious penis, threatening violent and explosive penetration. Many of these images represented bin Laden as feminine, clearly questioning his masculinity but also encoding a blend of racism, Islamophobia, and homophobia with an intense transmisogyny. When President Barack Obama announced that US troops had assassinated bin Laden, stories circulated that they'd found the leader inside his house, dressed in women's clothing. Puar and coauthor Amit Rai described such images as the "monster-terrorist-fag," arguing that it's important to pay attention to the inclusion of sexual perversity in Global North/Global West imaginings of the "terrorist" both because of its Orientalist roots and because of its departure from previous representations. [10]

Turning to people in the United States who were profiled as "terrorists" after 9/11, Puar points especially to Sikhs and Muslims, who bore the brunt of hate crimes and state persecution in the United States after the attacks. Curiously, she notes, the increasing persecution of Muslims and Sikhs coincided with an increase in gay rights activism, and with growing success in that activism within certain narrow parameters—all of them focused on the assimilation of cisgender, middle-class, and often white gay men and lesbians into the US mainstream through a narrative of patriotism. As we've seen, she termed this nationalist and assimilationist quest for rights *homonationalism*. Homonationalism, in the time of President George W. Bush's "War on Terror," included a commitment to that war and a willingness to decry the presumed "perversity" of terrorists and anyone associated with them; as homonationalism became increasingly adopted in certain gay and lesbian circles as the route to full inclusion in US society, Islamophobia and xenophobia traveled hand in hand with it. Muslim and Sikh communities, challenged often from all sides to "prove" their commitment to the United States against assumptions that their loyalties would automatically lie with everyone who shared their religion rather than with their fellow citizens, quickly adopted public displays of nationalism, flying US flags prominently outside mosques and gurdwaras and posting in their business and home windows the full-page flags that many newspapers printed in the days after the attacks, when stores quickly ran out of fabric ones.

So what of queer Muslims and Sikhs? Puar notes with interest that following the September 11 attacks, some Muslim and Sikh communities in the United States became more willing to engage in intersectional activism with their queer members. Like other queer folks and other Sikhs and Muslims in the United States during this time, queer Sikhs and Muslims also engaged in nationalism and homonationalism to the extent that they could. But the farther outside the apparent mainstream a person is, the more difficult it is to even have access to nationalism and homonationalism. While the United States was busy assimilating homonational queers and people willing to play by the rules of the "model minority," some queers, Puar argues, were perceived as being "too perverse to be queer"—too far outside the bounds of homonationalism and model minority status, that is, to be included in the queer rights to marriage and military service that were at the heart of gay and lesbian homonationalist activism in the years after 9/11. [11]

Similar rhetorics of perversity and danger pervade the Israeli and US governments' representations of Palestinians, as Puar demonstrates in her next book. As many have pointed out, popular discourse in Israel and even more so in the United States represents the conflict between Israel and Palestine as one between Jews and Muslims. Certainly some Muslims in the Middle East also see things this way; this is not to say that such rhetoric exists only in the United States and Israel, or only on one side of the tensions. But Puar is again especially interested in representations of racialized religious groups like Muslims as perverse. Even more, though, in *The Right to Maim* she's concerned with the ways that disability and disablement—the creation of inability—figure in representations of race, religion, and sexuality. By bringing together an analysis of transgender and disabled bodies in the United States with considerations of nationalism and rehabilitation (and which bodies are deemed capable and deserving of rehabilitation), and pairing these analyses with a careful evaluation of the use of bodily, emotional, and infrastructural debility as a strategy of war by the Israeli Defense Force, Puar offers an insightful and complex analysis of the interweaving of religion, race, and embodiment in the workings of power.[12]

Erin Runions's analysis of what she calls "theopolitics" in the United States builds on both Puar's work and the path-clearing writings of Janet Jakobsen and Ann Pellegrini, and connects us from poststructuralist theory and the study of power to the study of politics, the final topic in this chapter. As we discussed in chapter 2, in some ways Runions's book *The Babylon Complex* serves as an expansion of Jakobsen and Pellegrini's *Love the Sin*, in that Runions is also interested in how Christianity is threaded throughout the US state and what the political consequences of that fact may be.[13] A biblical scholar by training and an activist by experience, Runions pulls these two commitments together in her careful and detailed investigation of the metaphor of Babylon in contemporary US politics. Going a step beyond Jakobsen and Pellegrini's argument that the United States is not a secular state, as it claims to be (and as some conservative Christians complain it is), and building on Foucauldian models of power while refusing to relegate religion to long-gone forms of necropolitics, Runions argues that the United States is a theopolitical state. "This theopolitics," she explains, "facilitates biopolitical, market-oriented dynamics and seeks to maintain hierarchy and control in response to the proliferation of difference and the perceived potential for increased ungovernability in the new economic era." As Foucault anticipated before his death in 1984, the entwined forces of globalization and neoliberal capitalism have significantly impacted the nation-state as a form of government and have both drawn on and shifted biopower, challenging older forms of governmentality. In the United States, Runions argues, in the face of the uncertainties and anxieties caused by these developments "references to Babylon enable, manage, and occlude these contradictions; they cut across secular, religious, and political lines, revealing interdependencies of political positions, as well as the religious shaping of the entire political field."[14]

POWER AND POLITICS

This discussion of religion and politics in the US state brings us to two recent books that trace the intersections of Christianity and queerness in US politics: Heather R. White's *Reforming Sodom* and Anthony Petro's *After the Wrath of God*. These two scholars, both historians of US religions, focus on different topics and time periods but with similar goals: to complicate the standard narrative in the United States that all queer people are anti-Christian and all Christians are antiqueer. More specifically, each relates a complex history of the engagement of Christian leaders with the politics of homosexuality and, in Petro's case, of HIV and AIDS.

White begins her history with a story we've already considered at length: the entry of "homosexuals" into the Christian Bible through liberal Protestants' efforts to create a modern, scientifically informed translation. Within a few decades of this event, though, some liberal Protestant leaders were reconsidering that translation as the scientific consensus began to change and as gay men and lesbians in the homophile movement pursued activist strategies that sometimes included religious organizing. The most high-profile outcome of these changes in the mid-twentieth century was the Council on Religion and the Homosexual (CRH) founded in San Francisco in 1964 as a coalition of homophile activists and progressive Protestant leaders. The CRH worked on political and social issues such as police violence and entrapment, employment and housing discrimination, and the criminalization of same-sex sexuality. Homophile activists welcomed the engagement of Christian leaders with their cause, noting how often other successful rights movements, such as the civil rights movement, in the United States have been profoundly influenced by clergy. And although the stories we usually tell about the Gay Liberation Front and other radical gay activism of the late 1960s and early 1970s don't include religion, White demonstrates that it was there, too, in both symbolic and literal form.

"The untold story of Stonewall," White writes, "is that a movement sparked by a bar raid held most of its meetings in churches. Those spaces were available because of earlier networks developed by CRH-connected clergy who were also plugged in to ecumenical [multidenominational] programs geared toward facilitating urban outreach, young adult ministry, and community organizing."[15] The stories we tell and learn about Stonewall and the creation of the GLF as a radical break from the assimilationist past, a brand-new and unprecedented event, and a movement to which religion was irrelevant—these are all false. Not that GLFers were necessarily religious, but their movement built on previous forms of activism, emerged out of a rising tide of civil unrest among transgender and queer people in a number of countries and a number of US cities, and drew on preexisting networks of support, including religious support. Detecting religion in unexpected places, as religious studies scholars are skilled at doing, White also points out the religious structures of the GLF and of Stonewall remembrances themselves: "There are things strikingly *religionlike* about the pride commemorations, even something distinctly Christian," she writes. "They remember a Friday night act of violence with a triumphal Sunday ceremony that initiates newly transformed selves into a community of celebrants"—just like an Easter morning church service.[16] Religion is deeply intertwined with the history of queer and transgender politics, but not, White shows us, in the way many people expect. The oft-told story of Christians and gays being mortal enemies since the beginning of time is simply not true.

Petro offers a similarly nuanced analysis of the history of Christian responses to AIDS in the 1980s and the early 1990s. He argues that "religious leaders, organizations, and activists constructed AIDS as a *moral* epidemic, which has not only shaped cultural and political responses to the disease in the United States and abroad, but has helped draw the battle lines for the wider war over religion and sex."[17] As with the analyses of authors such as Jakobsen, Pellegrini, and Runions, Petro's study focuses largely on public discourse: representations and discussion of HIV and AIDS among dominant groups whose words, opinions, and initiatives had the power to impact large numbers of people. Like many scholars who study sexuality and the state, Petro also argues that sexuality and national identity were intertwined in this public discourse on AIDS, creating, he suggests, "a national sexuality"[18] that parallels in significant ways the national Christianity analyzed by Jakobsen, Pellegrini, and Runions.

Also like these scholars, and indicating his engagement with certain forms of poststructuralist theory, Petro perceives threads of religion—more specifically, of Christianity—running throughout ostensibly secular institutions and practices. Importantly, one of the key places where these threads are detectable in the context of HIV and AIDS is in the area of public health. Whether in the office of the surgeon general, among White House staffers, or in religious leaders' public advocacy for certain policies, religion, and especially dominant forms of Christianity, have been an influential force in shaping and sometimes even dictating ostensibly secular policies about science, medicine, public health, and the state.

In the final chapter of *After the Wrath of God*, Petro turns his attention from the opinions and policies of largely heterosexual religious and political leaders with regard to the work of AIDS activists; he focuses on the famous Stop the Church protest held by the AIDS Coalition to Unleash Power (ACT UP) and Women's Health Action and Mobilization (WHAM!). Held at St. Patrick's Cathedral in New York City, the December 1989 protest drew together a coalition of activists—including the brand-new New York house of the Sisters of Perpetual Indulgence—to protest the Roman Catholic Church's "public opposition to homosexuality, abortion, and safe-sex education."[19] The protest, and the individual protesters, are typically described by supporters and opponents alike as antireligious, but Petro argues that this interpretation depends on an understanding of religion as apolitical. Religion and politics, in this perspective, are like oil and water: They can be near each other but they can't actually mix, and if one or the other is too hot when you try to combine them, everything explodes. But both Petro and White, among a number of other authors we've considered in this book, have clearly shown us that religion and politics do intertwine, even if they often pretend that they don't. Furthermore, Petro argues that the Stop the Church protest wasn't just *against* policies and ethics the protesters found oppressive; it was also *for* alternatives. Stop the Church, he suggests, "was also a demonstration for an alternative ethics of sexuality, one that promoted safe sex, the right to sexual self-determination, and the political value of sexual pleasure."[20] Why should one group in this history—straight, cisgender Roman Catholics—have the right to declare their perspectives religious and ethical while that right is denied to the other groups?

Petro develops this argument even further with a thought-provoking question about the most infamous part of the protest. ACT UP and WHAM! welcomed affiliates, both individuals and groups such as the Sisters of Perpetual Indulgence, to take part in the action in their own way. In the middle of the portion of the protest that disrupted the Mass inside the cathedral, one of these affiliated protestors took a consecrated communion wafer from the altar and crumbled it onto the floor. Given the Roman Catholic doctrine of transubstantiation, which holds that consecration mystically turns the wafer into the actual body of Christ, this was a profoundly sacrilegious act. It is also often represented by both fans and opponents as a secular act, but Petro wants us to consider another interpretation. He argues that "if we stay within the Catholic vocabulary of sacrilege . . . , we might also read [the crumbling of the wafer] as a ritual of protest, . . . a devout—even Catholic—demonstration against the Church hierarchy. The young man," he remarks, "would hardly be the first in history—or even the first Catholic—to commit such an act. The visual history of ACT UP . . . suggests that Stop the Church was not only a battle between secular activists and the Catholic Church but also a struggle over competing claims to the true message of Jesus Christ."[21] So why is it rarely seen that way? In more recent work, Petro continues to explore the question of whose religious perspectives get to count as religion, and suggests that portraying nondominant perspectives as secular and even antireligious is a powerful tool that dominant groups—here, specifically high-profile, homophobic, and antifeminist Christians—use to discredit those who challenge their power.[22]

While most of the research on politics and power within queer and transgender studies in religion has so far concentrated on societies where Christianity is the dominant religion, and on the impact of dominant forms of that religion on everything from the workings of power to modes of understanding time, new research has also begun to ask such questions in other contexts. We've seen, for instance, how the intersection of Eurocentric models of modernity, anticolonial and anticorruption movements, and socially conservative perspectives on Islam have interwoven in Iran to produce a state that bans same-sex eroticism but pays for gender affirmation treatment. We've also seen how artists such as Alma López have used their work to comment on complex issues at the intersection of religion, gender, sexuality, race, and colonization. In a 2016 book entitled *Ghostly Desires*, Asian studies scholar Arnika Fuhrmann raises similar questions in the context of a predominantly Buddhist country: Thailand.[23]

Examining contemporary Thai films from both mainstream and experimental genres, Fuhrmann explores how art can both express and challenge dominant understandings of same-sex desire and gender variance. Like the authors we've discussed who analyze Christianity as a cultural force in Europe and North America, Fuhrmann considers Buddhism as a cultural force in Thailand that underlies these films. In other words, she isn't interested in Buddhist doctrine, in official Thai Buddhist teachings or questions of "what Buddhism says about queer and transgender people"—questions we've been steering away from throughout this book because of the problems with how they're framed. Instead, Fuhrmann is interested in the more everyday, what she calls "nondoctrinal," forms of Buddhism that underlie these films and provide resources for activist filmmakers. We might say that she's engaging with lived Buddhism through the films she's studying.

How do approaches to trans and queer politics change when the dominant religion is Theravada Buddhism (the oldest branch of the religion, and the predominant one in Thailand) rather than Protestant or Catholic forms of Christianity? For one thing, Fuhrmann explains, notions of reincarnation and karma come to play a role. In many cultures that understand existence through these concepts, one's current form of incarnation is the direct consequence of one's actions in previous incarnations. Aspects of one's existence that the culture considers negative, such as physical or mental disabilities or, traditionally, female embodiment, stem from negative actions in a previous lifetime. Same-sex desire and gender variance fall under this same set of explanations. Such perspectives produce an understanding of identity as inborn that, on the one hand, reinforces the idea that people can't change their gender or their sexuality (at least, not in this lifetime) and, on the other hand, marks them as having made unfortunate decisions in the past.

Ideas about reincarnation also suggest a different model of time. Unlike models of time in most forms of Christianity, Judaism, and Islam, which are linear and directed toward a timeless, eternal end-time of peace and perfection (or, in some cases and for some people, suffering and punishment), world concepts that center reincarnation often have a more cyclical or spiral view of time. If time is not understood to have an end, then the perspective is cyclical: Both individual lives and the universe as a whole cycle, slowly but continuously, through different stages of existence. If time does eventually end, then ideas of reincarnation produce a spiral model of time: It cycles repeatedly through the same phases, yet also moves ahead toward the final end point. We've already discussed the idea that models of time have profound social and cultural effects—a Christian model of time underlies Marx's very non-Christian ideas about economic progress, for instance—and Furhmann helps us to understand how such effects take shape under more cyclical concepts of time. Furthermore, another important aspect of time in Buddhism is the principle of impermanence and its corollary that desire causes suffering. Buddhist teachings stress the impermanence of all things—everything fades, dies, changes over time—and the inevitable suffering that results from attachment to things that are not permanent. In official Buddhist teachings, then, desire and the attachment that follows from it are sources of suffering to be avoided if at all possible. Yet Buddhists, just like followers of any other religion, still experience desire, attachment, longing, and loss. Fuhrmann, in her focus on lived Buddhism, describes what she calls "Buddhist melancholia" as a response to the tensions between Buddhist perspectives on impermanence and the realities of human existence. [24]

In turning to the concept of melancholia, Furhmann is drawing on the psychoanalytic tradition and on queer engagements with that tradition. In very basic terms, melancholia results from a refusal of loss: a refusal to grieve, let go, and move on and an insistence instead on holding onto the person or object lost. In the context of Buddhist understandings of desire and attachment, Fuhrmann argues, melancholia works in very specific ways; it also produces spaces for potential queer intervention. Furhmann argues that the use of film, in the context of Buddhist **temporalities** (understandings of time) and melancholia, can generate a uniquely Thai Buddhist intervention into the oppression of same-sex-attracted and gender-variant people, as well as those from other nondominant groups in Thailand, such as Muslims. Here, as in many of the contexts we've studied, art, politics, religion, and power intertwine in fascinating and provocative ways—so provocative, in fact, that one of the films Furhmann analyzes was banned in Thailand after its release.

QUEERING RELIGION/RELIGIONING QUEER

As the works we've discussed in this chapter have demonstrated, questions of politics and power offer especially generative opportunities for bringing together queer studies, transgender studies, and religious studies in ways that transform each of these fields at their intersections. Among the questions that have already arisen is why intersectional analyses don't typically include religion but instead ignore it as though it's not an axis of power but only a source—or as though, like some observers of the Stop the Church protest seemed to think, religion and politics are like oil and water instead of like water and wine.

Some of the studies we've covered in this chapter, especially the analyses that take up questions of politics as well as power, encourage us to ask whether there's a "compulsory Christianity," akin to the concept of compulsory heterosexuality, in Christian-based cultures like the United States. This question also returns us to the suspicion of the idea of secularism that has been an undercurrent in the last few chapters. If religion is central to the state, perhaps even more so in states that publicly deny its influence, then is the religious-secular divide as real as many of us think it is? *Are* there spaces, processes, governments, cultures, that are truly secular? What might they look like?

If a key concept of queer and transgender studies like compulsory heterosexuality has a religious corollary that might offer insights both to religious studies and to gender and sexuality studies, might there be other concepts for which this is true? Several of the authors discussed in this chapter, particularly in their more recent works, have engaged with the idea of affect, or feelings, as an important area of study, but in general religious studies hasn't yet taken up affect theory very much. Might the field benefit from building bridges to the work of affect theorists in queer and transgender studies?

What about temporality? World concepts—one of the key topics of religious studies whether or not they're explicitly religious—commonly include understandings of how time works. For instance, we've seen that Marx, despite his deeply rooted opposition to religion, understood time in a very Christian way as a linear process leading to an end point. Some queer studies scholars have focused their work at least in part on particular temporalities that are driven by heteronormativity, homonormativity, and homonationalism, and that also buttress the normative status of these forces. One that's gained quite a bit of attention is often termed *reproductive futurism*. This is a vision of the future—and, more than that, a focus on the future rather than the present—that centers on the expectation of biological reproduction. Reproductive futurism is a model of time that presumes that people will have children, and that having children is a central goal if not an imperative for a successful society. This temporality is marked by an intensive focus on protecting children, on encouraging and enabling biological reproduction even among those with same-sex partners, and on metaphors of generations and inheritance. Put differently, reproductive futurism is a form of biopolitics. But given that reproductive futurism has been predominant in the United States, we might ask whether it too is a Christian temporality. Does this form of futurism resonate with particular stories that Christianity tells about time? On the other hand, some queer theorists, especially those who were most heavily impacted by the height of the AIDS crisis, suggest that the wide-spread deaths from the disease created a uniquely queer temporality that rejected futurism because of the likelihood that death was just around the corner. Doesn't that idea sound a little like the perspective of apocalyptic branches of Protestantism, whose members believe that the final battle between good and evil that will usher in the eternal kingdom of God is just around the corner? Is apocalyptic temporality queer? If not, why not?

There are at least two more areas in which religious studies, queer studies, and transgender studies can inform one another when it comes to politics and power. One has to do with the ongoing resistance to what's commonly called *normativity* in religious studies. As we saw in the introduction, resistance to confessional perspectives on religion and a commitment to *Verstehen*—empathetically understanding people's religious lives and experiences even if we don't share them or if we find them repugnant—have been the expectation in the historical-descriptive-analytical side of religious studies for quite some time. Tied to this expectation, though, is the concept of normative values. These are values that claim that certain actions, goals, or outcomes are morally desirable while others aren't. Advocating for social justice is normative: antiracism is normative; anticolonialism is normative; feminism is normative. Feminist, queer, and transgender studies accept normative approaches to their fields as a matter of course, while some religious studies scholars continue to treat feminist advocacy, for instance, as though it's a form of religious reflection. Underlying this resistance to normativity, it seems, is a lingering positivism, or reliance on demonstrable and provable facts to determine the truth, as though religious studies is still seeking to make itself credible as an academic field, a "science of religion" or, as it was called in German in its early years, *Religionswissenschaft*. Can queer and transgender studies help religious studies to separate claims about the nature of the world beyond the human from claims about the immorality of sexism, transphobia, homophobia, and the like? Can it help religious studies to resolve its resistance to normative claims?

All three of the fields that feed into queer and transgender studies in religion are profoundly uncomfortable with theological advocacy, yet some scholars have objected that drawing a sharp line between confessional and nonconfessional scholarship marginalizes scholars of color. Currently in these three fields, claims to the existence of beings beyond the human, whether as ghosts, spirits, deities, "energies," or something else, are uneasily dismissed. A few nonconfessional religious studies scholars, though, most notably Robert Orsi and Amy Hollywood, have been pressing on that issue with explorations of what it might mean to simply accept that entities beyond the human exist, even if only for those whose religion we're studying. Anthropologist Lucinda Ramberg, who worked with Hindu women who were dedicated to the goddess Yellamma, went so far as to affirm that Yellamma exists, because she exists for the communities Ramberg works with. In queer and transgender studies we're more than willing to accept an individual's understanding of their own gender or desire, and their explanation for it. Are we equally prepared to engage in the same sort of acceptance with regard to the existence of the world (or worlds) beyond the human? Can a deity be real in the same way that lesbian identity, or being a transgender woman or a *bissu*, is real?

Lauren Berlant and Michael Warner conclude their landmark article "Sex in Public" with the argument that all forms of consensual sexuality and desire in public should be protected. Part of their point, and a perspective that's deeply relevant to the question of the existence of deities and spirits in religious studies, is that we shouldn't decide what we think deserves protection and what doesn't based on our own preferences for certain activities (or, we might add, our belief in certain less tangible entities). To illustrate their point, Berlant and Warner describe a public performance of erotic vomiting that they attended once in a bar. They make clear that neither of them is into erotic vomiting themselves; in fact, they even consider leaving before the performance begins. But they stay, and despite still not being into erotic vomiting by the end, they're intrigued by many aspects of the performance. It has value despite their own lack of attachment to it. Is there a parallel here between two queer theorists defending the world-altering value of an erotic practice they themselves have no interest in performing, and a religious studies scholar defending the actual existence—not just existence in the minds of her study participants—of a goddess? What can we learn from the answers to these questions, not only within queer and transgender studies in religion but in queer studies, transgender studies, and religious studies individually?

STUDY QUESTIONS

1. What did Karl Marx mean when he said that religion is the opium of the people? Why would he say this, and why would being like opium be bad?
2. What's hegemony? What about counterhegemony? What roles did Antonio Gramsci think religion played in these social forces?
3. What challenges does Marcella Althaus-Reid issue to liberation theology, and why?
4. In psychoanalytic theory, what's the difference between the phallus and the penis? How does the phallus figure into Daniel Boyarin's analysis of Sigmund Freud's interest in the early Zionist movement?
5. What are necropower and biopower, according to Michel Foucault? How did Achille Mbembe change the way that people were thinking

about necropower? What third mode of power did Jasbir Puar add to this analysis?

6. What do Jasbir Puar and Amit Rai mean by "monster-terrorist-fag"? What does this phrase refer to? Can you think of examples?

7. What is theopolitics, according to Erin Runions? Is it something you notice in the government where you live? In what ways? If not, why do you think it isn't there (or you aren't noticing it)?

8. Both Anthony Petro and Heather White argue that the story people often tell about the relationship between queerness, transness, and religion is simplistic and inaccurate. Explain their argument. What stories about this relationship are you aware of, other than what you've learned in this book? Do you think those stories are accurate?

9. According to Arnika Furhmann, how do Buddhist temporalities differ from Christian ones, and how do these differences impact understandings of same-sex desire and gender variance?

FOR FURTHER THOUGHT

1. Try applying a materialist analysis to an issue in queer or transgender studies in religion. Pick a particular movement, event, text, or question, and consider the impact of material reality—the availability of resources, the dominant economic system, and other material factors—on your topic.

2. What is an "Indecent Theology," for Marcella Althaus-Reid? Why does she call it this? What do you think of this approach to Christianity, and why?

3. How does psychoanalytic theory help Howard Eilberg-Schwartz to explain the Jewish avoidance of representing God and Daniel Boyarin to explain the early Zionist movement? What do you think of their analyses?

4. Consider Kent Brintnall's suggestion that realistic images of the male body in pain may help to challenge male dominance. Do you find it persuasive? Why or why not? Can you think of other examples beyond the ones he analyzes? Are there other images of the male body in pain that might not fit his argument as well? Are there specific male bodies that are the focus of his argument?

5. Try out your own Foucauldian analysis of something involving religion, sexuality, and/or gender. Trace the routes of power involved in what you're studying. What kinds of power do you think are involved, or does the answer depend on the context?

6. Use Jasbir Puar's ideas to develop an analysis of public representations of the Pulse nightclub shootings in Orlando, Florida. Many of the

victims were queer people of color, some of them immigrants and some of them undocumented. The man who shot them, Omar Mateen, was an American Muslim. Examine representations of the victims and of Mateen in traditional media, social media, and elsewhere. How can queer and transgender studies in religion help us to think not just about the shootings but about their aftermath and how people talk about them?

7. Anthony Petro's work raises questions we've been examining throughout this book, about whose religion and whose religious protest get to count as "real" or "true" religion and why. Consider a situation you know of, whether a public event or a lesser-known interaction, where different people's perspectives on religion mattered differently because of their gender or sexuality. What insights might Petro's analysis offer for this case?

8. Do you think apocalyptic temporality is a queer temporality? If so, why? If not, why not?

RECOMMENDATIONS FOR FURTHER READING

Althaus-Reid, Marcella. *Indecent Theology: Theological Perversions in Sex, Gender, and Politics*. New York: Routledge, 2000.

Boyarin, Daniel. *Unheroic Conduct: The Rise of Heterosexuality and the Invention of the Jewish Man*. Berkeley: University of California Press, 1997.

Brintnall, Kent L. *Ecce Homo: The Male-Body-in-Pain as Redemptive Figure*. Chicago. University of Chicago Press, 2011.

Eilberg-Schwartz, Howard. *God's Phallus and Other Problems for Men and Monotheism*. Boston: Beacon Press, 1995.

Fuhrmann, Arnika. *Ghostly Desires: Queer Sexuality and Vernacular Buddhism in Contemporary Thai Cinema*. Durham, NC: Duke University Press, 2016.

Jordan, Mark D. *Convulsing Bodies: Religion and Resistance in Foucault*. Stanford, CA: Stanford University Press, 2015.

Maduro, Otto. *Religion and Social Conflicts*. Translated by Robert R. Barr. Eugene, OR: Wipf and Stock, 2005.

Mbembe, Achille. "Necropolitics." Translated by Libby Meintjes. *Public Culture* 15, no. 1 (2003): 11–40.

Petro, Anthony M. *After the Wrath of God: AIDS, Sexuality, and American Religion*. New York: Oxford University Press, 2015.

Petro, Anthony. "Ray Navarro's Jesus Camp, AIDS Activist Video, and the 'New Anti-Catholicism.'" *Journal of the American Academy of Religion* 85, no. 4 (2017): 920–56.

Puar, Jasbir K. *Terrorist Assemblages: Homonationalism in Queer Times*. Durham, NC: Duke University Press, 2007.

Puar, Jasbir K. *The Right to Maim: Debility, Capacity, Disability*. Durham, NC: Duke University Press, 2017.

Puar, Jasbir K., and Amit S. Rai. "Monster, Terrorist, Fag: The War on Terrorism and the Production of Docile Patriots." *Social Text* 20, no. 3 (2002): 117–48.

Runions, Erin. *The Babylon Complex: Theopolitical Fantasies of War, Sex, and Sovereignty*. New York: Fordham University Press, 2014.

White, Heather R. *Reforming Sodom: Protestants and the Rise of Gay Rights*. Chapel Hill: University of North Carolina Press, 2015.

NOTES

1. See, e.g., Gustavo Gutiérrez, *A Theology of Liberation: History, Politics, and Salvation*, rev. ed., trans. Sister Caridad Inda and John Eaglson (Maryknoll, NY: Orbis Books, 1988); *The Power of the Poor in History*, trans. Robert R. Barr (Maryknoll, NY: Orbis Books, 1983); *The God of Life*, trans. Matthew J. O'Connell (Maryknoll, NY: Orbis Books, 1991).

2. Marcella Althaus-Reid, *Indecent Theology: Theological Perversions in Sex, Gender, and Politics* (New York: Routledge, 2000).

3. See Karl Bryant, "Making Gender Identity Disorder of Childhood: Historical Lessons for Contemporary Debates," *Sexuality Research and Social Policy* 3, no. 3 (2006): 23–39.

4. Howard Eilberg-Schwartz, *God's Phallus and Other Problems for Men and Monotheism* (Boston: Beacon Press, 1995).

5. Daniel Boyarin, *Unheroic Conduct: The Rise of Heterosexuality and the Invention of the Jewish Man* (Berkeley: University of California Press, 1997), 222, 229–31.

6. Kent L. Brintnall, *Ecce Homo: The Male-Body-in-Pain as Redemptive Figure* (Chicago: University of Chicago Press, 2011), 8.

7. Ibid., 62.

8. Achille Mbembe, "Necropolitics," trans. Libby Meintjes, *Public Culture* 15, no. 1 (2003): 11–40.

9. Mark D. Jordan, *Convulsing Bodies: Religion and Resistance in Foucault* (Stanford, CA: Stanford University Press, 2015), 123.

10. Jasbir K. Puar and Amit S. Rai, "Monster, Terrorist, Fag: The War on Terrorism and the Production of Docile Patriots," *Social Text* 20, no. 3 (2002): 117–48.

11. Jasbir K. Puar, *Terrorist Assemblages: Homonationalism in Queer Times* (Durham, NC: Duke University Press, 2007).

12. Jasbir K. Puar, *The Right to Maim: Debility, Capacity, Disability* (Durham, NC: Duke University Press, 2017).

13. Erin Runions, *The Babylon Complex: Theopolitical Fantasies of War, Sex, and Sovereignty* (New York: Fordham University Press, 2014).

14. Ibid., 7.

15. Heather R. White, *Reforming Sodom: Protestants and the Rise of Gay Rights* (Chapel Hill: University of North Carolina Press, 2015), 76.

16. Ibid., 139–40 (italics in original).

17. Anthony M. Petro, *After the Wrath of God: AIDS, Sexuality, and American Religion* (New York: Oxford University Press, 2015), 2 (italics in original).

18. Ibid., 9.

19. Ibid., 137.

20. Ibid., 139.

21. Ibid., 181.

22. See, for instance, Anthony Petro, "Ray Navarro's Jesus Camp, AIDS Activist Video, and the 'New Anti-Catholicism,'" *Journal of the American Academy of Religion* 85, no. 4 (2017): 920–56.

23. Arnika Fuhrmann, *Ghostly Desires: Queer Sexuality and Vernacular Buddhism in Contemporary Thai Cinema* (Durham, NC: Duke University Press, 2016).

24. See, for instance, ibid, 2.

Conclusion

Over the course of this book, we've considered many different approaches to transgender and queer studies in religion. We've learned the key concepts that ground this area of study, concepts rooted in all three of the fields that flow together into it. Using themes as tools or pathways for our explorations, we've analyzed the interconnections between religion, gender variance, and same-sex eroticism through stories, conversations, practices, identities, communities, politics, and power. We've seen how these interconnections change over time and across geographies, but also how they reoccur in different structures and forms in many cultures and traditions. We've attended to the perspectives of religious and spiritual people, of theologians and ethicists, of religious studies scholars who practice *epoché* and believe in keeping their personal world concepts separate from their academic pursuits, of normative and antinormative scholars. We've studied some of the various ways that scholars of transgender and queer studies in religion have already offered insights to all three of their formative fields, and we've explored new questions and possible new insights that might stem from their answers.

This is the end of the book, but it isn't the end of the story. In fact, it's just the first chapter. I wrote in the preface to the book that I wanted to leave readers not with all of their questions answered but with all of their answers questioned; I hope that's the point you've come to. What you've learned in this book gives you the knowledge and the theoretical tools to ask new questions. Maybe you'll want to pursue some of the new questions raised in the preceding pages, or maybe you'll come up with your own. Maybe you already have!

Queer and transgender studies in religion is an academic pursuit, a scholarly subfield of study, but it's also capable of being accessible and useful to a much broader audience. Since this is an introductory book, it's likely that most people reading it aren't scholars and aren't planning to become scholars. If that includes you, I hope you'll think about how this book might raise new questions for you and the world(s) in which you live. Maybe you'll consider news stories a little differently, think in new ways about sacred stories, or take a friend out for a meal and ask about their experiences with religion, transness, and queerness. If you're interested in learning more, go back and check out the lists of suggestions for further reading and the lengthier list in the following pages that offers a selected bibliography of book-length works in queer and transgender studies in religion. If you learn better from films, you might also want to explore the annotated filmography that follows this conclusion. There are a lot of films on transgender and queer studies in religion, and many of them are fascinating, informative, provocative, moving, and easy to access. If this book has done nothing else, I hope it's inspired you to keep learning and to keep asking questions.

I opened the introduction with a passage that Qwo-Li Driskill quotes from Malea Powell: "Theory and scholarship are always stories about how the world works."[1] Now that you've read all the way through this book, take a minute to consider what stories the book has told—not just the actual stories of specific people, movements, or sacred texts, but the stories that make the world in the way that Bruce Lincoln also talks about. What worlds are made in this book? What worlds are marginalized? Because I use ethnographic and historical methods to study religion in contemporary and recent times, the book focuses a lot on contemporary and recent religions and on ethnography and history. Because queer and transgender studies, and by connection queer and transgender studies in religion, are deeply rooted in the United States, there's more scholarship on that country than there is on other regions of the world, so at times the book has told stories that focus very specifically on the United States. This focus also means that there's less scholarship on queer and transgender studies in Asian religions, and in the Global South/Global East. Many of those stories have yet to be told, especially in English. Queer studies in religion, and transgender studies in religion even more so, are still emerging fields even though they've gotten big enough to write an entire textbook about and still have material left over that hasn't been covered. Whose stories are still missing? How can we add them in? What stories will you tell, through writing, art, speech, interviews, film, radio, theater, or even religious reflection during a service or ritual? It will take all of our contributions to write the next chapter. Let's get started!

NOTE

1. Qwo-Li Driskill, *Asegi Stories: Cherokee Queer and Two-Spirit Memory* (Tucson: University of Arizona Press, 2016), 4.

Annotated Filmography

Some of these films contain blatantly homophobic and transphobic language; I've tried to note where such language is prominent. There have been debates in the academic community over the topic of "trigger warnings"; however, it bears remembering that nearly every course on queer and transgender studies in religion attracts some queer and transgender students who've experienced religious rejection and persecution. Because of this, in my opinion films containing openly homophobic and/or transphobic content should be used with caution, and probably with forewarning. I say this because I have had students be directly impacted, sometimes severely, by this sort of content, especially when it came without warning. Each teacher will have to decide for themselves the ethics of including course content that inspires students to leave college and seek out conversion therapy; I have seen this happen, so I am cautious with homophobic and transphobic religious content in the classroom.

All God's Children. Dir. Dee Mosbacher, Frances Reid, and Sylvia Rhue. 26 mins. Woman Vision Films, 1996.

> *An early film discussing the experiences of black lesbians and gay men in the United States with Christianity; includes interviews with black lesbian and gay pastors. Woman Vision has made the film available for free streaming on its website.*

Altered Habits. Dir. Marjorie Newman. 3 mins. Stanford University, 1981.

> *It may be old, but this video is well worth screening, perhaps as an accompaniment to the final section of chapter 3. Essentially an unauthorized music video for Tom Lehrer's "Vatican Rag," the film follows the recently formed*

Sisters of Perpetual Indulgence in San Francisco as they dance in their traditional nuns' habits at the front of a church. Featuring Sister Missionary Position, Sister Homo Fellatio, Reverend Mother the Abbess, Sister Helen Damnation, Saint Thomas Bernina, and Father Mother as the celebrant with a bagel. The film is available on YouTube; because the Sisters have produced contemporary homages to it, look for the black-and-white version to see the original.

Angels in America, by Tony Kushner. Dir. Marianne Elliott. 352 min. HBO miniseries, 2003.

This TV adaptation of Kushner's famed play addresses religion, sexuality, AIDS, power, and US history in ways that often provoke engaged classroom discussion once students manage to understand what they're seeing. Some historical contextualization may be necessary; for instance, Ethel Rosenberg is a major character, but her history may be unfamiliar to students. It's quite long for classroom use but could be used as clips or screened in two movie nights.

But I'm a Cheerleader. Dir. Jamie Babbit. 85 mins. Lion's Gate, 1999.

A comedy that isn't funny when you know the context, this once-popular film tells the story of a feminine cheerleader who gets sent to a conversion therapy camp because her parents and friends suspect she's a lesbian. The camp turns out to be, well, camp, and the heroine discovers she really is a lesbian and that's okay. Students who watch this film sometimes have a hard time understanding that most ex-gay and conversion therapy programs are neither funny nor campy, but at the same time the film offers excellent opportunities for conversations about the larger issues that underlie its premises—including the use of religious parody in political commentary.

Call Me Troy. Dir. Scott Bloom. 100 mins. Tragoidia, 2007.

This documentary is a biography of Metropolitan Community Church founder Reverend Troy Perry. Containing interviews with family, church cofounders and leaders, and Perry himself, the film is a nice way to introduce this important religious organization to a class. Context regarding the contemporary issues in MCC can be added using David Seitz's A House of Prayer for All People, *portions of Heather White's* Reforming Sodom, *or, for an older perspective, my own* Coming Out in Christianity.

Conversation (Formation Remix). B.Slade. 4 mins. Suxxess Records, 2016.

This music video by singer B.Slade (formerly Tonéx) is covered in chapter 2 and is a great start to class discussion of the tensions and conversations— often one-sided ones—within religious communities.

Fire. Dir. Deepa Mehta. 104 mins. Trial by Fire Films, 1996.

The famous first film of Deepa Mehta's Elements *series portrays a relationship between two sisters-in-law provocatively named Sita and Radha. Some discussion may be required in certain classrooms to preclude an Orientalist reading of the film, not because the film itself is Orientalist but because students may import such readings into Mehta's thoughtful critiques.*

For the Bible Tells Me So. Dir. Daniel Karslake. 95 mins. VisionQuest, 2007.

A documentary about Christian rejection and acceptance of gays and lesbians, this film promotes the message that Christian homophobia is based in pseudoscience and misinterpretations of the Bible. Many audiences find it both disturbing (because of interviews with homophobic Christian leaders) and thought provoking. This film could be interesting to discuss in class in terms of its clear interpretive message—that is, in many ways it's a primary source.

God Loves Uganda. Dir. Roger Ross Williams. 83 mins. Full Credit Productions, 2013.

This documentary focuses on the role played by US evangelical Christian missionaries in the rise of virulent homophobia in Uganda; there is clear evidence that similar dynamics are taking place elsewhere in the world as well, so the film addresses a very pressing current issue. The documentary is well made and very teachable; in addition to discussing the neocolonial dynamics of evangelical homophobia, it's also useful to encourage students to think about the power dynamics involved in an exposé about evangelical exports of homophobia being made by non-Ugandans in the United States featuring a Ugandan religious leader living in exile as a refugee in the United States—especially if the classroom is also in the Global North/Global West.

Hedwig and the Angry Inch. Dir. John Cameron Mitchell. 95 mins. New Line Cinema, 2001.

This underground classic adapted from a stage musical by the same name tells the story of Hedwig, who fell in love with a US soldier when she was a German teenage boy and had gender affirmation surgery in the hope of remaining with her GI. The surgery was badly done, the GI left, and Hedwig started a career as a rock musician only to have her songs stolen by a rising cisgender star. Provocative in a number of ways, the film doesn't focus specifically on religion but features a vignette telling a story of intersex creation that will be familiar to intellectual and religious historians of European cultures from both Plato's Symposium *and the Talmud. Worth watching in entirety if you're interested in bringing transgender and queer studies in religion to the study of art and popular culture, or you can show just the vignette to illustrate the Stories theme in chapter 1.*

Hope along the Wind: The Life of Harry Hay. Dir. Eric Slade. 57 mins. Eric Slade Films, 2002.

This documentary covers all of Harry Hay's life, including his Communist Party work, his early involvement in worker's rights activism, his founding of the Mattachine Society, and his cofounding of the Radical Faeries. It's a well-made and engaging film, but some students who are expecting an entire film on religion may not give this one top ratings simply because it covers a lot of history that isn't about the Faeries.

I Exist: Voices from the Lesbian and Gay Middle Eastern Community in the US. Dir. Peter Barbosa and Garrett Lenoir. 56 mins. Third World Newsreel, 2003.

Although it isn't specifically about religion, this documentary is useful precisely because of that. In focusing on Middle Eastern gays and lesbians rather than on a specific religion, the film is one of the few in this collection to cover more than one religious tradition. For that reason, it's also useful for dislodging the racialization of Islam among students who have little exposure to that religion or to critical race studies.

A Jihad for Love. Dir. Parvez Sharma. 81 mins. Halal Films, 2007.

This documentary explores the lives and experiences of a range of queer Muslims, from an openly lesbian couple in Istanbul, to women struggling to determine the Islamic permissibility of same-sex sexuality, to men seeking asylum following arrests and beatings in their home countries, to openly gay Cape Town imam Muhsin Hendricks. A wonderful film for showing students a range of Muslim queer experiences and perspectives, but be prepared for many students to remember only the agony of the asylum seekers, which most directly match the assumptions that many students (including some Muslims) will bring into the classroom. Some discussion following the film can help to address this tendency.

Keep Not Silent: Ortho-Dykes. Dir. Ilil Alexander. 52 mins. Women Make Movies, 2004.

This documentary follows three Israeli women who are members of Ortho-Dykes, a support group for lesbian Orthodox Jews. Each navigates her Orthodoxy and her sexuality differently, demonstrating the diversity of approaches that even profoundly socially conservative communities may have to these issues.

Like a Prayer. 28 min. DIVA TV, 1990. Available online: https://vimeo.com/178261617

Not the Madonna music video! (Though that might also be interesting to use in class.) This film, made by the activist film collective DIVA TV, documents the Stop the Church protest and shows a number of religious themes that would surprise most supporters and detractors of the protest. The newly formed NYC

DisOrder of the Sisters of Perpetual Indulgence makes a fleeting appearance, as does activist Ray Navarro dressed as Jesus and playing a news reporter *(see Anthony Petro's article, cited in chapter 6, for more detail on Navarro). A great primary source.*

The Lost Tribe. Dir. Rachel Landers. 56 mins. Women Make Movies, 2005.

This documentary follows atheist and disfellowshipped Mormon comedian Sue-Ann Post as she travels from Australia to Salt Lake City to speak at an international meeting of Affirmation, the (not officially recognized) organization of and for queer and transgender Mormons and ex-Mormons. This film works well with chapter 5, since it shows the complex negotiations people make with religions that have rejected them but that are also a part of their heritage and culture.

The New Black. Dir. Yoruba Richen. 80 mins. Frameline, 2003.

This documentary is framed around the campaign for Question 6, a marriage equality referendum in the US state of Maryland, in the black community there. The film follows community organizers as they advocate for the referendum and talk with their families of origin about that advocacy. It also covers the perspectives of black religious leaders on both sides of the issue, so there is clear homophobic rhetoric in this film in addition to positive messages from Christians about queer and transgender people.

One Nation under God. Dir. Teodoro Maniaci and Francine Rzeznik. 83 mins. First Run Features, 1993.

Although this film is very dated, it's one of the few to cover the ex-gay movement. Marketed as a documentary, it's a bit of an exposé and has a clear message about the ineffectiveness of conversion therapy and the damage caused by the ex-gay movement. This isn't necessarily a bad thing—after all, numerous psychological and psychiatric professional associations have released statements on the harm caused by reparative therapies—but it may be worthy of discussion with students (if they ever pause in laughing over ruffled baby blue tuxes from the 1980s long enough to have a conversation). And while the film has a clear message, its treatment of ex-gay participants and leaders is human and empathetic. Worth watching if you can get past the fashion statements.

Tales of the Waria. Dir. Kathy Huang. 57 mins. ITVS, 2011.

There are few films available in English so far that address transgender studies in religion; this is the most recent—to my knowledge, anyway—at the time of this writing. The waria *whom Huang interviews are generally Muslim, but they preferred to focus their conversations with her on the challenges of finding a long-term cisgender male partner. Religion is therefore an undercurrent more than a focus in this film—which itself is an interesting subject for reflec-tion with students, since many viewers assume and the film's marketing im-plies that the biggest concern for* waria *will be Islam, not affairs of the heart.*

The Transformation. Dir. Susana Aikin and Carlos Aparicio. 58 mins. PBS, 1995.

A sequel to Aikin and Aparicio's 1990 film The Salt Mines *(the two can be usefully screened together or used separately), this film opens in a road salt storage facility on Manhattan's West Side Piers, home to a small community of Latinx transgender women, many of whom are first- or second-generation immigrants. A local church group, inspired by their pastor's understanding that "homosexuals" (how he understands trans women—here's the invert model again) have a special place in heaven, reaches out to the women and eventually builds a ministry in Texas to help them get off the street, at the price of both their gender and their sexuality. This sobering, moving, and profound-ly disturbing film raises provocative questions about transphobia, classism, and racism in community HIV/AIDS services; about immigrant rights; and about the role of Christianity in these oppressive systems. The film could be usefully paired with readings from Anthony Petro's* After the Wrath of God, *Lynne Gerber's* Seeking the Straight and Narrow, *or Tanya Erzen's* Straight to Jesus, *among others.*

Trembling before G-d. Dir. Sandi Simcha DuBowski. 94 mins. Cinephil, 2001.

A well-known film that covers the lives of a number of gay and lesbian Ortho-dox Jews in Israel and the United States. DuBowski took the film on the road, gaining permission to bring televisions into the most strictly observant com-munities to screen it, in an effort to create greater openness in Orthodox communities to their gay and lesbian members. The film Trembling on the Road *documents this effort, and can be usefully paired with* Trembling before G-d, *perhaps especially for chapters 2 or 5.*

Treyf. Dir. Alisa Lebow and Cynthia Madansky. 54 mins. Women Make Movies, 1998.

While the other two documentaries about Jewish gays and lesbians in this list focus on the Orthodox community, this somewhat more experimental film fol-lows the filmmakers—two secular Jews who met at a Passover Seder—as they explore their Jewish roots and their experience of being deemed treyf *(the opposite of kosher) by their own tradition. Engaging, provocative, and light-hearted, it's also useful for showing students that queer people sometimes come closer to religion rather than flee from it.*

Two Spirits. Dir. Lydia Nibley. 65 mins. Say Yes Quickly Productions, 2009.

This film traces the life and the murder of Fred "F.C." Martinez, a nádleehí *Navajo youth who was killed in a hate crime in 2001. Through interviews with his family and friends, the film builds a narrative of a young person who had struggled at times with self-acceptance but who was beginning to blossom. Though the film presents homophobia as the key issue in the hate crime, F.C.'s murderer was white and it's useful to raise intersectional questions with students in discussing the film (including why the murderer was focused on sexuality and not gender). Another resource the film offers is a series of interviews with Two-Spirit people, through which the director resists the typical structure of a memorial film where the only queer and trans people are dead and the only people speaking to the camera are straight and cis.*

Additional Films and Videos

The following is a list of additional films and videos used by various scholars who teach queer and transgender studies in religion. The list was collected in 2018 by Erin Runions, with whose permission I gratefully reproduce it here. Thanks to Kent Brintnall, Michael Campos, Elizabeth Castelli, Rhiannon Graybill, Jacqueline Hidalgo, Teresa Hornsby, Lynn Huber, Janet R. Jakobsen, Joseph A. Marchal, Ann Pellegrini, Anthony Petro, David K. Seitz, Max Strassfeld, Alexis Waller, and Heather Rachelle White for their contributions!

Benedetta. Dir. Paul Verhoeven. Expected 2020.

black enuf*. Dir. Carrie Hawks. 23 mins. 2017.

BPM (Beats per Minute). Dir. Robin Campillo. 143 mins. France 3 Cinéma, 2017.

Cutting Edge: The Virgin Daughters. Dir. Jane Treays. 48 mins. Granada Television, 2008.

Daughters of the Dust. Dir. Julie Dash. 112 mins. WMG Film, 1991.

Deepsouth. Dir. Lisa Biagiotti. 72 mins. 2014.

The Eyes of Tammy Faye. Dir. Fenton Bailey and Randy Barbato. 79 mins. Lions Gate, 2000.

Eyes Wide Open. Dir. Haim Tabakman. 91 mins. Pimpa Film Productions, 2009.

Frisbee: The Life and Death of a Hippie Preacher. Dir. David Di Sabatino. 105 mins. Jester Media, 2005.

Gender Revolution: A Journey with Katie Couric. 93 mins. National Geographic, 2017.

The Gospel of Healing, Vol. 1: Black Churches Respond to HIV/AIDS. Dir. Paul V. Grant. 43 mins. Ascender Communications, 2012.

Hell House. Dir. George Ratliff. 85 mins. GreenHouse Pictures, 2001.

I Know What You Want. Music video by Busta Rhymes. 5 mins. 2003.

Indecent (Paula Vogel play). 29 mins. Broadway HD, 2017.

Jesus Christ Superstar. Dir. Norman Jewison. 106 mins. Universal Pictures, 1973.

Kiki and Herb's Live at the Knitting Factory, last 1/3 of film. Dir. Gerard Schmidt. 96 mins. Kino Lorber, 2007.

The Life of Saint Death. 9 mins. AJ+ Docs, 2014.

Lenny Kravitz Tribute to Prince (Rock & Roll Hall of Fame Induction Ceremony). 7 mins. 2017.

Like a Virgin. Music videos by Madonna (4 mins; 1984) and Sister Cristina (5 mins; 2014).

Lilies. Dir. John Greyson. 95 mins. Triptych Media, 1996.

Prince's Super Bowl XLI Halftime Show. 2007.

Saturday Church. Dir. Damon Cardasis. 82 mins. Spring Pictures, 2017.

Sex Education: Last Week Tonight with John Oliver. 21 mins. HBO, 2015.

Silence. Dir. Martin Scorsese. 161 mins. SharpSword Films, 2016

Sister Act. Dir. Emile Ardolino. 100 mins. Touchstone Pictures, 1992.

Stop the Church. Dir. Robert Hilferty. 24 mins. Frameline, 1991.

The Ten Commandments. Dir. Cecil B. DeMille. 220 mins. Motion Picture Associates, 1956.

Tongues Untied: Giving a Voice to Black Gay Men. Dir. Marlon Riggs. 55 mins. California Newsreel, 1989.

Worshipping at the Altar of Saint Death. 14 mins. Journeyman Pictures, 2009.

A Partial List of Books in Queer and Transgender Studies in Religion

This list is incomplete by necessity, because the field of queer studies in religion has grown exponentially since the turn of the millennium, and transgender studies in religion is also starting to take off. However, listed below is a representative sample of books in English that contain significant content relevant to queer and transgender studies in religion. You can find additional books and articles by using search terms such as "religion and transgender," "religion and queer," and "religion and LGBT." Also try replacing the word "religion" with the word "spirituality" in each of these pairings, and using older terms like "homosexual" or "homosexuality" and "transsexual." Look carefully at the sources you find, especially using the older search terms; some may not be from gay, lesbian, LGBT, queer, or transgender studies in religion but instead may be homophobic or transphobic commentaries.

Afzal, Ahmed. *Lone Star Muslims: Transnational Lives and the South Asian Experience in Texas.* New York: New York University Press, 2015.

Ali, Kecia. *Sexual Ethics and Islam: Feminist Reflections on Qur'an, Hadith, and Jurisprudence.* Oxford: Oneworld, 2006.

Alpert, Rebecca. *Like Bread on the Seder Plate: Jewish Lesbians and the Transformation of Tradition.* New York: Columbia University Press, 1997.

Alpert, Rebecca T., Sue Levi Elwell, and Shirley Idelson, eds. *Lesbian Rabbis: The First Generation.* New Brunswick, NJ: Rutgers University Press, 2001.

Althaus-Reid, Marcella. *Indecent Theology: Theological Perversions in Sex, Gender, and Politics*. New York: Routledge, 2000.

———. *The Queer God*. New York: Routledge, 2003.

Armour, Ellen T., and Susan M. St. Ville, eds. *Bodily Citations: Religion and Judith Butler*. New York: Columbia University Press, 2006.

Babayan, Kathryn, and Afsaneh Najmabadi, eds. *Islamicate Sexualities: Translations across Temporal Geographies of Desire*. Cambridge, MA: Harvard University Press, 2008.

Bacigalupo, Ana Mariella. *Shamans of the Foye Tree: Gender, Power, and Healing among Chilean Mapuche*. Austin: University of Texas Press, 2007.

Belser, Julia Watts. *Rabbinic Tales of Destruction: Gender, Sex, and Disability in the Ruins of Jerusalem*. New York: Oxford University Press, 2018.

Best, Wallace D. *Langston's Salvation: American Religion and the Bard of Harlem*. New York: New York University Press, 2017.

Boellstorff, Tom. *A Coincidence of Desires: Anthropology, Queer Studies, Indonesia*. Durham, NC: Duke University Press, 2007.

Boisvert, Donald L. *Out on Holy Ground: Meditations on Gay Men's Spirituality*. Cleveland, OH: Pilgrim Press, 2000.

Boisvert, Donald L., and Carly Daniel-Hughes, eds. *The Bloomsbury Reader in Religion, Sexuality, and Gender*. New York: Bloomsbury, 2017.

Boisvert, Donald L., and Jay Emerson Johnson, eds. *Queer Religion*, Vols. 1–2. Santa Barbara, CA: Praeger, 2012.

Boswell, John. *Christianity, Social Tolerance, and Homosexuality*. Chicago: Chicago University Press, 1980.

———. *Same-Sex Unions in Premodern Europe*. New York: Vintage, 1994.

Boyarin, Daniel. *Unheroic Conduct: The Rise of Heterosexuality and the Invention of the Jewish Man*. Berkeley: University of California Press, 1997.

Boyarin, Daniel, Daniel Iskovitz, and Ann Pellegrini, eds. *Queer Theory and the Jewish Question*. New York: Columbia University Press, 2003.

Brintnall, Kent L. *Ecce Homo: The Male-Body-in-Pain as Redemptive Figure*. Chicago: University of Chicago Press, 2011.

Brintnall, Kent L., Joseph A. Marchal, and Stephen D. Moore, eds. *Sexual Disorientations: Queer Temporalities, Affects, Theologies*. New York: Fordham University Press, 2017.

Brooten, Bernadette J. *Love between Women: Early Christian Responses to Female Homoeroticism*. Chicago: University of Chicago Press, 1996.

Brown, Judith. *Immodest Acts: The Life of a Lesbian Nun in Renaissance Italy*. New York: Oxford, 1986.

Browne, Kath, Sally R. Munt, and Andrew K. T. Yip. *Queer Spiritual Spaces: Sexuality and Sacred Places*. Burlington, VT: Ashgate, 2010.

Burrus, Virginia. *Saving Shame: Martyrs, Saints, and Other Abject Subjects*. Philadelphia: University of Pennsylvania Press, 2008.

———. *The Sex Lives of Saints: An Erotics of Ancient Hagiography*. Philadelphia: University of Pennsylvania Press, 2004.

Cabezón, José Ignacio. *Buddhism, Sexuality, and Gender*. Albany: State University of New York Press, 1992.

———. *Sexuality in Classical South Asian Buddhism*. Somerville, MA: Wisdom Publications, 2017.

Carbajál, Alberto Fernandez. *Queer Muslim Diasporas in Contemporary Literature and Film*. Manchester, UK: Manchester University Press, 2019.

Cartier, Marie. *Baby, You Are My Religion: Women, Gay Bars, and Theology before Stonewall*. New York: Routledge, 2013.

Cheng, Patrick S. *From Sin to Amazing Grace: Discovering the Queer Christ*. New York: Seabury Books, 2012.

———. *Radical Love: An Introduction to Queer Theology*. New York: Seabury Books, 2011.

———. *Rainbow Theology: Bridging Race, Sexuality, and Spirit*. New York: Seabury Books, 2013.

Cobb, Michael. *God Hates Fags: The Rhetoric of Religious Violence*. New York: New York University Press, 2006.

Comstock, Gary David. *Unrepentant, Self-Affirming, Practicing: Lesbian/Bisexual/Gay People within Organized Religion*. New York: Continuum, 1996.

———. *A Whosoever Church: Welcoming Lesbians and Gay Men into African American Congregations*. Louisville: Westminster John Knox Press, 2001.

Comstock, Gary David, and Susan E. Henking, eds. *Que(e)rying Religion: A Critical Anthology*. New York: Continuum, 1997.

Conner, Randy P., with David Hatfield Sparks. *Queering Creole Spiritual Traditions: Lesbian, Gay, Bisexual, and Transgender Participation in African-Inspired Traditions in the Americas*. New York: Harrington Park Press, 2004.

Crawley, Ashon T. *Blackpentecostal Breath: The Aesthetics of Possibility*. New York: Fordham University Press, 2017.

Cruz, Daniel Shank. *Queering Mennonite Literature: Archives, Activism, and the Search for Community*. University Park: Pennsylvania State University Press, 2019.

Davies, Sharyn Graham. *Gender Diversity in Indonesia: Sexuality, Islam, and Queer Selves.* New York: Routledge, 2010.

De Alba, Alicia Gaspar, and Alma López, eds. *Our Lady of Controversy: Alma López's Irreverent Apparition.* Austin: University of Texas Press, 2011.

DeBlosi, Nikki Lyn. *Different from all Other Nights: A Queer Passover Haggadah.* New York: Bronfman Center for Jewish Student Life at NYU, 2013. Available at https://www.keshetonline.org.

Douglas, Kelly Brown. *Sexuality and the Black Church: A Womanist Perspective.* Maryknoll, NY: Orbis Books, 1999.

Driskill, Qwo-Li. *Asegi Stories: Cherokee Queer and Two-Spirit Memory.* Tucson: University of Arizona Press, 2016.

Dzmura, Noach, ed. *Balancing on the Mechitza: Transgender in Jewish Community.* Berkeley, CA: North Atlantic Books, 2010.

Eilberg-Schwartz, Howard. *God's Phallus and Other Problems for Men and Monotheism.* Boston: Beacon Press, 1995.

Ellison, Marvin M., and Kelly Brown Douglas, eds. *Sexuality and the Sacred: Sources for Theological Reflection.* Louisville, KY: Westminster John Knox, [2004] 2010.

Erzen, Tanya. *Straight to Jesus: Sexual and Christian Conversions in the Ex-Gay Movement.* Berkeley: University of California Press, 2006.

Faure, Bernard. *The Red Thread: Buddhist Approaches to Sexuality.* Princeton, NJ: Princeton University Press, 1998.

Fetner, Tina. *How the Religious Right Shaped Lesbian and Gay Activism.* Minneapolis: University of Minnesota Press, 2008.

Fielder, Bronwyn, and Douglas Ezzy. *Lesbian, Gay, Bisexual, and Transgender Christians: Queer Christians, Authentic Selves.* New York: Bloomsbury, 2018.

Frank, Gillian, Bethany Moreton, and Heather R. White, eds. *Devotions and Desires: Histories of Sexuality and Religion in the Twentieth-Century United States.* Chapel Hill: University of North Carolina Press, 2018.

Fuhrmann, Arnika. *Ghostly Desires: Queer Sexuality and Vernacular Buddhism in Contemporary Thai Cinema.* Durham, NC: Duke University Press, 2016.

Gaudio, Rudolf Pell. *Allah Made Us: Sexual Outlaws in an Islamic African City.* Malden, MA: Wiley-Blackwell, 2009.

Gill, Sean, ed. *The Lesbian and Gay Christian Movement: Campaigning for Justice, Truth and Love.* New York: Cassell, 1998.

Gilley, Brian Joseph. *Becoming Two-Spirit: Gay Identity and Social Acceptance in Indian Country.* Lincoln: University of Nebraska Press, 2006.

Goh, Joseph N. *Living Out Sexuality and Faith: Body Admissions of Malaysian Gay and Bisexual Men.* New York: Routledge, 2018.

Goss, Robert E. *Queering Christ: Beyond Jesus Acted Up.* Cleveland, OH: Pilgrim Press, 2002.

Griffin, Horace L. *Their Own Receive Them Not: African American Lesbians and Gays in Black Churches.* Cleveland, OH: Pilgrim Press, 2006.

Guest, Deryn, Robert E. Goss, Mona West, and Thomas Bohache, eds. *The Queer Bible Commentary.* London: SCM Press, 2006.

Habib, Samar. *Arabo-Islamic Texts on Female Homosexuality, 850–1780 A.D.* Youngstown, NY: Teneo Press, 2009.

Habib, Samar, ed. *Islam and Homosexuality*, Vols. 1–2. Santa Barbara, CA: ABCCLIO, 2010.

Hay, Harry. *Radically Gay: Gay Liberation in the Words of Its Founder*, ed. Will Roscoe. Boston: Beacon Press, 1996.

Herman, Didi. *The Antigay Agenda: Orthodox Vision and the Christian Right.* Chicago: University of Chicago Press, 1997.

Hunt, Stephen. *Contemporary Christianity and LGBT Sexualities.* Burlington, VT: Ashgate, 2009.

Isherwood, Lisa, and Mark D. Jordan, eds. *Dancing Theology in Fetish Boots: Essays in Honor of Marcella Althaus-Reid.* London: SCM Press, 2010.

Jacobs, Sue-Ellen, Wesley Thomas, and Sabine Lang, eds. *Two-Spirit People: Native American Gender Identity, Sexuality, and Spirituality.* Urbana: University of Illinois Press, 1997.

Jakobsen, Janet R., and Ann Pellegrini. *Love the Sin: Sexual Regulation and the Limits of Religious Tolerance.* Boston: Beacon Press, 2004.

Jordan, Mark D. *Blessing Same-Sex Unions: The Perils of Queer Romance and the Confusions of Christian Marriage.* Chicago: University of California Press, 2005.

———. *Convulsing Bodies: Religion and Resistance in Foucault.* Stanford, CA: Stanford University Press, 2015.

———. *The Ethics of Sex.* Malden, MA: Wiley-Blackwell, 2002.

———. *The Invention of Sodomy in Christian Theology.* Chicago: University of Chicago Press, 1997.

———. *Recruiting Young Love: How Christians Talk about Homosexuality.* Chicago: University of Chicago Press, 2011.

———. *The Silence of Sodom: Homosexuality in Modern Catholicism.* Chicago: University of Chicago Press, 2000.

———. *Telling Truths in Church: Scandal, Flesh, and Christian Speech.* Boston: Beacon Press, 2004.

Kolodny, Deborah R., ed. *Blessed Bi Spirit: Bisexual People of Faith.* New York: Continuum, 2000.

Krutzsch, Brett. *Dying to Be Normal: Gay Martyrs and the Transformation of American Sexual Politics*. New York: Oxford University Press, 2019.

Kugle, Scott Siraj al-Haqq. *Homosexuality in Islam: Critical Reflection on Gay, Lesbian, and Transgender Muslims*. London: Oneworld, 2010.

————. *Living Out Islam: Voices of Gay, Lesbian, and Transgender Muslims*. New York: New York University Press, 2014.

Ladin, Joy. *Through the Door of Life: A Jewish Journey between Genders*. Madison: University of Wisconsin Press, 2013.

Leong, Pamela. *Religion, Flesh, and Blood: The Convergence of HIV/AIDS, Black Sexual Expression, and Therapeutic Religion*. Lanham, MD: Lexington Books, 2015.

Lewin, Ellen. *Filled with the Spirit: Sexuality, Gender, and Radical Inclusivity in a Black Pentecostal Church Coalition*. Chicago: University of Chicago Press, 2018.

Leyland, Winston, ed. *Queer Dharma: Voices of Gay Buddhists*, Vol 1. San Francisco: Gay Sunshine Press, 1998.

————. *Queer Dharma: Voices of Gay Buddhists*, Vol 2. San Francisco: Gay Sunshine Press, 2000.

Linneman, Thomas J. *Weathering Change: Gays and Lesbians, Christian Conservatives, and Everyday Hostilities*. New York: New York University Press, 2003.

Loughlin, Gerard. *Alien Sex: The Body and Desire in Cinema and Theology*. Malden, MA: Blackwell, 2004.

Loughlin, Gerard, ed. *Queer Theology: Rethinking the Western Body*. Malden, MA: Blackwell, 2007.

Manalansan, Martin F. IV. *Global Divas: Filipino Gay Men in the Diaspora*. Durham, NC: Duke University Press, 2003.

Martin, Dale B. *Sex and the Single Savior: Gender and Sexuality in Biblical Interpretation*. Louisville, KY: Westminster John Knox, 2006.

Melton, J. Gordon. *The Churches Speak on AIDS*. New York: Gale, 1989.
————. *The Churches Speak on Homosexuality*. New York: Gale, 1991.

Mollenkott, Virginia Ramey. *Omnigender: A Trans-Religious Approach*. Cleveland, OH: Pilgrim Press, 2001.

Mollenkott, Virginia Ramey, and Letha Scanzoni. *Is the Homosexual My Neighbor?* San Francisco: Harper and Row, 1978.

Moon, Dawne. *God, Sex, and Politics: Homosexuality and Everyday Theologies*. Chicago: University of Chicago Press, 2004.

Morgensen, Scott Lauria. *Spaces between Us: Queer Settler Colonialism and Indigenous Decolonization*. Minneapolis: University of Minnesota Press, 2011.

Murray, Stephen O., and Will Roscoe, eds. *Islamic Homosexualities: Culture, History, and Literature*. New York: New York University Press, 1997.

Najmabadi, Afsaneh. *Professing Selves: Transsexuality and Same-Sex Desire in Contemporary Iran*. Durham, NC: Duke University Press, 2014.

Nanda, Serena. *Neither Man nor Woman: The Hijras of India*. Belmont, CA: Wadsworth, 1990.

Nugent, Robert, ed. *A Challenge to Love: Gay and Lesbian Catholics in the Church*. New York: Crossroad, 1983.

Nynäs, Peter, and Andrew Kam-Tuck Yip, eds. *Religion, Gender, and Sexuality in Everyday Life*. Burlington, VT: Ashgate, 2012.

Pattanaik, Devdutt. *The Man Who Was a Woman and Other Queer Tales from Hindu Lore*. New York: Harrington Park Press, 2002.

Petro, Anthony M. *After the Wrath of God: AIDS, Sexuality, and American Religion*. New York: Oxford University Press, 2015.

Peumans, Wim. *Queer Muslims in Europe: Sexuality, Religion, and Migration in Belgium*. New York: I. B. Tauris, 2018.

Pritchard, Elizabeth, and Kate M. Ott, eds. *Special Issue: Transing and Queering Feminist Studies and Practices of Religion*. *Journal of Feminist Studies in Religion* 34, no. 1 (2018).

Puar, Jasbir K. *The Right to Maim: Debility, Capacity, Disability*. Durham, NC: Duke University Press, 2017.

———. *Terrorist Assemblages: Homonationalism in Queer Times*. Durham, NC: Duke University Press, 2007.

Rambuss, Richard. *Closet Devotions*. Durham, NC: Duke University Press, 1998.

Reddy, Gayatri. *With Respect to Sex: Negotiating Hijra Identity in South India*. Chicago: University of Chicago Press, 2005.

Roden, Frederick, ed. *Jewish/Christian/Queer: Crossroads and Identities*. Burlington, VT: Ashgate, 2009.

Rudy, Kathy. *Sex and the Church: Gender, Homosexuality, and the Transformation of Christian Ethics*. Boston: Beacon Press, 1997.

Runions, Erin. *The Babylon Complex: Theopolitical Fantasies of War, Sex, and Sovereignty*. New York: Fordham University Press, 2014.

Sanchez, Melissa E. *Queer Faith: Reading Promiscuity and Race in the Secular Love Tradition*. New York: New York University Press, 2019.

Seitz, David K. *A House of Prayer for All People: Contesting Citizenship in a Queer Church*. Minneapolis: University of Minnesota Press, 2017.

Shah, Shanon. *The Making of a Gay Muslim: Religion, Sexuality, and Identity in Malaysia and Britain*. New York: Palgrave MacMillan, 2018.

Shallenberger, David. *Reclaiming the Spirit: Gays and Lesbians Come to Terms with Religion*. New Brunswick, NJ: Rutgers University Press, 1998.

Sheridan, Vanessa. *Crossing Over: Liberating the Transgendered Christian*. Cleveland, OH: Pilgrim, 2001.

Shipley, Heather, ed. *Globalized Religion and Sexual Identity: Contexts, Contestations, Voices*. Leiden: Brill, 2014.

Shneer, David, and Caryn Aviv, eds. *Queer Jews*. New York: Routledge, 2002.

Shokeid, Moshe. *A Gay Synagogue in New York*. New York: Columbia University Press, 1995.

Sneed, Roger A. *Representations of Homosexuality: Black Liberation Theology and Cultural Criticism*. New York: Palgrave MacMillan, 2010.

Stone, Ken. *Practicing Safer Texts: Food, Sex, and Bible in Queer Perspective*. New York: T&T Clark, 2005.

Stone, Ken, ed. *Queer Commentary and the Hebrew Bible*. Cleveland, OH: Pilgrim Press, 2001.

Strongman, Roberto. *Queering Black Atlantic Religions: Transcorporeality in Candomblé, Santería, and Vodou*. Durham, NC: Duke University Press, 2019.

Stuart, Elizabeth. *Gay and Lesbian Theologies: Repetitions with Critical Difference*. Burlington, VT: Ashgate, 2003.

Stuart, Elizabeth, ed. *Religion Is a Queer Thing: A Guide to the Christian Faith for Lesbian, Gay, Bisexual, and Transgender People*. London: Cassell, 1997.

Swidler, Ann, ed. *Homosexuality and World Religions*. Valley Forge, PA: Trinity Press International, 1993.

Talvacchia, Kathleen T., Michael F. Pettinger, and Mark Larrimore, eds. *Queer Christianities: Lived Religion in Transgressive Forms*. New York: New York University Press, 2015.

Tanis, Justin. *Transgendered: Theology, Ministry, and Communities of Faith*. Cleveland, OH: Pilgrim Press, 2003.

Taylor, Yvette, and Ria Snowdon, eds. *Queering Religion, Religious Queers*. New York: Routledge, 2014.

Thumma, Scott, and Edward R. Gray, eds. *Gay Religion*. Walnut Creek, CA: AltaMira Press, 2005.

Tinsley, Omise'eke Natasha. *Ezili's Mirrors: Imagining Black Queer Genders*. Durham, NC: Duke University Press, 2018.

Tonstad, Linn Marie. *God and Difference: The Trinity, Sexuality, and the Transformation of Finitude*. New York: Routledge, 2016.

———. *Queer Theology: Beyond Apologetics*. Eugene, OR: Cascade Books, 2018.

Udis-Kessler, Amanda. *Queer Inclusion in the United Methodist Church*. New York: Routledge, 2008.

Vanita, Ruth, ed. *Queering India: Same-Sex Love and Eroticism in Indian Culture and Society*. New York: Routledge, 2002.

van Klinken, Adriaan. *Kenyan, Christian, Queer: Religion, LGBT Activism, and Arts of Resistance in Africa*. University Park: Pennsylvania State University Press, 2019.

White, Heather R. *Reforming Sodom: Protestants and the Rise of Gay Rights*. Chapel Hill: University of North Carolina Press, 2015.

Wilcox, Melissa M. *Coming Out in Christianity: Religion, Identity, and Community*. Bloomington: Indiana University Press, 2003.

———. *Queer Nuns: Religion, Activism, and Serious Parody*. New York: New York University Press, 2018.

———. *Queer Women and Religious Individualism*. Bloomington: Indiana University Press, 2009.

Wilson, Nancy. *Our Tribe: Queer Folks, God, Jesus, and the Bible*. San Francisco: HarperSanFrancisco, 1995.

Wolkomir, Michelle. *Be Not Deceived: The Sacred and Sexual Struggles of Gay and Ex-gay Christian Men*. New Brunswick, NJ: Rutgers University Press, 2006.

Yip, Andrew Kam-Tuck. *Gay Male Christian Couples: Life Stories*. Westport, CT: Praeger, 1997.

Yip, Andrew Kam-Tuck, and Sarah-Jane Page. *Religious and Sexual Identities: A Multifaith Exploration of Young Adults*. Burlington, VT: Ashgate, 2013.

Young, Thelathia Nikki. *Black Queer Ethics, Family, and Philosophical Imagination*. New York: Palgrave MacMillan, 2016.

Glossary

agender: An adjective describing someone who doesn't identify with gender.

aromantic/arrow: Someone who doesn't experience romantic attraction. People who identify as arrow may also be ace, or may have any number of other sexual identities.

asexual/ace: Someone who doesn't experience sexual desire.

baklâ: A traditional gender-variant role in the Philippines for feminine people assigned male at birth.

BDSM: Standing for bondage, discipline, dominance, submission, and sadomasochism (or sadism and masochism), BDSM refers to both practices and communities that engage with the connections between power and desire, pain and pleasure. Some BDSM communities are strictly same-sex oriented, but for many others desire focuses less on the physical attributes—including genitalia and other sexual characteristics—of a potential partner and more on compatibility in terms of the roles the person enjoys in BDSM play.

biopower/biopolitics: A Foucauldian term referring to the mobilization of power through state control over life.

Black Atlantic traditions: The traditions of black communities and cultures connected by the Atlantic Ocean, in particular those West African cultures from which people were taken into slavery during the transatlantic slave trade and the cultures those people formed in the Americas and the Caribbean during and after slavery.

Bori: A traditional Hausa form of communicating with the spirits through possession.

charismatic: A term describing a movement within twentieth- and twenty-first-century Christianity, and the movement's organizations and adherents. Drawing from an experience that Jesus's closest followers had after his death, as described in the book of Acts in the Christian Bible, the charismatic movement holds that the "gifts of the Holy Spirit" experienced by Jesus's early followers can still be experienced by Christians today.

cisgender: An adjective describing someone who identifies with the gender they were assigned at birth based on their perceived embodiment.

cisnormative: Based in the presumption that all people are cisgender and that being cisgender is the normal way to be. *See* **cisgender**.

compulsory heterosexuality: The cultural assumption that all people are naturally heterosexual; a cultural insistence that all people live out that "natural" heterosexuality.

constructivist theory: A body of theory exploring the social construction of various aspects of human experience, such as gender, sexuality, race, and religion. *See also* **social construction**.

counterpublic: A public that resists the dominant public's norms and values.

cultural genocide: The process of killing off the culture of a group of people.

diaspora: A situation in which people from a shared homeland are scattered to live in distant places.

discourse: Verbal, written, or symbolic communication about a topic.

doctrine: Official religious teachings.

epistemology: The study of, and theories about, knowledge.

epoché: A term proposed by Dutch scholar Gerardus van der Leeuw, meaning a suspension of our own beliefs (*epoché* means "suspension" in Greek) when we study those of someone else.

essentialism, essentialist: An understanding of certain characteristics, typically those of categories such as gender, race, class, or sexuality, as permanent, innate parts of a person's essence, either through biology (chromosomes, hormones, etc.) or through irreversible psychological changes brought about in infancy and early childhood. The former theory is called biological essentialism and the latter is psychological essentialism.

fatwa: A formal legal opinion in Islamic law.

franchise colonialism: Colonizing a group of people primarily for the purposes of resource extraction and importation to the colonizing country (whether the "resources" in question be minerals or human bodies, as with the transatlantic slave trade).

gender: Identity and/or expression as woman, man, genderqueer, feminine, masculine, nonbinary, transgender, and the like.

genderqueer: An adjective describing someone who combines aspects of multiple genders.

governmentality: A Foucauldian idea referring to the processes for creating a docile and highly governable population.

hajj: The pilgrimage to Mecca that all Muslims are encouraged to undertake at least once in their lives, if their life circumstances allow.

hegemony: A term developed by Italian Marxist theorist Antonio Gramsci to describe a form of power so complete that it appears natural and normal even to those who suffer under it.

hermeneutic of suspicion: An interpretive strategy that refuses to accept the narrative at face value and instead asks "suspicious" questions about how the narrative came to be and why it's influential.

hermit: A person who lives alone in an isolated place by choice, often for religious reasons.

heteronormativity: The cultural assumption that only particular forms of different-sex desire and eroticism are normal, natural, and beneficial to society.

hijra: A person assigned male at birth who dedicates herself to a goddess, lives as a woman, is often sexually active with men, and typically undergoes at least certain aspects of medical transition such as the removal of male genitalia.

homonormativity: The application of heteronormative standards to gays and lesbians.

homonationalism: Nationalist, patriotic homonormativity.

homophile movement: Mid-twentieth-century gay rights movements and organizations, especially in the United States. These groups named themselves "homophile" in an effort to move heterosexuals' focus away from same-sex *sex* and toward same-sex *love* (*philos* in Greek). The members of homophile groups were often middle-class and white; some, such as the Daughters of Bilitis, required their members to follow cisnormative gender codes at meetings.

homosociality: Socializing primarily with members of the same sex.

identity compartmentalization: The practice of keeping identities separate from one another.

identity politics: A narrow approach to justice based solely on identity, wherein all people who share a particular identity are considered to have the same or at least very similar experiences.

imam: A Muslim religious leader.

intentional communities: Shared, residential, and typically long-term communities that people enter into voluntarily. Many, but not all, intentional communities are religious.

intersectionality: A methodological approach that stresses the inextricability of various analyses of power, such as race, class, gender, sexuality, and ability.

intersex: An adjective describing people whose bodies express aspects of both femaleness and maleness through chromosomes, hormones, sexual organs, and/or secondary sexual characteristics. An older term for intersex people, which is now considered by many to be offensive, is *hermaphrodite*.

inversion model: A system for understanding same-sex desire and gender variance that was invented by nineteenth-century sexologists, mostly in Europe. This model retains compulsory heterosexuality by interpreting same-sex desire as what the sexologists termed *gender inversion*; that is, a man attracted to other men is "really" a woman in a man's body, and vice versa for a woman attracted to other women.

Latinx: A gender-inclusive way of describing people of Latin American heritage.

lay: Not religiously ordained.

liturgy: The script for a ritual, as written down or as enacted.

lwa: A deity or spirit in Haitian Vodou.

madrassah: A Muslim religious school.

materialist analysis: An analytical approach associated with Karl Marx that focuses on the impact of material conditions such as wealth, poverty, and economic systems.

monotheism: The principle that only one deity exists in the world.

necropower/necropolitics: A Foucauldian term referring to the mobilization of power through state control over death, expanded upon in recent years by Achille Mbembe.

nonbinary: An adjective describing someone whose identity resists the binary of "man" versus "woman" or "feminine" versus "masculine."

Orientalism: Racist assumptions about people from the Middle East, North Africa, and Asia, sometimes also applied to Native American and First Nations people. As described by the path-clearing scholar Edward Said, Orientalist perspectives often include the idea that a culture was once great but has since fallen into ruin, that men are either lazy and feminine or violent and tyrannical, and that women are sensuous and alluring. Some Orientalist fantasies also imagine religions (generally with the exception of Islam) as mystical and spiritually advanced.

pansexual: Someone who is sexually attracted to people regardless of sex or gender.

pederasty: A form of same-sex eroticism in which adult men form sexual and often amorous relationships with male adolescents.

polity: The organizational structure of a group, here specifically a religious group.

populism: A focus on everyday people.

public: As a noun, an "imagined community," in historian Benedict Anderson's phrase, of people who don't necessarily know one another or even live in the same place but imagine themselves to all share the same norms and values.

Qur'an: The sacred text revealed to the Prophet Muhammad, which forms the cornerstone of Islam.

rabbi: A Jewish religious leader.

renunciants: People who renounce worldly comforts and pleasures, usually for religious purposes.

sangha: A community of Buddhists.

settler colonialism: A form of colonization in which land is the most important resource. Because land cannot be shipped back to the colonizing country, the colonizing country sends its citizens to the land. Settler colonialism therefore often lasts for centuries.

sex: Biological, or embodied, assignment to categories such as male, female, or intersex.

SGL: Same-gender loving, a term for same-sex desire that focuses on what a person *does* rather than what that person *is* and that focuses on love rather than sex.

social construction, social construct: An aspect of human experience that is not inborn but is fundamentally shaped, even created, by society; social construction is the process of this shaping and creation. Scholars of gender and sexuality typically consider these two aspects of human experience to be socially constructed. This does not mean that there is no physiological aspect to these parts of human experience, but rather that even those physiological aspects are shaped by social norms and social structures. Religious studies scholars commonly hold that the idea of religion as a universal human phenomenon that can be compared across cultures and that perhaps has roots deep in the human psyche is also a social construct. Importantly, to say that something is a social construct is not to say that it isn't real; most social constructs have very real effects in the world and in people's everyday lives.

soteriology: Understanding of salvation, especially in a Christian context.

Talmud: A collection of commentaries on the Torah written by ancient rabbis in the early centuries of the Common Era.

teleological: Focused on the end-time.

temporalities: Understandings of time.

Torah: Jewish scriptures. The word can refer either to the first five books of the Hebrew Bible, or to its entirety.

transcorporeality: A term used by Roberto Strongman to describe a Black Atlantic understanding of the psyche.

transgender: An adjective describing someone who identifies with a different gender from the one they were assigned at birth based on their perceived embodiment. The term sometimes includes people who are genderqueer, nonbinary, or agender.

transmisogyny: A combination of transphobia and sexism experienced by transgender women.

Two-Spirit: A term used by some Native people, mostly in North America, to describe their identities as same-sex-desiring and/or gender-variant people who identify with their ancestral traditions.

unmarked category: The dominant, or assumed, category, such as men in a male-dominant culture or white people in a white-dominant culture.

***Verstehen*:** A term proposed by Dutch scholar Garardus van der Leeuw, meaning empathetic understanding (*Verstehen* means "understanding" in German) of world concepts and experiences different from our own.

womanist: A term coined by scholar and novelist Alice Walker in 1984 to describe the inextricably intertwined commitments to racial and gender justice among women of color. The term is used today especially by African American women, but also by other women—and some men—of color.

***'yan daudu*:** People who identify with a traditional gender/sexual role among the Hausa in Nigeria that is historically associated with spirit possession.

Index

Abraham, Ibrahim, 119, 120, 120–121, 122, 137

academic stories, 48, 55–57, 57, 64

ACT UP (AIDS Coalition to Unleash Power), 31, 189–190

Affirmation (Mormon group), 156

After the Wrath of God (Petro), 188, 189, 206

agender status, 9, 221, 226

AIDS, Christians viewing as a moral epidemic, 189

Ali, Kecia, 56–57, 63, 67

Alpert, Rebecca, 39–40, 42–43, 67

Althaus-Reid, Marcella, 31, 175–176, 195, 196

Anderson, Benedict, 163, 225

apocalyptic temporality, 194, 197

aromatic (arrow) status, 22, 221

asexuality (ace) status, 22, 30, 95, 107, 221

Austin, J. L., 20

The Babylon Complex (Runions), 187

Babylon metaphor in US politics, 84–85, 187

baklâ of the Philippines, 100–101, 221

Bataille, Georges, 180, 181, 184

BDSM practices and communities, 22–23, 51, 58, 104–105, 221

Bean, Carl, 166

Beauvoir, Simone de, 15, 20, 21

beguinages in the European Christian tradition, 144

Benedict XVI, Pope, 78–79

Berlant, Lauren, 84, 163, 195

Bernice, Carol, 95, 145

Beth Chayim Chadashim (BCC), 155

Bhabha, Homi, 120

bin Laden, Osama, 185

biopolitics, 182, 183, 193, 221

biopower, 182, 183–184, 187, 195

bisexuality, 22, 81, 104, 125, 135–136, 136, 144, 151, 152, 157

bissu of Indonesia, 68–70, 73, 93, 99, 151, 153, 195

Black Atlantic identity, 117, 137, 221, 225

Black Leather Wings group, 104

Blackpentecostal Breath (Crawley), 143

Black Pentecostalism, 143–144, 152, 158, 166

black population: black churches, marginalization in, 81, 86, 143; black liberation theology, 175; black queer religious leaders, 158, 166; black religious communities as safe havens, 141–142; black women's writing, womanists inspired by, 80–81; chosen families of black queer people, 145–146; *quare*, as term used by black queer folk, 23; transcorporeality concept and, 117–118

227

About the Author

Melissa M. Wilcox is professor and Holstein Family and Community Chair of Religious Studies at the University of California, Riverside. She is the author or editor of several books and journal issues as well as numerous articles, on gender, sexuality, and religion. Her books include *Coming Out in Christianity: Religion, Identity, and Community*; *Sexuality and the World's Religions*; *Queer Women and Religious Individualism*; *Religion in Today's World: Global Issues, Sociological Perspectives*; and *Queer Nuns: Religion, Activism, and Serious Parody*.